ROSCOE "FATTY" ARBUCKLE

"FATTY"

Also by Andy Edmonds in Macdonald

HOT TODDY

"FATTY"

The Untold Story of
ROSCOE 'FATTY' ARBUCKLE

Macdonald

A Macdonald Book

First published in Great Britain in 1991 by
Macdonald & Co (Publishers) Ltd
London & Sydney

Printed and bound in Great Britain by
BPCC Hazell Books
Aylesbury, Bucks, England
Member of BPCC Ltd.

British Library Cataloguing in Publication Data
Edmonds, Andy
  Fatty.
  1. California. Los Angeles. Hollywood. Cinema films.
  Acting. Stars. Social life, history
  I. Title
  791.43028092
  ISBN 0-356-19194-X

Macdonald & Co (Publishers) Ltd
Orbit House
1 New Fetter Lane
London EC4A 1AR
A member of Maxwell Macmillan Pergamon Publishing Corporation

To Joe Rock:

Who always gave so much,
yet asked for so little in return

FOREWORD

There's an old story about three blind men and an elephant. Each was positioned at a different part of the animal and asked to describe the elephant as best he could. One blind man felt only the tusks and described the elephant as short, smooth, and hard with a razor-sharp point at the front. The second grabbed the ear and believed the animal was flat and thin, rather floppy and weak. The blind man at the end of the beast thought the elephant must look more like a snake, with a clump of rough hair at its tail.

Every story I read about Roscoe Arbuckle reminded me of the story of the three blind men and the elephant – each described an aspect of the man and his ordeal, but none seemed to present the complete picture. Each book provided certain insight, but none left me with a feeling that I really knew the comedian millions called "Fatty" or why he fell victim to the treacherous scheme that destroyed his career and his life.

In 1976 I met Joe Rock, a silent-film comedian, stunt man, and producer, who became a dear friend and greatly affected my life. On one of my first visits to Los Angeles, Joe told me a story I had never heard before, the story of what really happened at the Arbuckle party where a bit-part actress named Virginia Rappé died. As it turned out, Joe knew Roscoe Arbuckle quite well and told me the story he had heard from Arbuckle himself, a story that was not even allowed under oath in the courtroom during Arbuckle's three trials! I was a little skeptical at first, but any doubt was erased

7

after Joe introduced me to a woman who knew Arbuckle better than anyone else, his former wife Minta Durfee.

Minta was a very gracious lady who had been staying at the Motion Picture Country House and Hospital, a health and rest facility in Woodland Hills for those in the film industry. Together, Joe and Minta talked about the early days of film and about Hollywood, gossiped a bit about some of the old crowd, then chatted in great detail about Roscoe. It seemed that reminiscing with someone from the "old days" jogged Minta's memory and she began to open up. During the conversation she recalled a story Roscoe had told her on one of her visits to him in jail—his version of what happened at the party. Independently Minta confirmed the very story Joe had told me, the story Arbuckle's defense attorneys fought to keep off the record. Minta admitted she had given many interviews but had never told anyone this story before. I sensed then that I had stumbled on to something that no one else had the privilege of knowing.

At that time, I wasn't sure if there was enough information to pursue a book. I heard that another author was coming out with a book that promised to be a comprehensive look at Arbuckle's career and the trials. Though it went into great detail about those aspects, it did not contain much of the information I had learned from Minta and Joe. In fact, Minta's story of Roscoe's early life, the records I uncovered, and the newspaper accounts of the trial contradict a great deal of the information in that book.

I chose to rely on my extensive interviews with Minta, whom I considered a first hand source and who also offered greater detail about Roscoe's beginnings, details that tend to lend more credibility to Minta's version. I also relied on the records I found, as well as the newspaper reports written by people who were actually there—again firsthand sources.

I also believed there was much more to the story of why Roscoe fell from grace and became the scapegoat for the moral "housecleaning" of Hollywood.

I could not understand how it all came about—what happened to spark Arbuckle's downfall? Why, if he was making a million dollars a year, did he run up bills and amass so many debts? Why didn't his tax records jibe with stories of his supposed income? There were too many whys that needed an answer. Not knowing what would lie at the end of the trail, I started digging and uncovered a wealth of startling new information.

When combing through boxes of records and artifacts at the Hollywood Museum Archives for research on another book, I came across a small pile of canceled checks from the Paramount Studios. Out of curiosity I thumbed through them and found two checks were ten-thousand-dollar bank drafts to the San Francisco district attorney drawn on the Paramount account and signed by Adolph Zukor. I made a note and tucked it away.

Other files in the facilities provided more missing pieces of the Arbuckle story. I found letters to and from Will Hays that kept hammering away at Arbuckle long after he was cleared of any wrongdoing. I uncovered documents that indicated a plan to frame Arbuckle, masterminded by several people for purposes of control and political gain. I searched through long-closed police files and discovered more than fifty counts including bigamy, fraud, and racketeering against the prosecution's star witness, Maude Delmont. Through private sources I managed to find old tax records for Arbuckle for the years just prior to the scandal and gained insight into how he was left bankrupt and deeply in debt to the IRS though he was allegedly making one million dollars a year.

The court transcripts of the first two trials were believed destroyed long ago, but they were turned over to me in fairly complete form by someone connected with the case. These are believed to be among the only copies in existence. I found files from Adolph Zukor and Joe and Nick Schenck that laid out in detail the terms of the contracts between Roscoe and Zukor, and Roscoe and Schenck, contracts that many people claimed never existed.

Finally, I came across the "ace"—the original memo, written by Will Hays on Zukor's interoffice stationery, that banished Roscoe Arbuckle from the screen. This is the first time this memo has ever appeared in public.

With the help of those listed in the acknowledgments, I formed another picture of Roscoe Arbuckle, a man who many called a naïve baby yet one who was considered a comic genius. Arbuckle was more popular than Charlie Chaplin at one time and was the highest-paid movie star in his day. He was a complex man with a gentle nature, yet he would go to great lengths to plot out a practical joke, rarely concerned for the victim's feelings. He was shy and easily embarrassed, yet flashed a powerful temper and sharp tongue when crossed. He was an alcoholic and workaholic who never understood why he was banned from the screen. Arbuckle was an abandoned child from a broken home who never believed he was loved and searched for love in three marriages. He was an innocent clown who died of a broken heart.

Much of what follows appears here for the very first time—new information on Arbuckle's family and early struggles, his dealings with Schenck and Zukor, his work and life at Warners shortly before his death, the real story, in Arbuckle's own words, of what happened at the infamous party, new information on the underhanded deal making of Adolph Zukor and the overt campaign by Will Hays to keep Arbuckle as a pariah long after he was cleared and the ban lifted, an explanation for Virginia Rappé's cryptic accusation of Arbuckle as the perpetrator of the crime, and finally why Arbuckle was actually singled out as the scapegoat for all of Hollywood's moral decay.

How, after seventy years, would never-before-published information be found? The answer, I believe, is simple—no one had ever looked in many of the files and archives. When I went into these sources I broke the seals on many records, indicating that I was the first one to comb through these documents since they were assembled: documents detailing secret negotiations over Arbuckle between the Schencks and other studios, which possibly triggered Zukor's actions, as well as memos of conversations with Zukor that give a strong indication of a hidden setup at the San Francisco party. I carefully went through the San Francisco and Los Angeles newspapers—one page at a time—searching for every published detail of the story from Roscoe's arrest to his return to the stage.

Through this painstaking research a new and shocking story has been uncovered.

I began this book as a writer interested in a good story. During my research I developed a fondness for Roscoe and many of his comedies. Through the support and generosity of friends I was able to see a retrospective of Arbuckle's comedies. I saw his frustration during his Keystone days, his zest and genius during the Comique years, the sensitivity and subtleness of the Paramount features, and finally, the struggle of the final years with Warner Bros. Seeing these films, many of which were believed "lost," helped me gain an insight into Roscoe the man and Roscoe once the most-loved comedian in the world.

I also found a group of people who had either known Roscoe or been familiar with his life or with the era. It was in conversations with these people that the full story fell into place.

When I first sat down next to Minta Durfee I asked her why "Fatty" was falsely accused of such a terrible crime and literally hung out to dry in Hollywood. When she answered that question she gently put her hand on my knee and very politely said, "My dear, we never called him 'Fatty.' " So, for Minta, and in this book, neither will I.

ACKNOWLEDGMENTS

M any people have generously given their time and help in putting this book together, opening their files and their doors, many for the first time. The late Joe Rock and the late Minta Durfee Arbuckle provided the initial spark many years ago. I wish also to thank Eleanor Keaton, Betty (Mrs. Alf) Goulding Saunders, Bill Heyes, Lois Laurel Hawes and Tony Hawes, Adela Rogers St. Johns, June Chase Hargis, Mike Hawks, Joe Rinaudo, Lorraine Saunders, writer/researcher Randy Skretvedt, Diane Schrader, A.C. Lyles, Deborah Rosen of the Paramount Studios Archives, "Doc" Dougherty, Michael Yakaitis, Dino Castro, Malcolm Willits of the Collector's Bookstore, Michael Redmond of the Santa Barbara Historical Society, Ann Calixton of the San Francisco County Superior Court office, Donald Lee Nelson, Ned Comstock, Leith Adams, and the staffs of the UCLA, USC, and Academy of Motion Picture Arts and Sciences Libraries and Special Collections, the staff of the San Francisco District Attorney's Office, and the staffs of the Glendale, San Francisco, Santa Barbara, and downtown Los Angeles libraries.

Thanks also to Paulette Lee for her wonderful photography and her tremendous work in obtaining some of the photos for this book.

I would also like to thank Sam Gill, archivist at the Academy of Motion Picture Arts and Sciences, a wonderful person to share information and flesh out previously undiscovered gems. He also provided the updated filmography at the end of this book, the only complete listing of the films of Roscoe Arbuckle known to exist.

A major note of appreciation must also go to filmmaker/director Brian Anthony who, through his tireless energy in tracking down information and bringing to the surface a wonderful retrospective of Arbuckle's work, helped round out this book to a great degree. I was "tickled to death" for his help.

My only regret was that I was unable to interview Arbuckle's last wife, Addie O. McPhail Arbuckle Sheldon.

Finally, a very big "thank you" to Robert Gottlieb of the William Morris Agency for his continued encouragement. And to Lisa Drew, my editor, who first suggested there might be enough new information on the Roscoe Arbuckle story to warrant this book. It was a pleasant surprise to learn how right she was!

QUOTES

"The evidence in my possession shows conclusively that either a rape or an attempt to rape was perpetrated on Miss Rappé by Roscoe Arbuckle."

—San Francisco D.A. Matthew Brady—

"Arbuckle's weight will damn him. He will no longer be a roly-poly, good-natured comedian. He will be a monster. If he were an ordinary man his spotless reputation would save him. But he is not. He is Roscoe Arbuckle. They'll never convict him, but this will ruin him and maybe motion pictures for some time. God help us all."

—Attorney Earl Rogers—

"I directed Arbuckle for a year and a half at Sennett. Virginia worked with him, too. She disliked him. She said he was cheap and vulgar. I will make any financial sacrifice to see Arbuckle punished. He came up a beast from saloons."

—Henry "Pathé" Lehrman, Virginia Rappé's fiancé—

"In all the years Fatty worked for me he didn't do a thing anyone could point a finger at. Fatty wouldn't hurt a fly. He was a kind, good-natured fat man and a good comic."

—Producer Mack Sennett—

"Roscoe Arbuckle is as guilty as I am. And I wasn't even at that party. He wouldn't hurt a fly. He was a gentle man to whom I owe everything. He is innocent. Those who are out to

14

destroy him should be ashamed for what they're doing to this wonderful man."

—Comedian Buster Keaton—

"We thought we would make a fortune on Roscoe—for years. I never guessed it would all end like this."

—Producer Jesse Lasky—

"I tried to get Arbuckle the best representation Paramount could afford, which is considerable. The affair is out of my control and out of my hands. As far as the ban on Mr Arbuckle's films, Paramount stands to lose a lot, too.'

—Paramount president Adolph Zukor—

"Every man in the right and proper time is entitled to his chance to make good. The public will decide if Roscoe Arbuckle had endured punishment enough."

—Movie czar Will Hays—

"The evidence showed a depravity entirely independent of the question of actual murder. As long as his character must be measured by such orgies . . . there is no reason why he should be given another chance."

—Attorney William Jennings Bryan—

"Acquittal is not enough for Roscoe Arbuckle! We feel a great injustice has been done to him."

—Verdict of third manslaughter trial—

"As Arbuckle walked out of the courthouse acquitted—a free man legally—he was stabbed repeatedly by women using their hat pins. It's a wonder how he escaped alive."

—Arbuckle publicist Harry Brand—

"Fatty sold me more newspapers than the sinking of the Lusitania."

—Publisher William Randolph Hearst—

"I've no resentment against anybody for what has happened. My conscience is clear, my heart is clean. I want to go back to the screen. If I do get back it will be grand. If I don't—well, okay. If the public doesn't want me, I'll take my medicine. But after the vindication I received, I am sure the American people will be fair. I am due for a comeback. I only want to make people happy once again."

—Roscoe Arbuckle—

"My husband lived for 12 years after the San Francisco trial, but he died in that courtroom. He died of a broken heart. He was denied an audience by bigoted people who thought three trials to prove your innocence wasn't enough."

—Minta Durfee Arbuckle—

1

To friends he was "The Balloonatic," "The Prince of Whales," "Big Otto," "Rosc," "Buckie," "My Child the Fat." To millions around the world he was "Fatty," a rotund comedian who starred in his own two-reelers, who weighed between 250 and 300 pounds depending on appetite and publicity releases. When his career reached its zenith in 1921 he was signed to a deal that no other comedian, not even Charlie Chaplin, had achieved—having complete control in every aspect of film from direction to casting as well as starring in his own feature-length comedies. His salary was one million dollars per year at the time when the average Los Angeles home cost two thousand dollars and the average income was something near six dollars per week. In 1921 Roscoe Conkling Arbuckle was among the wealthiest, most popular, most loved movie comedians in the world. And in 1921, he also became the most hated.

Murderer! Rapist! Degenerate! Pervert! In one evening it seemed the entire world had turned from a fan club to a lynch mob. The initial perception was that Arbuckle had murdered a young starlet named Virginia Rappé during a violent sex orgy in a San Francisco hotel. Years later that perception changed through a number of books and articles portraying Arbuckle as a naïve and somewhat dull-minded dupe who happened to fall prey to a ruthless San Francisco district attorney. In truth Roscoe Arbuckle was a bright, ambitious, creative, but all too trusting practical joker who fell victim to one of the most intricate frame-ups and diabolical conspiracies

17

ever launched in Hollywood—a town notorious for back-stabbing and blind ambition and run by power-hungry moguls who often cared little for their stars and had no regard for any consequences of their actions for others as long as they achieved their purpose.

Roscoe often joked about his birth. He said, "Two big things blew Smith Center, Kansas, off the map—my birth and a cyclone. No one heard of the place since." But in reality his early years were nothing to laugh at. One of five children, Roscoe was born at home into extreme poverty on March 24, 1887. His mother delivered her sixteen-pound son three days prematurely without the aid of a midwife. The delivery nearly killed her; she remained in frail health until her death twelve years later. In one of his many drunken rages Arbuckle's father accused the boy of secretly trying to kill his mother and never failed to blame her tenuous condition on his son. Arbuckle's father, William Goodrich Arbuckle, a hard-drinking and luckless wheat farmer with a violent temper, named his son after a prominent Kansas politician, Roscoe Conkling. His mother, who Roscoe called "Dee," peppered her conversation with biblical quotes as a somber "hellfire and Brimstone" Baptist and prayed for instead of fighting against her husband, her "preaching" often serving to escalate the hostility.

William Arbuckle was among the hundreds of thousands of easterners who believed prosperity and opportunity lay in the open fields of the Great Plains. They arrived with little more than their families and the basic necessities. They built crude homes on land they claimed as their own as homesteaders. And they battled against nature which refused to give way to the newcomers. Many soon found out they were ill equipped for the extremes of the midwestern seasons. The Kansas soil was cracked and hard, the roots of the wild plains grasses dug in too deep to relinquish their stranglehold. The wind continually howled.

The Arbuckles lived in the squalid and desperate conditions of many early American Homesteaders. Lumber was scarce on the Plains, and what little could be had was usually of poor quality or very expensive. Most homesteaders on the Kansas Plains built huts—nothing more than crude one-room cabins blanketed with thick clods of sod. Cows often grazed on the roofs and the settlers took the brunt of the elements—the icy-cold winters that left many families dead of exposure, the fierce windstorms that howled through the huts and ravaged meager crops planted as a family's only source of food, and torrential rains that turned cracked, dry plains into gully washers sweeping away unprotected cabins.

The huts, built miles apart, forced families into quiet isolation and desperation. The huts had no privacy. The sleeping area was cordoned off with a ragged sheet or home-made scrap quilt. There was no indoor plumbing and only essential furniture. The children slept on the floor or crammed together in beds made of rope with mattresses stuffed with dried grass or straw. Often, children were not raised for love of a family unit but bred to work and were out into the fields or out on the streets as soon as they were able to swing an ax or push a broom. While the men dragged wood and steel plows behind horses and oxen, the women remained prisoners inside, raising their large families and cooking over the only source of heat—a large open fireplace. Men often died in the fields; women went slowly insane from the confinement and the moaning wind, which never seemed to stop.

Wheat farming in the late 1880s was nearly impossible. Severe drought had withered what few shoots had emerged from the ground. His spirit broken and his dreams decayed, William Arbuckle consoled himself with whiskey and took out his frustrations in violent beatings on Dee and the children. Roscoe usually bore the brunt of those whiskey-induced rages.

The California gold rush had been under way for nearly forty years, and by 1889, the trek west with its promise of gold and fertile soil ripe for the grabbing had lured thousands of homesteaders across the Rockies. The Arbuckles packed a few chairs, beds, and cooking utensils and abandoned their hut for the promise of the new horizon. Picking up odd jobs in towns across the way, they had scraped enough money together by the time they arrived in Santa Ana to rent a small, run down two-flat home. The upper floor and part of the bottom floor were divided and rented out, and the Arbuckles lived in the front half of the home on North Birch Street.

Santa Ana was a small, ramshackle, dusty town at the turn of the century. The sidewalks, if any, were built of warped boards. The streets were dirt and littered with horse manure. Most of the residents were cowboys, worked as hands on the nearby citrus ranches, or were newly arrived families from the East. Though the old-timers were clannish, the town had a sense of community and the Arbuckles were welcomed as neighbors.

But despite the promise of a fresh start, the drinking and beatings continued. That winter, William Arbuckle walked out on his family and headed to the northern California town of San Jose. There he reportedly found work as a crop picker and eventually scraped enough together to buy a small hotel. He succeeded in starting a new life, sending no money and little correspondence to his family in Santa Ana.

The Arbuckle children immediately went to work. Roscoe was barely five, but picked up odd jobs sweeping stores and delivering light groceries. When he enrolled in school, he continued his delivery routes and cleaning jobs. He had few friends, partly because his after-school jobs left no time for play and partly because he was so painfully shy in front of strangers. Roscoe later confessed that a main reason for his awkwardness was his early isolation in Kansas; he had never met anyone outside his family until they moved to Santa Ana and he did not know how to act in front of strangers.

Another reason was his abandonment by his father. Roscoe often said he never felt loved as a child and therefore never really knew how to love in return. He chased after his father for attention and went out of his way to try to win his love. But each effort was returned with a beating or an abrupt rebuff. Often William Arbuckle denied Roscoe was his son. Finally, Roscoe was conditioned to believe the response to showing love was receiving pain.

Another reason for Roscoe's early shyness was his size. Continually reminded that he was often double the bulk of his playmates, he watched quietly instead of joining in schoolyard games. Teasing, his classmates nicknamed him "Fatty," which Roscoe vehemently hated. The name calling so desperately embarrassed Roscoe that he finally refused to return to school. He dropped out in the second grade, without telling his mother.

He lived the lie for several months and pretended to go to school every weekday. But instead of sitting in a classroom he would hide backstage at one of the neighborhood theaters and watch the current stock company rehearse its series of vaudeville sketches and short plays, ducking the manager, who liked to bounce nosy young boys out into the back alley. Several times Roscoe sneaked in, pretending he was a member of the company, only to be caught and bounced out. After a while the sneaking in and bouncing out became a game with the manager.

Santa Ana was considered a "B" stop on the vaudeville circuit. In fact, Los Angeles at this time was still a cowboy town. The movie industry that would make Los Angeles into a boomtown was still in the experimental stage. The acts that stopped in Santa Ana were small, usually ragtag troupes that picked up and dropped players as finances and bookings allowed. The town had its share of vagabonds and ruffians who tumbled in and out of the troupes. Overall, the actors were looked down upon by the local residents, who considered them crude and vulgar, usually nothing more than no-talent bums and whores who could not find a more honorable profession.

Roscoe was only eight years old, and probably realized the common perception of actors, but he could not have cared less. He was mesmerized by the makeup and the costumes and, most important of all, the applause. To Roscoe, it meant affection, and he said that as a boy, he often fantasized about being on stage at the receiving end of the applause. In September of 1895, Roscoe happened to be in the right place at the right time. Fate intervened.

The Frank Bacon Stock Company was a traveling troupe that often used local talent for the bit parts in its show. Only the featured performers stayed on with the company. The show was cast and about to open in Santa Ana when it suddenly needed one player—a young black boy. Desperately Frank Bacon took to the streets for a replacement and found a cherubic-faced, pudgy boy chasing after him, eager to do the part. Bacon thought Roscoe would be mildly amusing in the role but told him that if he was going to play the part of a "pickaninny," his white legs could not show. Bacon ordered Arbuckle home to get some black stockings to cover his legs. Roscoe knew he could not explain to his mother why he needed the stockings, especially when he was supposed to be in school. Not knowing what else to do he cried, not letting on that his mother had no idea of what he was really up to and would wallop him if she found out. Bacon succumbed and not only painted Roscoe's face black with greasepaint, but his legs and arms as well. The boy earned fifty cents a week for three weeks, which was considered pretty good for an eight-year-old in a bit part. He didn't tell his mother about his newfound career and said he earned his first week's pay sweeping stores.

School at the turn of the century was not mandatory, nor was it considered important when weighed against finding gainful employment. Dee held to that conviction unless it involved the theater, which went against her strong religious convictions. Fortunately she never questioned her son, and never let on if she was suspicious about Roscoe's real job. So he gleefully went to the theater every night, smeared himself head to toe with the greasepaint and did as he was told. The women in the company fawned over him, tweaked his cheeks, and brought snacks backstage (which Roscoe carefully loaded into his pockets to take home). For the first time in his life he felt not only accepted but loved by strangers. As Roscoe later told friends: "I knew that was it. I was bit by the old show business bug . . . and overnight I was eight going on eighteen."

Arbuckle quickly graduated into more "sophisticated" roles, his next acting job being the guinea pig for a traveling mindreader and hypnotist named Melvor Tyndall. Tyndall's reputation as a mystic often preceded him and crowds usually gathered in the streets to greet him upon his arrival, which was never dull. His trademark entrance was by way of a speeding horse-drawn carriage, which he drove while blindfolded. Using his "mystic" powers he would tell the horse to stop by telepathy (or so he claimed), then whip off his blindfold and announce the time of his show.

Looking for a "victim," Tyndall adressed the crowd: "Is there any boy who will permit me to hypnotize him and sleep in a store window until I wake him up? I will pay him ten dollars and treat him and his mother to three meals in one of your town's fine restaurants." Roscoe seized the opportunity before any other boy could speak out. Again he was told to ask his mother. But this time he didn't cry. Instead he lied and said his mother had already said it was okay.

That night, when Roscoe did not return home for supper, Dee became upset. Fearing the worst, and by now suspecting Roscoe's ambitions in the theater, she headed out for the local opera house. But on the way, she was sidetracked by a crowd pointing and shouting in front of a department-store window. She elbowed her way through the crowd and saw her chubby little boy sleeping soundly with a half-eaten apple resting in his hand. Dee pounded on the window, but could not awaken Roscoe.

"It's the power of the Great Tyndall," someone shouted from behind. With anger in her eyes, Dee scurried off to find the mystic and give him an unasked-for Bible lecture. Instead of clashing, the two became friends; she felt sorry for the man who was obviously only trying to earn a living. He never expected the crowd to keep watch on Roscoe all night and promised to send him home as soon as the crowd left.

When Roscoe arrived home that morning, he handed his mother a ten-dollar gold piece and a note good for three dinners for two at the Golden Ox, one of Santa Ana's best restaurants. Though they enjoyed the restaurant dinners (which were considered a very rare treat in 1899), Roscoe was admonished by his mother to stay away from the theater. She warned him that nothing but trouble would come from that type of life. He promised to return to school and forget his theatrical ambitions. Roscoe kept to that promise until that winter, when Dee, the only person he felt really loved him, died.

By this time, most of the children had either left home to find work or had gotten married. Roscoe moved in with his older sister Nora and her husband, Walter St. John, for several months. Both Nora and Walter had been working fairly steadily in vaudeville and their son Al (who later co-starred in many of Roscoe's comedies and later became a top comedian in his own right) often appeared on stage with them. In fact Roscoe later credited his sister with encouraging him toward the stage. But when Al grew out of the toddler stage and needed more room, the St. John house was too cramped for four and Roscoe was shipped off to live with his father, William, and brother Arthur in San Jose.

A group of local churchwomen packed a lunch for the youngster, rounded up a secondhand suitcase full of ill-fitting clothes, and put Roscoe on the train north. He later told his future wife Minta it was one of the loneliest and most heart-wrenching trips of his life; a trip that left him with a haunting fear of abandonment and made him distrustful of any closeness.

2

The last thing Roscoe wanted to do was travel to San Jose to see his father. William Arbuckle had always teased, ridiculed, and snickered at his youngest son's weight, forcing Roscoe to withdraw and become very self-conscious about his appearance. He remembered the drinking and the beatings that always followed a half bottle of whiskey. The youngster sensed he was moving away from the only happy times in his life—with his mother, on stage, and earning that gold piece in Santa Ana. He was actually terrified of what might await him with his father in San Jose.

When Roscoe became nervous, he got hungry—ravenously hungry. Less than a half hour after pulling out of Santa Ana, Roscoe wolfed down the fruit and sandwiches meant to last the duration of the five-hour trip. When the train finally pulled into the San Jose station, Roscoe stayed in his seat, clutching his suitcase, until the conductor escorted him off the train. There was no one there to meet him.

Roscoe sat on the station bench, alone. Every time he heard a man's footsteps he winced, half wishing it would be his father, half hoping it was not. After several hours' wait, a railroad worker approached the boy and asked if he could help.

"I'm waiting for my father."

"What's his name?"

"Arbuckle, sir. William Arbuckle. He works at a hotel here with my brother."

The man gave Roscoe a puzzled look. At first, Roscoe was concerned that he would miss his father, who would finally show up and become angry at not finding his son at the station. His anger usually triggered a beating. But Roscoe also sensed that his father was not going to show up. The man took Roscoe's suitcase and together they walked to the hotel to meet the desk clerk, a man named Bill, who informed the child that his father had not only worked there but owned the hotel as well. He had sold the hotel in a hurry three days before and left town to head north somewhere. There was no forwarding address. There was also no word about Roscoe's older brother. It seemed that once again William Arbuckle had skipped out on his family. Roscoe had the very real sense that his father had heard about his arrival and run out to avoid the responsibility of taking care of his son, especially a son whom he hated, abused, and denied.

At twelve years old Roscoe was broke (he had only two dollars in his pocket—the money his sister and brother-in-law had given him) and was alone in a strange town.

The desk clerk felt sorry for the youngster and offered him a place in the hotel as long as he was willing to work for his keep. Eager, and used to hard work, Roscoe agreed to the deal. He saw no other possibility. Roscoe recalled that he followed the clerk into the kitchen, which was rather old and dilapidated but clean. He sat down at a long wooden table near the kitchen stove alongside several other hotel employees who were having their dinner. They were all so friendly, swapping stories about the guests, telling jokes and gossiping, that Roscoe had the immediate impression of a happy family. He desperately wanted to belong.

They welcomed the boy by piling huge helpings of food on his plate. A few of the employees made "Fatty" jokes while dishing out the food, but Roscoe was so hungry and so lonely that, for the first time in his life, he did not mind the ribbing. He chowed down as fast as they could pile it on, entertaining the crew with his voracious appetite.

After dinner, the bellhop showed Arbuckle to his room, about the size of a closet with barely enough room for the bed and a small dresser. But it was home. Here, he thought, he could stay forever! His own room, all the food he could eat (which was considerable), and friends. Arbuckle finally was his own man.

The clerk enrolled Arbuckle in school the following Monday and after school he worked doing odd jobs in the hotel, from kitchen duty to sweeping and cleaning out rooms. He never played much with other youngsters, partly because of his workload at the hotel and partly because of his size. Though he was only twelve, he appeared and acted much older. Roscoe often took on more work than should have been required of a boy his age. He withdrew into his chores at the hotel, filling any free time with work. He later said he did it to avoid social contact and out of fear they would find him a burden and send him back to Santa Ana if he didn't pull his weight.

Occasionally he wrote his sister to boast about how well he was doing (the truth embellished with a great deal of exaggeration) and to let the family know where he was staying in the faint hope that one day his father would surface and ask about his youngest boy. Sadly, William Arbuckle never enquired about Roscoe, though Roscoe never gave up hoping.

The hotel was becoming one of the most popular in San Jose and catered to travelers who liked to socialize in nightclubs. Several months after Roscoe moved in, a piano player and singer were hired to entertain in the dining room. The singer's name was Pansy Jones. She was a sweet teenager who felt sorry for Roscoe and often lectured the other employees when they teased him about being "the fat kid." Roscoe said she always smelled of lilac perfume.

One afternoon she heard him singing while he was sweeping the kitchen and thought he had a decent, though somewhat frail-sounding voice. Pansy taught Roscoe some popular songs and encouraged him to sing in public. The thought of doing anything before an audience fascinated, yet terrified him. But Pansy held firm in her conviction about Roscoe and acted as both teacher and friend.

When Roscoe was not needed to fill in as a bellhop or janitor, Pansy let him sing in the dining room for tips and let him keep every cent of his money. She also offered the boy some sound advice—to learn everything about every aspect of

27

the theater if he wanted to make it as a performer. She warned him that too many people relied on only one talent, and when that talent failed they were left with nothing. Heeding her advice, Roscoe practiced juggling pots and pans in the kitchen, somersaults in the yard, and pratfalls in the hall—an odd sight inasmuch as he was well on his way to his infamous proportions of six feet and 275 pounds.

Typical of every twelve-year-old boy, Roscoe became smitten with the first "older" woman who showed him any attention. Though Pansy was eighteen, she was sophisticated and appeared worldly and Roscoe was head over heels. This, he thought, was the girl he was going to marry!

One evening the man who had initially helped Roscoe at the railroad station came into the hotel for dinner. He heard Roscoe sing and persuaded Pansy to speak with the desk clerk, Bill, about letting Roscoe perform at amateur night at the Empire Theater. Bill agreed to the night off. It changed Roscoe's life forever as it was his first real stage experience.

The show was of the old-fashioned variety type that is still spoofed in cartoons and revival houses—where the unpopular acts were literally dragged offstage by a large hook that the manager slid out from the wings. If the audience did not like an act, mixed in with "boos" and jeers would be cries of "get the hook," and out it came. Roscoe was petrified of the hook but bolstered his confidence with thoughts of pleasing Pansy and the five-dollar prize awarded each night for the best act.

Roscoe sang one or two ditties of Pansy's and went over big—so big that the audience demanded an encore. Roscoe froze. He had not prepared another number and did not know what else to sing so he danced a crazy jig, waved his arms, jumped across the stage, and did somersaults. Roscoe never did find out if he was really that good or if it was because the audience had never seen such a big, chubby boy doing such frantic stunts on stage, but the more he jiggled around, the louder the applause. Caught in the frenzy, Roscoe kept going. But slowly from the stage wing came the hook. He shimmied and jumped out of the hook's grasp and finally did a somersault and bellyflopped into the orchestra pit to escape. He won the five-dollar prize and the request that he return whenever he was able.

Arbuckle was the talk of the hotel and apparently of the town as well. Word of his theatrical shenanigans reached one of the most important theater moguls, who happened to be staying in San Jose on his regular route to San Francisco, David Grauman. (His son, Sid, would later open the Chinese and Egyptian theaters in Los Angeles, making the name famous worldwide.)

Roscoe had been swimming at a local creek when word arrived that Grauman had requested a meeting in the hotel lobby. Apprehensive and still distrustful of strangers, Arbuckle defiantly trekked through the lobby dripping wet to meet the biggest man in the theater business. He thought his casualness about his appearance would indicate confidence. Grauman never said a word, as if such a waterlogged look was routine. Grauman later said he had seen it all with theater people so nothing ever surprised him.

'You that fat kid who did the crazy act in the show last night?'

"Yes, sir."

"I liked the way you sang. You've got a good voice. Better still, I liked the way you danced. I'm staying at the Victory Hotel. One day, kid, you and I are going to do business."

The next morning, Arbuckle was ordered to drive the hotel's new horse-drawn butcher wagon on its rounds. For reasons that were never clear, a young woman named Betsy hopped on board. Roscoe said he was not paying much attention, just minding his business and singing while steering the wagon. Suddenly, the horse spooked and raced out of control. Taking a corner too fast, the wagon toppled over, threw Betsy in one direction, Roscoe in another, and scattered the meat across the dirt road. The meat was tainted, Betsy stormed off and Roscoe took the brunt of the blame for the accident. Though he offered to work off the loss of the meat, small-town gossip forced fate's hand.

Word quickly spread around town that Roscoe was caught "alone in the wagon with a girl," and Bill was forced to fire him to avoid a scandal. To make things worse, Bill told him that Pansy had left with some salesman who offered to take her out for a night on the town. Once again, Roscoe lost both his home and the love of the one person he cared for. This time he vowed to himself that he would never again open up emotionally to anyone.

Dejected and disillusioned, Roscoe packed what few clothes he had and headed to the Empire Theater, where he hoped to be working steadily in the Friday night amateur shows.

He knocked on the theater door and heard a racket—chairs breaking, glass smashing, and a good peppering of language that Roscoe had previously heard only during his father's drunken rages. Sheepishly, Arbuckle opened the door, ducked a shattering light bulb, and asked for the manager. Still in a rage, the manager explained that the opening act, a unicyclist named Weber, had gone out on a bender the night before and had not been seen since. The wheels turning, Roscoe quickly volunteered to fill in as a singer. The manager was skeptical.

"The opening act is always some kind of animal act or acrobat or something. I don't think anyone will go for some fat kid standing there singing."

But Roscoe was determined. He needed the money.

"I do acrobatic stunts. Remember the amateur night last night! That was me!"

"Tell ya what. Just sing in front of the screen and get the audience to sing. That usually warms 'em up."

Roscoe got the nod and was told to go on in as the lead act. Singing the song that had helped win him the prize the night before, "Believe Me If All Those Endearing Young Charms," he also worked a deal to live in one of the dressing rooms. The marquee was changed, and a new strip of paper was pasted over WEBER-UNICYCLIST. The new opening act was formally launched. ROSCOE ARBUCKLE: BOY SINGER (SINGER OF ILLUSTRATED SONGS).

But both the vaudeville performers and the audience were cool toward Roscoe. Some of the performers were upset that an upstart had walked in and stolen top billing. And the audience expected an acrobat. While Roscoe tried to get the audience to sing along to the illustrated slides that projected lyrics on a screen, stagehands moved scenery and props behind him. Every once in a while, a table or prop flew out into the back of the screen, once almost bumping Arbuckle off the stage in a deliberate attempt to force him to lose his place. It was his initiation as an official member of the troupe. The excitement and anticipation of star billing was quickly tainted, but it was a job. And Roscoe learned a key lesson about entertaining. In a later newspaper interview, he said he "understood that everyone likes to be entertained but that no two audiences were ever alike. A joke that went over big one night might die the next. So a performer had to learn to think on his feet and have enough backup material to ride the flow." He also learned a lesson about jealousy and pecking order in the theater. Words of advice that trailed back to Pansy Jones.

After the show Arbuckle stayed up all night to try to expand his repertoire to five or six songs. Once he had the songs memorized he decided to take David Grauman up on his offer. Remembering Grauman was staying at the Victory Hotel, near the Unique Theater which he owned, Arbuckle left a note explaining that he was the opening act—the illustrated singer—at the theater down the street.

Grauman did not respond. Roscoe continued to send notes to Grauman night after night but never saw him in the audience. So much for big talk from big people.

Within a few weeks, the audiences warmed up to Arbuckle and his songs, and he found himself the subject of hot gossip among some of the more "worldly" female members of the troupe. One very brazen woman made several unsuccessful attempts to seduce Roscoe, causing him to lock himself alone in his dressing room. He became the butt of several jokes from the women, who questioned whether or not he was still a virgin and had a standing bet among themselves to see who could discover the answer by sleeping with him first.

Arbuckle also received his share of well-wishers, especially older women who sent cakes and pies backstage in an effort to "adopt" him as their own son. He enjoyed the food and was always cordial but somewhat aloof out of his cautious regard for strangers.

One night after the show he heard two men talking in the hall outside his dressing room and heard his name clearly mentioned. Arbuckle recognized one voice as that of the manager. The other seemed vaguely familiar. He listened for several minutes. The words were slurred and the voice grew louder. When Roscoe realized whose voice it was he got sick to his stomach and vomited. It was his father.

3

"**I** heard you were here. Saw your name on the poster. Singer, huh?"

Roscoe could barely look at his father, who seemed oblivious to his son's revulsion.

"So here we are."

Roscoe noticed the emphasis on the word "we." He also noticed a thin and homely woman grabbing at William Arbuckle's arm. He kept brushing her away crudely and with great hostility. Roscoe refused to speak.

"Why the hell weren't you at the hotel where you were supposed to be? Why don't you ever do what you're told?"

The boy looked up.

"I waited for you. That was a long time ago." Roscoe looked at the woman who was obviously trying to include herself in the one-sided conversation. "Who's that?"

"Your mother."

"My mother died."

"Your new mother and I have started a new life, we've got three kids living with us now. We want you to come live with us on a little farm we bought on the edge of town."

Roscoe was in shock. It was the second marriage for both. Mollie had seven children of her own from a previous marriage. Now Willie Arbuckle and Mollie had two children together, making fourteen between them. Roscoe believed they had come to see him for two reasons—he was making money and he was big enough to handle a fair amount of heavy farm labor. With no place to go, he packed his bags and left with his father, a man who abused his son and bled him dry of any emotional attachment and feelings of affection. Roscoe felt as if his gut had been kicked in, but he also felt he had no alternative.

Arbuckle reportedly labored on the farm for several months, then worked as a cook, cashier, and janitor when his father and stepmother opened a restaurant in nearby Santa Clara. Though the Arbuckles were making solid money in their restaurant venture, William's heavy drinking and verbal and physical abuse continued. It became so regular that after several months, Roscoe learned not to react to any outburst from his father. His hatred seethed quietly inside. He had not yet learned to speak out against his father. After each tirade, Roscoe calmly walked out and stayed out most of the night. Often, he went to local theaters to either watch a show or participate in amateur nights against his stepmother's strong objections.

One evening in the spring of 1902, Roscoe was singing at one of the local theaters when he received a note backstage. It was from David Grauman, offering him a permanent job singing in his theater in San Jose—the Unique Theater—for a salary of nearly eighteen dollars a week. Grauman kept his word. That "someday" he promised several years back had finally arrived.

Elated, Roscoe saw the job as a chance to get away from his father, the beatings, and the near-slave labor imposed by his family. Roscoe had been working hard in the family restaurant, supposedly on a steady salary of seven dollars a week, but William Arbuckle rarely if ever paid his son, instead pocketing the cash and accusing Roscoe of trying to steal from him when he demanded his weekly wages. Mollie usually intervened and slipped her stepson a few dollars when William was not in the restaurant. The fifteen-year-old lad finally had his freedom.

As it turned out, Grauman had followed Arbuckle's singing all along. He had watched as the boy grew through puberty and waited until the teenager's voice developed and was strong enough to project to a full theater. Roscoe now knew dozens of songs, and when he was stumped for a tune or the slide projector jammed, he was comfortable enough with the spotlight to improvise. Grauman liked what he saw.

Arbuckle trouped on at Grauman's Unique Theater for nearly two years with considerable success. He opened the show each night as an illustrated song man, and even filled in as a backup comedian—his first, real starring role on stage! No one in the audience caught on that the hefty kid feeding one-liners and the chubby boy singer were one and the same. Roscoe enjoyed the intrigue as well as his first opportunity to do comedy.

He was soon known throughout San Jose as a solid singer with a sweet tenor voice. And he also worked hard at odd jobs in the theater, from taking tickets to sweeping floors after the show for extra money. Roscoe proved himself eager and ambitious, which pleased Grauman. He also saved quite a bit of his salary, which he kept tucked away "just in case." Arbuckle's desperately poor childhood was never far from his thoughts and he had a gnawing fear those grim days were only one step away. But Grauman saw a bright future ahead for the talented teenager.

"Pack your bags, kid. You're heading north."

Never one to question authority, Roscoe followed orders. By seven o'clock the following morning, Grauman, Arbuckle, and a small contingent were standing on a train platform heading to San Francisco. Arbuckle dutifully sent a hurried note back to his father and stepmother, but was afraid they would show up at the station and demand he stay in San Jose. Luckily, either William Arbuckle never read the note or no longer cared. Roscoe boarded the train in the same manner he had stepped off more than five years earlier—with no family present to wish him well.

But things were different on this trip. Grauman arranged to treat the group to a first-class breakfast in the dining car. It was after the meal that Roscoe learned his plans. They were to open at the Portola Café in San Francisco, which Grauman had recently purchased. The café featured singing waiters and it needed a boy who could serve as both head-waiter and solo artist. Since Arbuckle had proved himself dependable as an entertainer and a worker, Grauman believed he could be trusted to handle the job without much supervision.

Being a singing waiter at such an exclusive restaurant as the Portola was considered a major step up from a small vaudeville stage. The café catered to the monied San Francisco theater crowd that was known for its generous tips. Roscoe was given the best tables and often raked in ten dollars a night in tips—a handsome salary in 1904.

Roscoe was happy, but David Grauman proved to be even more of a benefactor and mentor. He believed Roscoe's destiny was as a headliner on stage and again set destiny in motion.

While Roscoe was making his usual rounds as a waiter, Grauman entered the café and waved Roscoe over to a secluded table in the back of the restaurant. Rarely did Grauman appear there, so Roscoe sensed the importance of the signal. Sitting with Grauman was a middle-aged man with a thick Greek accent. He had an obvious air of importance but even after the introduction Arbuckle still did not fully realize who this gentleman was.

He was also in the theater business, Grauman explained to Arbuckle. In fact, he had a chain of big theaters across California and in New York. He was looking for a singer and had expressed an interest in a private audition. Roscoe sheepishly sang a short tune for the man, who was not immediately impressed.

Roscoe shrugged his shoulders and sang again, receiving applause from restaurant patrons, a grin from Grauman, and an approving nod from the stranger.

"When you're ready, you talk to me."

It did not take Roscoe long to figure out who the great man was—Alexander Pantages. Roscoe understood that when you signed on with Pantages, you signed on for a circuit, moving across the country from one Pantages theater to another, not working in one theater for one vaudeville show. The Pantages Circuit was considered one of the most popular and prestigious of the shows. In addition to the theaters, Pantages also owned several nightclubs and cafés which usually attracted wealthy and influential customers.

Roscoe knew that hooking up with such an organization would put him on the inside track to steady and well-paying work as a performer.

With encouragement from Grauman, Roscoe extended his chubby hand and sealed his future as a personal protégé of the great Alexander Pantages.

The troupe headed north of San Francisco to Washington and Oregon, then south to Arizona; small theaters, large houses, crowded dressing rooms, sizable suites, Arbuckle played them and stayed in them all. His salary was gradually increased from twenty-five dollars a week to fifty. Best of all, he no longer had to take tickets, clean dressing rooms, and sweep out the theaters between shows. He was a star, a featured performer on the Pantages Circuit, hobnobbing with everyone from great stage thespians to bit-part fill-in comics, dignitaries to stage-door fans who could not afford a ticket. For the first time in his life he had an actual following —fans who wrote letters, bought advance tickets, and even asked for autographs between shows.

In early September of 1906, Roscoe formed his own small group from the larger Pantages Circuit. The group returned to Portland to work in a small theater in a job obtained through a local booking agent. Arbuckle led the troupe as a featured singer, fill-in comedian, and road manager. The group was required to perform a matinee and two nightly shows every day but Sunday for two weeks; an exhausting schedule that left no time for backstage visitors.

After one of the weekday matinees two men pounded on Arbuckle's dressing-room door, and startled him out of a catnap. One of the men had an accent Roscoe had never heard before—not quite British. He soon discovered the gentleman with the odd speech was Australian, the manager of the Orpheum Theater down the street, who was moonlighting at a nearby nightclub, a club Roscoe called a "nickel and dime tavern for actors on the skids."

The pair introduced themselves as Pete Gerald (an American) and Leon Errol (an Australian who was soon to become a major stage star with the Ziegfeld Follies and later a movie comedian). Errol explained that they had teamed up several months back and had been experimenting with new burlesque comedy routines but could not get any decent bookings—the tavern was the only place that would have them.

37

Arbuckle appreciated their spunk but was taken aback by their boldness when they laid out the purpose of their visit. They believed they could get bookings if they had a singer and Arbuckle was just the man they needed. Before Arbuckle could usher the pair out the door, Errol went into a whirlwind diatribe about the benefits of an up-and-coming close-knit group over a ragtag troupe of performers working for a circuit. Roscoe had never seen such energy and such conviction from anyone before and was captivated.

"Well, where do you intend to get bookings if I join your group?"

"Boise, Idaho."

Roscoe laughed good and hard. He had tears in his eyes when he settled down. Anyone who could make him laugh that hard had to be good. But in addition to the laughter, Errol promised something that Arbuckle had secretly desired—to branch out from illustrated songs. He wanted to juggle, dance, and do comedy onstage. Roscoe agreed that such an opportunity was worth the cut in pay. When his two-week tour with Pantages ended, he found a train ticket to Boise tucked in an envelope under his door.

When they arrived there, the trio settled into a dank building that was more of a honkey-tonk than an actual theater. They were literally let loose to do anything and try everything before an audience eager for entertainment.

The audience was composed primarily of gold miners who were tired, a bit ornery, and looking for a good time. The group's pay was in gold dust, a bag dropped on the stage at the end of the show. The dust, called "poke," had to be turned in for real cash.

The first night in the dressing room, Errol caught Roscoe from behind and slapped black greasepaint all over his face, shades of his first job so many years ago. The unsuspecting Arbuckle was apprehensive about parading as a black man until Errol put his cards on his table.

"In this group you're Negro. Greek. Yiddish. Whatever fits the bill. You'll learn accents and you'll have to dress like a dame if we need one."

A woman? Arbuckle insisted he'd draw the line there.

Eventually the group grew to add a woman to the show—a

hefty lady who fancied herself somewhat of a diva but who was actually closer to an overweight madam. She was a soprano who waved scarves and belted out opera and love songs, and enjoyed her liquor and her men. One night she was nowhere to be found and Errol and Gerald were frantic. Arbuckle went on in her place and did some song and dance routines, filling time until the diva returned. No luck. The crowd wanted the woman. Then Errol and Gerald took their turn onstage while Roscoe turned the building upside down. Still no diva and the miners were pounding on the tables and banging the chairs on the floor. The crowd was turning ugly and the situation escalating out of control. Panicked, Errol started to improvise some routines that he hoped were bawdy enough to please the crowd.

During the act, the audience broke out into a raucous yell and a round of whistles. The diva had arrived! The band started into her opening song of "The Last Rose of Summer" and a very sensuous, hefty woman strolled out to center stage one step at a time. Errol exited the stage to let the long-awaited lady take over. But when the whistles turned to howls, Errol took a closer look.

The diva was Roscoe, dressed in the woman's dress complete with crumpled paper stuffed in the bodice, red wig, and "street corner" makeup. Roscoe quieted the men down and signaled the band to start once more. As a soft falsetto of "The Last Rose of Summer" echoed through the theater, Arbuckle did one of the funniest female impersonations that ever hit Boise. Some of the miners never suspected they were wolf-whistling at a man. When the real diva saw what was happening, she tore onstage, wobbling drunkenly and threatened to kill Arbuckle. She chased Roscoe across the tables, through the aisles, ducking Errol and the other performers who tried to catch her, determined to get the man who was ridiculing her on stage. The miners thought the chase was part of the act and it received a standing ovation. The bit was so popular that it became a draw in itself and one of the most popular acts in the show.

The group worked its way across the farm belt through Idaho and Montana and finally west toward California, hitting most of the small theaters and roadhouses along the way. The burlesque tour was quite different from the prestigious Pantages Circuit, which was vaudeville; burlesque was more daring, a bit bawdy, and quite a bit looser than the more structured and refined vaudeville. Roscoe gained a wealth of knowledge about comedy and the business from Leon Errol who was still the star and mainstay of the group.

After wrapping up a two-night stand just north of San Francisco, Errol sat Gerald and Roscoe down for a chat. He had been approached by a man representing Florenz Zeigfeld, who had seen the act and wanted to incorporate part of it into the world-famous Ziegfeld Follies in New York. Errol continued speaking before his friends could jump to the wrong conclusion. The offer was extended only to Errol, not the others, and Errol had agreed to accept it with his wife. Roscoe's "theatrical" family was shattered.

Roscoe continued on with Pete Gerald, taking over many of the parts Errol had created onstage. Errol was an agile comic with a keen sense of timing. Arbuckle had not yet developed his agility or his timing and was ill-suited for the role. Though Roscoe was a trouper he was no fool. He knew he was out of his league, forcing himself into a role that was tailored for another man. Gerald and Roscoe eventually split the act, Gerald teaming up with another comedian, Roscoe alone again with no place to go.

He wired Alexander Pantages to ask for his old job back with the West Coast troupe. Hoping that an eager Pantages would allow him to remain in California, he never expected the reply he received via telegram.

"Begin work immediately in Vancouver, British Columbia."

He packed his bag, bought a thick fur coat (which made him look like an immense grizzly bear) and headed for cooler climates and cold cash. The troupe took him through Alaska into subzero temperatures before it finally folded. Once again Roscoe was out of work. But this time he was determined to stay put in the state he liked the best, California, where he could thaw out and live cheaply, now a necessity because Arbuckle was flat broke.

Roscoe headed straight to San Francisco and in February of 1908 signed on with the Elwood Tabloid Musical

Company as a featured singer. Roscoe enjoyed the sophisticated San Francisco audiences who knew how to appreciate a good performance. He promised himself he would never return to the crude and vulgar crowds of down and dirty roadhouses. He blended well with the Elwood group and determined he was willing to stay as a member as long as they would have him. He was ready to dig in and settle down.

By summer the contract between the Elwood Company and the theater had expired and the leader of the group, Jack Elwood, was looking toward greener pastures in Southern California. He offered Roscoe a chance to stay on with a skeleton crew from the company and sing at a theater in Long Beach.

Roscoe was now twenty-one years old. He was to receive star billing at the Byde-A-While theater in the Virginia Hotel. He would earn a steady income, become a star in a closed circle for friends, and believed he had life figured out. No emotional attachments to anyone or any group and definitely no romantic entanglements. Or so he thought.

4

Roscoe packed his bags for what he hoped would be the last time. The hellish childhood of extreme poverty, brutal beatings, and drunkenness, the hard knocks of trial and error before audiences hungry for any excuse for an outburst, promised to be part of the past. Roscoe was heading to Long Beach to headline in a respectable hotel-theater with a nice, private room to call his own.

The train trip to Los Angeles was in itself uneventful. But a dramatic turn happened as Roscoe tried to board the streetcar to the theater in Long Beach.

He was just about to climb onto the car's steps when a petite, dark-haired young woman inadvertently lowered the boom.

"Excuse me, can I help you, miss?" Roscoe reached for the suitcase which was far too heavy and awkward for the young lady who was trying to board in front of him. As he grabbed the bag the girl snapped back.

"Don't touch my suitcase. I can handle it myself."

Roscoe turned red with embarrassment, not at the rejection but over the spectacle he believed he had made of himself in front of a dozen passengers also waiting to climb on board the streetcar to Long Beach.

The girl continued to battle with the bag on her own, vainly struggling to get it up the stairs and onto the streetcar, blocking passage for the mob now shoving behind her. Roscoe stood to the side and watched until the conductor descended the steps through the crowd to help. The girl turned to Arbuckle for one last remark.

"By the way, I don't like fat men and I don't like blonds!"

Roscoe looked away and hoped none of the others had heard the remark. He boarded the car in silence. Though he thought the young woman was extremely rude, he also found her captivating, unlike anyone he had ever met before. He had to get to know her!

Arbuckle stood at the back of the car for a while, then mustered up the courage to walk to her seat. She was staring out the window, a dogeared hardcover book barely resting in her lap.

"Um, I guess that book is no good, huh?"

He startled the girl, who dropped the book on the floor. They both reached for it at the same time.

"Do you always sneak up on women like that?"

"I'm sorry, I didn't mean to scare you . . . "

"Stop apologizing! Everyone's looking at you."

Roscoe sat down in the seat across from her and started a conversation. As it turned out, the girl was also a stage performer who, coincidentally, was also headed to Long Beach to appear at the Byde-A-While. They were both under contract to the Elwood Company and would be performing together.

"I'm Minta Durfee. I'm a professional actress. I just finished a tour with the Morosco Stock Company. I don't believe I know your name."

"Roscoe Arbuckle. I'm a singer and dancer."

The young woman who had been so cold at the beginning of the ride had now warmed. For Roscoe, this was no Pansy Jones infatuation—this was the real thing, love at first sight. Though Minta kept up a good front, she sensed she was also becoming attracted to the chubby fellow sitting near her.

Minta remembered being struck by how incredibly neat Roscoe was—a brand-new suit, a bow tie, a bowler derby, shined shoes. He smelled of soap and his hair was smooth and shiny. Minta had just finished her first tour away from home, and though she was only eighteen years old and fresh out of the Morosco chorus line, she felt very grown-up and mature. She was a working girl with no time for schoolgirl flirtations and small talk. She also thought she was very progressive in letting a man know she was neither frail nor a lady to be trifled with.*

On opening night Minta realized what a treasure she'd stumbled into on board that streetcar. As she stood in the stage wings with the other chorus girls, a beautiful, rich tenor voice echoed through the theater. The audience was unusually quiet, entranced with the singer performing before it. As Roscoe sang the last chorus he turned to Minta and directed the lyrics to her.

"I love you as I loved you . . . when you were sweet sixteen."

It was one of the few times in Minta's life that she was speechless. As Roscoe left the stage to thunderous applause, Minta and the other chorus girls took over. When she passed Roscoe offstage she looked away and refused to make eye contact. She was caught completely defenseless, afraid her interest in the "boy singer" was obvious.

When Roscoe went on the second time the audience howled and stomped and cheered, quite a different reaction from the opening number. This time their favorite "fat boy" (as he was known by word of mouth) was doing Irish jigs, affecting a German accent, and singing raucous songs. Once again he held the crowd in his hands.

After the show Roscoe, still a loner, walked out to a bench on the beach to relax. Minta saw him sitting quietly and walked up to him from behind, startling him. Roscoe expected another reprimand about the incident on the streetcar, but instead he received a much more gentle woman who looked at him with much softer eyes.

Minta told Arbuckle how impressed she was with his voice; it was something she had never heard coming from a man, let alone such a big man. Then she abruptly switched gears

* There are at least five conflicting versions of how Roscoe met the woman who was to become his first wife, ranging from a chance meeting on the beach, to Arbuckle's seeing Minta in the Elwood show and asking for date, to a version similar to the one mentioned above except the streetcar was a train out to Long Beach from San Francisco. The version related here was the one Minta offered shortly before her death and appears the most plausible.

and scolded Roscoe for wasting his talent in small touring companies when he should be making records or singing with opera companies or in New York shows.

Roscoe did not know what to say. Was she encouraging him or was she angry with him? He never could understand Minta's intentions and often misunderstood her purpose because of her sharp tongue and iron-willed personality. It was a dilemma that would continue to threaten the budding romance and eventually shatter their subsequent fragile marriage.

The stroll to the beach after the last show became a nightly routine for Roscoe and Minta. Usually Minta did most of the talking, about her childhood in Los Angeles and her Baptist upbringing, how the family would go to the theater each weekend to see the vaudeville matinees, how she eventually worked her way into the chorus. She also peppered the conversation with ideas to push Roscoe into bigger and bigger shows. Roscoe rarely spoke. He was usually exhausted from the show and thinking about ways to better his performance. But one evening Roscoe interrupted Minta in midsentence.

"How about you and me doing a show together . . . as a team?"

"You know I don't sing that well."

"I'll carry it. You join in. The audience will love it. Two sweethearts singing to each other on stage."

It was the first mention of "sweethearts" from Roscoe, a subject that embarrassed him to no end. It was apparent the word caught in his throat as he looked at Minta for her reaction to both the offer of performing together and the idea that they were a couple.

"Why not? I'll try it if you think it will work."

"I've already set it up with Mr. Elwood. He's all for it."

Roscoe wasted no time. That same evening the "fat boy" and the "chorus girl" stood side by side on stage and sang "Let Me Call You Sweetheart," held hands, and courted before a full house. It was Roscoe's way of warming Minta up to the big question—marriage. In Roscoe's mind, if Minta was going to turn him down, he would know it from her reaction to the song. They barely knew one another but Roscoe had already made up his mind and was gingerly finding ways to approach an awkward situation. Minta refused to play the game and avoided an answer. She believed if a man was to ask for a woman's hand in marriage, he had better be direct about it.

The two continued performing their specialty number as well as their previous solo routines, Roscoe as a specialty singer, Minta as the soubrette, until the show folded at the end of July. Because the troupe was assembled specifically for the run at the Byde-A-While, there were no future touring plans. Mr. Elwood released the players.

Minta planned to head to San Francisco where there was the possibility of work with the Kolb and Dill vaudeville circuit, a highly successful company at the time. Roscoe had no plans except to keep Minta in Los Angeles as his wife. Their last night together they walked down to the beach. Minta remembered that night as frightening, confusing, and magical.

Roscoe popped the question.

"Are you going to marry me or not? Yes or no!"

"I just don't know."

Roscoe scooped Minta in his arms and playfully threatened to toss her in the ocean if she turned him down—the kidding was Roscoe's way of working out his embarrassment.

"Well? I love you. I want to marry you."

"I love you, too. Now put me down!"

"You haven't answered my question."

"Of course I will marry you."

On August 6, 1908, the Byde-A-While theater was transformed into a quaint country chapel filled with flowers, fans, and friends.* The ceremony began with Roscoe stepping out from behind the stage curtain to greet everyone and then sing a love song. But the reception from the audience upon seeing Roscoe was so overwhelming that it was five or ten minutes before the applause quieted enough for him to begin. A twelve-piece orchestra accompanied Arbuckle in a chorus of "An Old Sweetheart of Mine." Minta's father gave the bride away in a romantic, turn-of-

* Previous accounts gave August 5 as the date of the wedding, but the official document in the Los Angeles County Hall of Records gives the date as the sixth.

the-century ceremony presided over by the Reverend P.J. O'Reilly.

The newlyweds received numerous gifts, from silver, china, and cut glass to lace and linens, which were put on display in the window of the Buffum's department store in Long Beach. A heart-shaped sign below the display announced the trove as some of the presents of "local stage stars Roscoe C. Arbuckle and Arminta E. Durfee, married at the Byde-A-While Theater." The reception was held in the Virginia Hotel. It was a romantic end to an unusual five-month courtship in which Roscoe chased, cajoled, and finally convinced the girl he loved to marry him. It was also a seemingly ideal beginning to a marriage that would take the couple to the summit of Hollywood fame and fortune and plummet the pair into the depths of depression and anguish.

Their honeymoon offered a strong indication of Roscoe's embarrassment about sex and his respect for women. During the reception some of the men and women teased the newlyweds about "the wedding night" and joked about Roscoe's weight against Minta's small body. There were also insinuations about other matters even more personal. Though Minta ignored the remarks as crude party jokes, Roscoe was humiliated. He never said a word about the joking until after the reception when he was alone with Minta in the hotel suite.

Roscoe stepped out of the bathroom wearing a tan Chinese-style pajama outfit, very well-tailored and very proper. Minta had previously changed into a frilly, white chiffon nightgown and robe, but had changed once more into a short pink gown while Roscoe was in the bathroom. Roscoe questioned her actions and Minta explained the pink nightgown was better for lovemaking. Roscoe sat on the edge of the bed and withdrew into frozen silence.

"Minty." Roscoe had given Minta the nickname during their courtship and he remained the only person allowed to address Minta by that name. "I can't."

Roscoe told his new bride that the people at the reception said they would know that he and Minta had made love and they would surely tease him about it the next morning. He said that if it was true, that they could tell, he would not be able to face them.

He kissed Minta on the cheek and Minta held his hand.

That night the newlyweds slept together in the same bed, side by side, hand in hand. It was more than a week before Roscoe felt comfortable enough to formally consummate the marriage.

Very few couples, except for the very rich, ever took honeymoon vacations in the early part of the century. Very few men even took time off from work after the wedding. Honeymoon vacations did not become possible for the working class until well into the 1920s, and then became a luxury once again during the Great Depression. The Arbuckles were typical of the average couple in this regard; their "honeymoon" was spent working on the road.

Roscoe had been earning fifty dollars a week as the lead singer with the Elwood Company, Minta between fifteen and twenty dollars. After room and board and what he called "walkin' around money," Arbuckle managed to pocket about one third of his salary and had a small nest egg at the end of the five-month engagement at the Byde-A-While. Minta saved virtually nothing. The Arbuckles needed to get back to work and hooked up with a new stock company that had just formed in San Bernardino, at that time a very rural desert town. Once again, Roscoe performed as a singer, dancer, and comic, Minta as Roscoe's partner and soubrette, eventually working her way up as solo performer.

Everything appeared to be going well for the newlyweds: a new show, a steady income with two performers apparently headed for stardom, and love. That all threatened to come to an abrupt end in October. Only three months into the marriage Roscoe and Minta faced their first serious crisis.

Minta contracted pleurisy during the first month of the run in San Bernardino and went back home to her family in Los Angeles. Roscoe and Minta had received an offer to travel throughout the Northwest with another stock company, which offered a considerable raise in pay for the couple, but over his wife's objections, Roscoe turned the offer down without explanation. During Minta's convalescence, Arbuckle announced they would be traveling instead to Bisbee, Arizona, to tour with Walter Reed.

Minta was dumbfounded. She refused to travel to a town that offered nothing more than dust, snakes, spiders, and cowboys. She also refused to believe her husband would make such plans without consulting his wife. During their first argument as a married couple Minta learned the truth. Roscoe had already agreed to tour with Reed and had signed a contract while he was still in Long Beach with the Elwood Company. It was after their marriage that he also worked the deal to get Minta into the show. He felt obligated to honor the contract and never suspected Minta would not want to tour with him; therefore he had never mentioned it.

Having been alone since he was twelve, Roscoe was used to traveling on his own and making his own way. It was obviously going to take some time before he became accustomed to sharing his life with another person. His secrecy continued to be a sore point in their marriage.

Hurt at the thought that Roscoe had not been entirely honest with her, and angered at what she believed was "second class" treatment by her husband, Minta refused to go, and tested Roscoe to see if he would travel without her. As he left for the train to Arizona, Minta questioned whether she had made a serious mistake in marrying Roscoe Arbuckle, who, she believed, espoused love with his words but through his actions showed he cared only for himself.

Minta's mother, Flora, insisted her daughter remain by her husband's side, no matter what the circumstances. She scolded her daughter and told her that they would never work out their problems if they were not together to talk them out. Minta initially objected out of stubbornness and claimed it would appear as if Roscoe was right and she was chasing after him. But she gave in to her mother's pressure, and when she was well enough, boarded the train.

Bisbee was exactly what Minta expected—and worse. As she stepped off the train she was "greeted" by the local contingent of prostitutes who regularly waited at the station to check out potential customers and new "stock" for their stable.

Roscoe shoved his way through the mob and grabbed Minta's arm. He was smiling the widest smile Minta had ever seen. He was clearly enthralled to see his new bride and she was overjoyed to be in her husband's arms once again. But the enthusiasm was shortlived.

"I have a room for us at a boardinghouse. It's all set."

"A boardinghouse?"

"The hotel is too expensive. You wouldn't like it anyway."

The show was a great success, with a packed house every night. But in the short time Roscoe had been separated from Minta, alone in the Arizona mining town with Reed and the troupe, he seemed to have changed. Minta noticed exaggerated mood swings—teetering from jovial husband to quick-tempered adversary after several drinks of whiskey. At first she put it down to the dust, mosquitoes, and cowboy mentality of the town where men were required to out-drink one another to show their "manliness." But then something else became all too apparent—Roscoe drank excessively almost every night. The two worst traits of his father were now beginning to emerge in Roscoe—drunkenness and a violent temper.

Roscoe had gotten his first taste of the demon that destroyed his father and touched off the violent childhood beatings . . . and apparently had become addicted. Because Roscoe had been close-mouthed about his brutal childhood, Minta had yet to understand and realize the potential impact of alcohol on her husband. Though she was frightened by his alcohol-induced mood changes, Minta remained silent to avoid an argument, hoping the fun-filled sober times would outweigh the drunken rages. Minta was witnessing the beginning of a Jekyll and Hyde personality—a sweet, caring sensitive husband turned into a foul-tempered man, but she did not yet have an inkling of the agony that awaited both her and her husband because of alcohol, its effects, and the people who flourished in its vicinity.

5

In many ways Minta blamed herself for the widening emotional gap between her and her husband; she had been sick in bed and away from Roscoe for nearly five months, almost the same length of time as their courtship. As a married couple they had only been together a short while before Roscoe headed to Bisbee. There were many times while she was home alone in bed in Los Angeles that she thought the entire affair with Roscoe at the Byde-A-While had been a dream. It was real for such a short time, then it vanished.

"Roscoe was the most gentle man I had ever known. Everyone loved him, such a dear soul. When he sang onstage it was just as if he reached into the heart of every man and woman in that audience. He just had this kind way about him. And he was always very funny to strangers and audiences. Around me he was not the clown that he was on stage. He was very sensitive. Until he started drinking. Then he changed. He became dour and would pick fights with me —argue about anything—and storm out. A changed man. Everyone drank, so no one really thought much about it in those days."

Minta also suspected Roscoe's withdrawal from her might have been triggered by a personal tragedy.

"Several months after we were in Bisbee I suffered a miscarriage. It was awful. Roscoe was so disappointed. He never talked about it to anyone but somehow he thought it was his fault. He always thought that when bad things happened it was his fault. I believe his father made him feel that way from babyhood on and he never shook it."

After the miscarriage Roscoe became very aloof with Minta and focused his energies on his routines. He was nothing but drive and energy onstage, and quiet and somewhat sullen at home. Their sex life also withered after the miscarriage. Roscoe rarely made love to Minta. More often they would simply lie side by side, Minta curled in Roscoe's arms with no more physical affection than a kiss and a hug. Minta sensed she was losing her husband, and as for the marriage itself, it never seemed to get back on track after the initial parting when Roscoe left for Bisbee; in retrospect Minta admitted leaving her husband alone at that early, critical stage in their marriage was clearly a mistake. The union seemed doomed from the outset though they clearly loved one another, yet neither Roscoe nor Minta would face the prospect of failure. Especially Roscoe, who came from a broken home and still expected rejection with each emotional outreach.

The Arbuckle-Reed troupe traveled on to Tombstone, Arizona; still a real Wild West town, then to El Paso, Texas, where they stayed in a rooming house. An outrageously funny accident with a pullout Murphy bed happened while they were in El Paso, and it later became a popular sight gag in Arbuckle's silent comedies.

Exhausted from the trip to El Paso, Arbuckle teased Minta that he was going to race her to flop into bed the second they got to the rooming house. He pulled the bed down and Minta heard a loud "thwack"! When Roscoe hurled all his 275 pounds onto the bed, his bulk crammed the mattress through the bed boards and somehow wedged his head between the edge of the mattress and the headboard. With his hips and buttocks pinned in the bed frame, and his head under the headboard, he was stuck. Minta was too small and too weak from laughing to pull him out. Even in his pretzeled position Roscoe saw the silliness of his predicament and joined in the laughter, shaking the bed and wedging himself further between the boards. The commotion was so loud that it drew a good-sized crowd—miners, fellow performers, and other guests. As they entered the room, their view was of a gargantuan pair of pants sticking out of a bed, flailing madly in the air. Pretty soon the room was crammed with people making jokes and roaring at the sight—the loudest laughter of all coming from Arbuckle. Several of the miners helped free Roscoe from the bed and it became a running joke on the tour.

While in El Paso, the Arbuckle troupe found itself smack in the middle of the Mexican Revolution, in hand to hand "combat" with Pancho Villa, the most famous revolutionary/bandit south of the border.

One hot summer afternoon the troupe took the day off for a picnic on the banks of the Rio Grande. Suddenly, across the river, a horde of rifle-brandishing Uralees lined the banks, with their sights clearly set on their gringo targets. Cool-headed Roscoe tried to hail them over to join the picnic, but no soap; the army stood its guard.

"Well, if the fight won't come to us, I guess we'll have to go to the fight!"

With that, Roscoe loaded bunches of bananas and apples under one arm, and with slingshot accuracy fired away—a direct hit caught one fighter square in the stomach. The Uralees howled and Roscoe got into the spirit of the game, hurling the fruit at the men.

Suddenly, the soldiers stopped laughing and came to attention. A dignified man rode to the bank and dismounted, yelling something in Spanish. He turned to the gringos across the river.

"Who are you, sir?"

"Arbuckle. Roscoe Arbuckle. And you, sir?"

"Pancho Villa."

The two chatted and struggled to communicate in each other's language as if they were old comrades. During the conversation either Villa or Roscoe must have commented on the food throwing because moments later Roscoe picked up a fruit pie and flung it at Villa, who caught it and tossed it back in somewhat sorrier shape than it had originally been. The two laughed uproariously and parted with mutual respect.

There are several footnotes to the story. Some in Hollywood have claimed that the food fight between Roscoe and Villa's men was the inspiration for the infamous food war in the battle scene from the Marx Brothers' movie *Duck Soup*, in which the Marx Brothers hurled fruits and vegetables from their bunker onto the battlefield.

Arbuckle himself claimed the food fight was the first time that pie throwing was done in public. Though many comedians have tried to claim the gag as their own, Arbuckle is credited with "inventing" pie throwing in pictures because he initially introduced the gag on the Sennett lot, and it was used on film there for the first time. Arbuckle even said his scene with Villa was the inspiration for his movie gag. The routine became a mainstay for Sennett and scores of other comedians who adopted it and perfected it.

By an odd coincidence, Roscoe and Villa later would switch roles in life; Roscoe would become an outlaw after his involvement with the Rappé case; Villa would try his hand at the movies. In 1914, five years after the pie-throwing incident at the Rio Grande, the Mutual Film Company (which later hired Charlie Chaplin) offered Villa a juicy contract to star in a film about the Mexican Revolution. But the film was so bogged down by Villa's star-struck antics and mugging that it never really got off the ground, ending any film aspirations that the outlaw may have had.

A long, rugged, and unusual road trip over, Roscoe and Minta returned to Los Angeles, which thrilled Minta but left Roscoe with some serious doubts about his future. He now had a name (the Fat Boy) and a reputation, he earned fifty dollars a week when he found work, and picked up jobs in local theaters doing vaudeville sketches with Minta as well as performing solo. But Roscoe was tired. He was twenty-two-years old and had been hustling jobs for more than fifteen years.

By 1909 Los Angeles was beginning to attract attention as a prime location to shoot movies. The East Coast and Midwest winters and unpredictable summers had become a hindrance to some companies, which were discovering the wonders of outdoor (location) shooting over the confines of one-room, three-walled indoor stages. Scores of local real-estate agents bombarded the stage and movie trade newspapers with enticing ads extolling the virtues of Southern California's warm and accommodating temperatures and predictable climate.

A handful of East Coast movie corporations sent small

companies west to explore the fantastic claims espoused by the Los Angeles publicity mills. All found the claims of sunshine and beautiful scenery true. The desert was a short driving distance, the mountains had snow in winter and were a day's trip away, citrus groves and farms were around the corner. Soon companies connected with Selig (a Chicago-based company), Biograph, Kessel and Bauman, Centaur, and Nestor established permanent West Coast operations for their one-reel dramas and comedies. It was the first of these companies, Selig, that initially lured Roscoe Arbuckle to film.

Selig built its studio at 1845 Allesandro Street in an area called Edendale, now the southeastern part of Glendale near Echo Park, an area that also sprouted the Bison Studios of Kessel and Bauman (later to become the Mack Sennett/Keystone Studios). The company was formally known as Selig Polyscope Company and a man named Francis Boggs had been sent by Selig to work his way west with a touring company to crank out one-reelers, usually dramas, along the way.

If stage actors and performers were considered lowlifes by those outside the business, movie actors (called players in the early days of film) were held in even less regard, considered vermin by almost everyone, even stage actors. In fact, most rooming houses in Los Angeles posted large notices over their vacancy or rooms-for-rent signs: NO ACTORS OR DOGS ALLOWED. Although it was difficult to find a paying job in legitimate theater or vaudeville and burlesque, few performers would admit to considering a job as a film player, which usually offered five dollars a day, considered fair wages. When performers did accept film work they usually did it on the sly. To act in film was to admit failure as a stage performer. Because there was no screen credit given, and the names of the actors were not released by mutual consent (to keep the "stars" in line by the movie companies and to keep the actors' misfortune at accepting such work a secret), it was possible to moonlight and have no one the wiser.

In June of 1909, Arbuckle was out of work. With only odd jobs since the El Paso tour, he needed money to support himself and his wife. When he heard Selig was looking for extras for its one-reelers, he applied. He earned five dollars for his appearance in *Ben's Kid*, a one-reeler, and then in *Mrs. Jones' Birthday*, a half-reel filler that was released with another short. (He worked for Selig sporadically until 1913, including one on-screen appearance dressed as a woman, when he reportedly moved to the Nestor Studios for one month before finally landing a permanent movie job with Keystone.) Like so many other things that cropped up in their marriage, Roscoe never told Minta about his early film work. In fact, it was not until after Roscoe's death decades later that she even learned her husband had worked at Selig and Nestor.

Eventually Roscoe and Minta hooked up with the Ferris Hartman Company, which was based in San Francisco, a town that was becoming a familiar stomping ground to the 275-pound comedian. He jumped at the chance to get out of the Los Angeles dust bowl, away from film work and back on the road. The company was young, and Roscoe, who had a big name on stage, would be the star attraction again as a singer and dancer. They opened to a very receptive audience at the Grand Opera House and then headed east to Chicago. A big mistake.

The musical blew into the Windy City with a trunk filled with outstanding reviews, sold-out performances, and a cast eager to repeat its success. But the show was not even received coolly; the audience thinned between breaks and those who remained until the end apparently did so only to get their money's worth. No one in the cast understood the reason for the abrupt change from the San Francisco audience to the Chicago audience, but it was enough to force the show to fold after two performances. Broke again, Roscoe and Minta worked a series of one-night stands (known as pickups in vaudeville circles) to pay their way back to Los Angeles, where they moved in with Minta's family until they hooked up with another company.

One would imagine that after life on the road as a married couple, moving in with the wife's parents would be nothing short of dreadful, but it was not. In fact, the move may have helped put the marriage back on its unsteady feet. The Durfees adored Roscoe who never failed to make them laugh or charm them as a doting son-in-law.

Even though Roscoe was hovering near the six-foot mark and tipping the scales at close to three hundred pounds, he was graceful and agile and appeared more like a playful cherub fluttering around the house than a big man stomping through the living room. He sang for the Durfees, took Minta out dancing, and regained the spark and zest that had slipped away somewhere in Bisbee, Arizona. He also slowed his drinking down to an occasional glass of beer or whiskey. For Minta, life was looking good again and she cast off her doubts about her marriage. But once more, that happiness was short-lived.

Roscoe never failed to make a good impression. He was impeccably clean and neat, well-dressed, polite, and always made a joke or witty remark. He was a charmer. So much so that often the Durfees took Roscoe's side in an argument with Minta. Minta would have preferred they remain out of the quarrel completely. After several months the interference was so constant that Minta contacted Ferris Hartman to find work. The timing was right on the money.

Hartman was assembling a troupe to tour the Orient with a production of *The Mikado*. It was a chance to see the world and get paid handsomely to do it!

After one very successful season in Honolulu, the group set sail for the Far East. Everyone in the show was extremely apprehensive; they were Americans playing Orientals, in a show satirizing the Orient, and doing it all in the Orient. They believed they had pushed their luck in Hawaii; it was not yet an American state and some of its ethnic groups were not particularly Americanized. They expected to get booed off the stage in China—and more than booed if they were unlucky. Nevertheless, forty-three nervous Americans packed their bags and costumes and waved Hawaii good-bye.

The first stop was in Tientsin, China. They played it safe and performed before American oil-company executives and their friends. The show went smoothly and a select group (including the Arbuckles) staged a command performance for the Dowager Empress, who enjoyed the show.

The Chinese people had never seen anything like the Hartman troupe before—Americans doing superb impersonations of Orientals and spicing up the show with some

American songs and dances for an encore. The reception was a significant ego boost for the company whose spirits had bottomed out in Chicago. The elation quickly took a downturn for Roscoe and Minta when an old problem returned—Roscoe's drinking.

While in China Roscoe went out with "the boys," cruising local night spots without Minta, who was sick once again. It was also considered improper there for women to enter places where liquor was served. As Roscoe drank he became outgoing and the life of the party. When he returned to the hotel he was belligerent toward Minta, and violent arguments often followed a night on the town.

The group had been in the Orient about a year and a half when Roscoe turned on his wife, accusing her of destroying his life by forcing him to leave the United States and making him work for what he called "slave wages."

"He had been drinking heavily. He was angry and shouting about how miserable his life was and blaming it all on me. He missed America and said that it was my fault we signed on with the tour, that he was happy living in Los Angeles until I insisted we travel with Hartman. I couldn't figure out why he was so angry about everything because, as far as I knew, he hadn't been working in Los Angeles. He never told me he picked up work in movies. Then he finally told me what bothered him. It was money."

In a drunken rage, Roscoe accused Minta of corralling him into a small contract in which he believed he was not being fairly compensated for the amount of work required of him. In many ways Roscoe was correct—he felt he was carrying the whole show and he was not being paid much more than the other members of the cast.

When Minta appealed to Hartman for a raise, Hartman agreed but Arbuckle refused to back down. He was still dour with Minta, and the party boy with everyone else.

The troupe worked its way through Hong Kong and the Philippines, wrapping up in Manila. Roscoe pushed himself and continued to work hard with the show and then stay out all hours of the night drinking with the male members of the crew.

Several days after they arrived in Manila, Roscoe's

carousing caught up with him. He contracted a viral throat infection and lost his voice. He was unable to go on and he had no understudy. The show was forced to fold for three weeks until he recuperated. No show, no pay for the rest of the crew, though Hartman agreed to pay Roscoe's salary. When the cast found out that Roscoe had, in effect, brought about his own illness, and that he continued to draw a salary, he was persona non grata. The crew not only resented him but ostracized him for the remainder of the tour.

He was anxious to get back to California, mainly to San Francisco, where he had worked so many times before and felt quite comfortable. Roscoe believed he could take a much needed vacation and get his marriage back on track. Minta looked toward Los Angeles and her family. They struck a compromise and sailed from the Philippines to northern California, did some sightseeing, and took a relaxing train ride back south.

When the Arbuckles stepped off the train in downtown Los Angeles the entire Durfee clan was on hand to greet them. They were bombarded with questions about their tour, details about the infamous "houses of ill repute" in China, the exotic food in the Philippines, and the souvenirs in Hong Kong. Roscoe had never seen such warmth, caring, and excitement from a family, certainly not from his family, and he was deeply moved. He was overwhelmed and remained silent the entire streetcar trip home.

The last leg of the tour left Roscoe bitter about vaudeville. The troupe had turned on him and blamed him for the three weeks' salary cut. Although this was somewhat justified, the hostility took a hefty toll on Arbuckle, who was accustomed to receiving adoration and affection from cast members and audiences. When he settled back into the Durfee home he completely withdrew.

Minta landed a bit part in the chorus of a local theater; the work was sporadic and the wages were low, only three to five dollars a day, barely enough to allow the married couple to believe they were paying their way and not living off Minta's parents.

If there was any resentment from the Durfees it was never expressed, but after several months of self-imposed hiatus,

Arbuckle mustered the enthusiasm to pursue a job. Unfortunately, none of the local theaters was hiring singers and there were no vaudeville or burlesque troupes in town with openings. He once again turned to film.

It had been nearly three years since his last clandestine work in moving pictures, work Arbuckle considered humiliating and loathsome. But now, either because of his dire financial straits or because public opinion of the mushrooming film industry was changing, Roscoe took a second look at film acting. He heard that the Selig Polyscope Company was looking for a female player. Somewhat in jest and probably still hoping that he would not be recognized "just in case", Arbuckle donned his stage makeup and dress and arrived in the studio in full female regalia. He got the part and *Alas! Poor Yorick* is believed to be Arbuckle's first on-screen appearance as a woman, a routine he would soon adopt as one of his on-screen trademarks.

Around the same time, spring of 1913, Arbuckle also picked up work with Al Christie at the Nestor Studios and the Universal Film Manufacturing Company in Hollywood. He was still secretive with Minta about his initial involvement with film, but found the process fascinating. He was intrigued by the whirring of the hand-cranked camera, the sets and lights, the unusually dark makeup, and the exaggerated pantomime. He could not shake the experience from his mind. He missed the response of a live audience, but the process of actually recording a story on film made stage work trite. He became obsessed with learning more about moving pictures, from directing to the mechanical intricacies of the camera.

One afternoon, he stepped onto a streetcar that set him on the fast track to international fame and wealth beyond his imagination. Impeccably dressed as always from his straw hat to his white shoes, Roscoe sat next to an unusual-looking man who told him that there was a "shindig" going on over on Effie Street, near Allesandro in Edendale. Roscoe was familiar with the area from his stint at Selig and rode to the end of the line to check out the commotion. He stepped off the car and into his future with the Keystone Studios.

6

There are countless versions of how Roscoe met Mack Sennett, some clearly publicists' fantasies, others related with conviction by those who knew Roscoe, all of them different. One popular story has no basis in fact but took on tremendous credence when reported in newspapers as fact during Arbuckle's later manslaughter trial.

According to the story, Arbuckle had been working as a plumber's apprentice in a shop owned by A.G. Rushlight, the Mayor of Portland, Oregon. In an extensive newspaper interview, Rushlight claimed there were many workers in the shop and Arbuckle was "just one of the boys, singled out," he said, "only by his ridiculous roly-poly appearance." The young man was called "Fatty" by the group and he was put to work in the basement with the other "beginners."

Rushlight claims "Fatty" did not like to work and found it more fun to climb up the basement stairs, stick his head out a window, and make faces at people passing by. He said he remembered how "Fatty" used to run frantically down the stairs when he heard Rushlight coming. Rushlight stated the fat boy decided the work was "too fatiguing" and quit when he ran into a man named Larry Keating at the Lyle Theater in Portland. Rushlight said this was Arbuckle's first stage work (in 1913). The interview continued with Keating calling Arbuckle "utterly hopeless." He said he only took him on as a performer because of his atrocious appearance. But eventually Arbuckle caught on and the upper society of Portland threw what the interviewer called a beef party, and convinced

Arbuckle that he belonged in movies in California. During the farewell party the crowd was so certain "Fatty" would become a star that they ripped off his shirt as a souvenir. Keating claimed Arbuckle left for California with no shirt and only twenty cents in his pocket.

This story is outrageous, especially in light of the fact that Roscoe had already toured the world in vaudeville and nearly worked himself to death by 1913, but important here only because it ties in with one of two stories Sennett liked to tell about how he discovered "Fatty" Arbuckle. Sennett said he was in his office and this fat plumber's assistant started hammering away under his sink. Sennett said he had been searching for a "good, fat boy to round out his players" and asked Arbuckle if he could do somersaults. He said Arbuckle did a flip, a somersault, and a perfect pratfall and landed a job.

Sennett also spun another yarn about Arbuckle. In his autobiography, *King of Comedy*, Sennett wrote that Arbuckle walked up to him and flippantly introduced himself. "Name's Arbuckle . . . Roscoe Arbuckle. Call me Fatty. I'm a funny man and an acrobat. Bet I could do good in pictures. Watcha think?"

This story is also suspicious because Arbuckle was far too shy to pull off such a bold move as an introduction to anyone, let alone the head of a studio. He also detested the nickname "Fatty" when he was called that as a boy, so he would not, and never did, introduce himself as such to anyone.

Minta offered another version. She believed Roscoe got off the trolley car at Effie Street and merely walked through the gates of the Keystone lot. He wandered around carrying his portfolio of photographs and press clippings, hoping to find someone in a position to hire comedians. He found everyone too busy to talk until a gray-haired, rumpled man scurried by with a mouthful of tobacco. As he spit out the juice, he shouted at Arbuckle, "Be here tomorrow at eight o'clock," and raced back inside his office.

Roscoe laughed off the man as a stock player playing a joke. He wandered around most of the afternoon without success. He was about to leave the lot when the same gray-haired man shot out of an office. "Be here at eight tomorrow. You might be a star someday." The gray-haired man was Mack Sennett and Roscoe arrived at eight the next day for work. The rest, Minta said, is history.

Another version is probably closer to the truth. It was told by several people who claim they heard it from Roscoe himself. It picks up with Roscoe on the streetcar, hearing about the "shindig" on Effie Street. (Minta, Roscoe, and others often referred to Keystone as being on Effie Street. Effie Street was actually the streetcar stop nearest the lot, which was located on Allesandro Street.) The fellow who was sitting next to Roscoe on that streetcar was Fred Mace, a comedian with Sennett's Keystone stock company. Mace gave Roscoe an earful about Keystone—a lot run by a madman named Mack Sennett who paid lunatics good money to run wild in front of cameras. Mace waved his arms, jumped in and out of his seat, acted out gags and routines the group had done for its one-reelers. Roscoe initially had no intention of looking for a job in movies, especially after his last stint at Nestor. But by the time he arrived at Effie Street, Roscoe wanted in. It sounded like a great way to have fun and get paid for it; the first time in his life he had ever associated work with fun.

Mace escorted Roscoe onto the lot and introduced him to Mabel Normand, who was not only Sennett's leading lady but his girlfriend as well. Mabel was the only one allowed the privilege of entering Sennett's office unannounced. In spite of Mabel's introduction, Sennett initially turned Roscoe down. He thought Roscoe's appearance was too polished. (Arbuckle was dressed in a crisp white suit, straw hat, and white shoes and smelled of soap and cologne. At best Sennett smelled of sweat, his hair was never combed and rarely cut, and his shirts were usually tobacco-stained. Many suspect Roscoe's appearance intimidated Sennett, who believed anyone so well-groomed could not be funny.) But Mabel was persistent and eventually convinced the boss of this young fat boy's potential. Roscoe was formally listed as a stock player with Keystone on April 16, 1913. He was to report directly to Mack Sennett for his instructions.

Mack Sennett began his film career as a stock actor in New

York with D.W. Griffith's Biograph Company. In her auto-biography, *When the Movies Were Young*, Griffith's wife Linda Arvidson remembered Sennett as a loner who rarely blended with the others in the company. He was usually argumentative and not the least bit funny. He played straight dramatic roles and there was no sign of the comic genius who seemed to be hidden just below the surface. On location, when the cast relaxed with fishing or camping, Sennett usually went off by himself and read.

Arvidson also recalled Sennett's behavior as erratic—calm one minute and angry and hostile the next. She suspected a drug problem, possibly cocaine, which had been working its way into the lower-class and gangster element shortly after the turn of the century, but she did not elaborate. Sennett was not liked by the Griffith company because of his aloof-ness and tendency to complain about working conditions, which were usually abhorrent. When he finally left the company in the summer of 1912, Arvidson said Griffith and the crew wished him no ill, but were not sorry to see him go.

Sennett, it seemed, had a penchant for comedy. The books he had been reading instead of socializing with the Griffith company were humorous short stories, comic plays, and collections of articles on directing comedies for the stage. He was not aloof, but absorbed. He never blended with the seriousness of the Griffith company because most suggestions for spicing up the dramas with humor were turned down. Sennett was planning his future, whether he realized it at the time or not.

Even as head of his own studio, Sennett was considered an oddity—he had dead aim when spitting tobacco juice, he wore ill-fitting clothes, he donned a straw hat with a cutout brim (he believed the sunshine was a good way to prevent baldness), and in his ramshackle Keystone office, he installed a massive Turkish bath, which he considered the mark of a wealthy man. His office was located on the upper floor of a tower-type building to allow him a bird's-eye view of the entire lot and company—to, as he put it, "keep close watch so the kids won't goof off." Sennett was highly suspicious of every employee on the lot, convinced everyone was out to cheat him by drawing a salary without working for it.

He ate green onions and radishes for breakfast and chugged shots of whiskey all day (for his health, he claimed). He was the last person one would pick out of a crowd as the head of a studio, but he knew what was funny. And that was the key to his success.

When he was not watching his players from his office, he spent hours watching the dailies in the projection room. Sennett was his best audience and his worst critic. When something struck him as funny, he laughed harder and louder than anyone on the lot, which usually brought out even wilder performances from his stars. If he failed to laugh at a scene, it was abruptly cut and either discarded altogether or reworked. His authority was never questioned and he rarely missed the mark.

Sennett called himself a common man who reflected the taste of his audience—"the average working guy," as he put it. He believed that his sense of humor was a pretty accurate barometer of what would go over on the screen.

The Keystone lot had two entrances—a front gate for visitors and a side door for employees. The first building near the employee's entrance was a long shiplap building used for dressing rooms. Though the men and women were divided, they were anything but private. In 1913 there was one wooden stage in the center of the lot that consisted of nothing more than three exterior walls and muslin diffusers to let the sun in for the cameras. (Artificial lighting was rarely used.) Sennett used this only when necessary; he found most of his inspiration on the streets of Los Angeles, in small neighborhoods or from current events.

He paid homeowners ten dollars a day to shoot in front of their houses, fifteen if his group actually set foot on the property, and twenty-five dollars to shoot inside homes. He even paid the owners a dollar a day plus a studio box lunch if they picked up extra work in the film. When word spread around Edendale (Glendale) of Keystone's generous pay scale, homeowners advertised and solicited the studio.

Mack Sennett also had a talent for hiring men and women who would subsequently earn a place in history as masters of their crafts, some even labeled geniuses. Sennett's folly was that he usually failed to recognize the potential of those he was fortunate enough to "discover" until they went on to other studios. Over the years he hired Harry Langdon and made him a star, but lost him in a dispute over control. He hired Frank Capra as a gag writer but never allowed him to direct.

He put a little-known actress named Gloria Swanson to work on a Mack Swain/Chester Conklin comedy *The Pullman Bride*, put her in a bathing suit for publicity stills, and placed her among comedians doing pratfalls. Swanson considered Sennett little more than a good opportunity and a stepping-stone and eventually left to work at Paramount.

He had a talented young man under contract and used him as a stock player, gag writer, and unit director in more than thirty comedies in less than three years. But when Sennett refused to give the man a well-deserved raise in pay and move him into a permanent directing spot, he left for a contract at Fox Films. Charley Chase (at that time using his real name of Parrott) later became one of film's brightest directors and most popular two-reel comedians.

Sennett later brought a popular English music-hall comedian to the studio and taught him the techniques of film acting and directing. He thought the comic was eccentric but a good performer. When the comic asked for more money and more control, Sennett released him in the belief the young man would come back hat in hand. The comic was Charlie Chaplin.

Sennett was a hard taskmaster and demanded complete and unquestioned loyalty from his stars. When they left his studios he considered their departure treason and the stars traitors. Once they left he never spoke to them again, even in social situations where his abrupt silence was considered rude. In Gene Fowler's *Father Goose*, Sennett was described as a "tenacious and forthright hater . . . loyalty, however, won from him a never-failing friendship and affection." There was never any question where one stood with Sennett.

Though he began his movie career as an actor, and even appeared in many Keystone comedies as a company player, he considered the "stars" second to the writers and script editors. He claimed that if a story was strong enough, anyone could adequately perform the role, but if a story was weak or incoherent, no actor could help it. He personally worked on every story, from inception to final draft, and saw every production through until distribution.

Story conferences at Keystone were often nothing more than someone tossing out an idea, with the next person playing off that idea until a story evolved. The shooting scripts varied from ad-libbing ideas to working around stock footage to writing out elaborate shooting scripts complete with scenes and camera moves. Much depended upon Sennett's mood as well as the comedian for whom the story was written. And all of his comedies depended on pacing, timing, and quick-moving sight gags from pratfalls to car crashes to seemingly death-defying jumps.

Though Sennett was a master of original gags, he was also a master of plagiarism. Once, during his stint with D.W. Griffith, he tried to sell Biograph several stories for twenty-five dollars apiece. Biograph purchased the stories, then quickly realized they had been stolen from O. Henry. Sennett was forced to return the money. After that experience he freely admitted he "borrowed" from foreign writers because their work was more difficult to trace and most likely not as widely read in America. Later, of course, many comedy producers, writers, and actors stole from Sennett.

Arbuckle immediately disliked his new boss. He found him crude, slovenly, and vulgar, and completely disorganized and disrespectful—unlike anyone he had ever met before in his life. Roscoe detested anyone who swore, especially when women were present, and Sennett had no compulsion to curb his tongue. He put Arbuckle on the company payroll at three dollars a day but gave him nothing to do but watch, listen, and stay out of the way. For Sennett to pay someone without an honest day's work meant he obviously had an ulterior motive. He was likely hoping the hefty young man would become discouraged and quit, thereby proving Mabel Normand wrong.

Roscoe's spirits sagged his first week at Keystone and he continued to look for stage work without avail. He was ordered to remain an observer for several days, not a participant, in a world he had only brushed against briefly at Selig and Nestor. This was a world of comedy spoofs and auto chases by a band that was to become world famous as The Keystone Cops, a first-rate group headed by Ford Sterling and Fred Mace. The group's primary director was Henry Lehrman, who was called "Pathé." (He was given the name by his first boss, D.W. Griffith, who detested Lehrman, believed him to be incompetent, and pinned the label on him after he claimed he had experience directing "in the French cinema." The name "Pathé" was taken from the successful French movie company.) Though Lehrman's directing skills often fell under sharp criticism from his co-workers, he proved himself to be generally adequate, though boastful and crude, and he was kept on as Sennett's primary director. He later directed Arbuckle's first three films at Keystone. Their teaming up was stormy at best. Several years later they would clash again. Henry "Pathé" Lehrman was soon to become the boyfriend of actress Virginia Rappé.

Minta was wrapping up a six-week engagement at Clune's Auditorium in Los Angeles in which she performed as a singer and actress. The strain nearly destroyed her voice and she was forced to rest before accepting more stage work. Minta planned on taking time off and relaxing at her parents' home. The last thing she ever expected was for her husband to try to persuade her to pick up work in motion pictures.

Roscoe had been with Keystone one week and came home virtually grinning from ear to ear. "He was just beaming," Minta said. "He said that Sennett had finally come around and it looked like he was actually going to do some work. Roscoe said that Sennett heard him laughing, that hearty, robust laugh of Roscoe's, and that laugh caught his attention. Sennett told him he'd 'never heard anyone laugh like that before . . . you laugh in all languages, fat boy . . . and that's what we need.' "

Sennett had ordered him put to work as a stock player in a Ford Sterling/Fred Mace comedy titled *The Gangsters* for which a rough shooting script had been sketched out. Roscoe knew Sennett was always on the lookout for new talent and suggested Minta and his nephew Al St. John (who by this time had done extensive work in vaudeville). Again, he relied on Mabel Normand, who was becoming a close ally, to approach the boss. This time Sennett did not balk at her suggestion and hired the two of them at the same pay scale as Roscoe—three dollars a day. The job was ideal for Minta. In silent pictures she was not required to speak so she could rest her voice as planned. She did expect to return to the stage, assuming she would not remain at Keystone longer than a week or two.

Roscoe and Minta were once again working together and Roscoe's spirits were high. His dour mood vanished and he rode the streetcar to and from the studios each day with Minta. The work was hard—one-reelers were cranked out at a hectic pace, sometimes three per week. Often actors would run from one production to another. But few ever really considered it hard work. For the cast and crew the Keystone lot was fun, crazy, and one big party.

The Gangsters was completed at the end of April for release about one month later. When Sennett saw Arbuckle's work he thought little of his new hire and kept him on only at Normand's insistence. "If you like him so much, you work with him!" And with that command, Arbuckle was assigned as Mabel's co-star in subsequent half-reelers and one-reel comedies.

Once again it seemed that genius arose from Sennett's anger. Sennett's order to Mabel was meant as "punishment," a way of washing his hands of Arbuckle and proving to his girlfriend that she had made a serious mistake in backing the comedian. Instead, he had unwittingly created the comedy team that would launch both Mabel Normand and Roscoe Arbuckle as major film comedy stars and earn Sennett even greater acclaim in history as one of the greats of the film comedy. Fame and fortune would soon be Roscoe's for the taking . . . if he could overcome several significant obstacles: He needed to improve his acting technique, gain the confidence of the boss, and smooth over a hostile relationship with a man who was to become one of his most outspoken adversaries.

7

"You don't register on film, Arbuckle. If you can't cut it with Mabel, you'd better look somewhere else for a job. I got enough gagmen and I don't need another director."

Arbuckle's blond hair and creamy-white skin did not photograph well on early black-and-white film. His acting was far too broad and exaggerated for film and he could not get the hang of working before the camera. Henry Lehrman complained to Sennett that Roscoe was impossible to work with, that he refused to listen to direction and had no sense of timing. But Mabel never lost faith in her rotund co-star and coached him. She taught him when to ignore the camera and when to play to it to win audience sympathy or set up an "inside" joke with the audience. She also gave him a nickname, "Big Otto," because he looked "German" like "someone named Otto would look," she joked. By this time others on the lot had already started calling him "Fatty," Fred Mace dubbed him "Crab" as a joke because he was usually good-natured in public, and comedian Charlie Murray (the "court jester" of the lot) called him "My Child the Fat." He was listed in the cast on the title cards as Roscoe "Fatty" Arbuckle.

To most everyone on the Keystone lot, Roscoe "Fatty" Arbuckle had become one of the gang; except to Henry Lehrman, who reportedly refused to work with Arbuckle unless ordered to do so by Sennett. The boss intervened on several occasions, stepping behind the camera to direct when he was not busy with other productions. But when he could not take the helm, Lehrman was ordered to direct with Mabel serving as go-between.

This greatly depressed Roscoe, who was not used to disagreements and avoided any argument or quarrel at all costs. He tried to keep his frustration inside, which usually made him sick to his stomach. He knew he had to get on Sennett's good side and believed the best way to achieve that was through honest, hard work. But he could not find a common ground with Lehrman who openly resented the newcomer. Every misstep of Arbuckle's was an excuse for Lehrman to vent his hostility. Fortunately for Roscoe, he was a quick study and soon gave Lehrman little cause for an outburst.

Though still not a favorite of Mack Sennett's, Arbuckle felt somewhat secure in his position at the studio. He still envisioned returning to the stage, where he believed he belonged, but found work at Keystone enjoyable (when not working with Lehrman who continued to be dictatorial if not hostile) and financially rewarding. By June of 1913, Arbuckle's salary was upped to five dollars a week with what Sennett called an "open contract," meaning the salary could be negotiated when an actor's output increased, though Sennett was very slow and usually reluctant to agree to any such pay hikes.

Minta recalled this as one of the happiest times in her home life—her husband was steadily employed and working among people he felt were true friends, especially Mabel Normand with whom he found his first real friend and professional ally. Minta was earning a steady salary and, along with her husband, gaining a small following among early moviegoers. Most important, the marriage was finally on steady ground. Roscoe brought bouquets of flowers home for Minta several times a week. They took long walks together after dinner hand in hand. Roscoe even became more affectionate and romantic in bed. But best of all, he had completely stopped drinking. This was finally the man Minta had fallen in love with on the pier in Long Beach, a romantic, passionate man who was beginning to display an air of confidence and self-esteem. The scars of emotional abuse as a child were healing. Roscoe was finally evolving into a husband and a man.

In July of 1913, Roscoe's career took a major upswing when a bit of film history was made. According to legend, one of the most famous, and most repeated, sight gags in the world was created during the filming of *A Noise from the Deep*, a Normand/Arbuckle one-reeler. Mabel and the crew were searching for a gag to break a sequence in the comedy. Seeing a batch of pastries on a nearby tray, Roscoe grabbed a creamy custard pie and called Mabel off to the side. Waving the pie about, he explained to Mabel the routine he had in mind, out of earshot of the rest of the crew and Mack Sennett, who was directing and did not like to be left in the dark about anything. As Sennett approached the two, barking orders to return to work and accusing the pair of plotting, Roscoe called over to his boss. "Keep a close eye on us. We've got an idea." In a newspaper interview, Sennett jokingly said it was when Arbuckle yelled out "trust us" that he knew something was brewing.

Suspicious, and betting that whatever they were scheming would be good for one take only, Sennett ordered the camera to shoot wide to get both Arbuckle and Normand. Mabel winced her face, grabbed the pie, pulled back her arm, and let the custard fly. "Splurch!" Sennett's word for the squishing sound the custard pie made when it splattered dead center in Arbuckle's face. The gag was a hit and Sennett was forced to take another look at his hefty comedian. "The kid's got something."

Arbuckle gladly taught the rest of the cast to hurl custard pies. He tossed pies in ways no one had ever seen before— behind his back, with both hands, or in opposite directions— and could catch them without spilling a drop. Gene Fowler's *Father Goose* described Arbuckle as " . . . the greatest custard slinger of all time, the mightiest triple-threat man . . . the All-American of All-Americans, the supreme grand lama of the meringue, the Hercules of the winged dessert, the Ajax of the hurling fritter . . . the unconquerable and valiant flinger of open and closed minced models . . . Roscoe Arbuckle! When Fatty threw a pie it stayed thrown . . . He could deliver a bake-oven grenade from any angle, sitting, crouching, lying down with a good book, standing on one leg or hanging by his toes from a pergola . . . ambidextrous he could hurl two pies at once in opposite directions." Roscoe was also quick to give credit in part to Mexican bandido Pancho Villa who unknowingly helped create film history during that river encounter several years ago in El Paso, Texas.

The pie-throwing routine went over big with film audiences and early reviewers, who mentioned the Normand/Arbuckle film primarily for the gag. It was rapidly perfected and the crew found that pies with such dark fillings as blueberry or blackberry photographed better than light-colored pies when dripping down a victim's face. Though the gag was clearly associated by film audiences with Keystone, other studios had no qualms about stealing it for their own comedies. (Sennett himself freely admitted stealing gags and jokes from other comedians, especially French comedians such as Max Linder.) Local bakers grew rich off orders for hundreds of pies from studios across Los Angeles and the rest of the country. Custard pies became the rage in dinners and posh restaurants around the world.

Keystone comedies now billed Roscoe in front of Mabel Normand and in September released the first official "Fatty" comedy, titled *Fatty's Day Off*. It was clearly Roscoe's picture and the plot centered around the hefty young man, a wayward love, a Keystone Cops chase, and a reunion between lovers Fatty and Mabel. Along with the world-famous Keystone Cops (of which Roscoe was an active member), the Fatty/Mabel comedies were one of the mainstays of the Keystone studios and helped set it far above any other comedy producer in the early silent era. Sennett's "Fun Factory," as it was now called in public, in the press, and on the lot, was "the" studio for comedy.

As Arbuckle's popularity grew among his co-workers and fans, and he perfected his technique before the cameras, Lehrman's attitude toward Roscoe softened and the two were able to work together without any major disputes, though they never became friends on the lot. The Fun Factory was clicking as a company and cranked out as many as six one-reelers and split-reelers of various quality per week—an astonishing output for a single studio.

As for Roscoe, his popularity extended through all classes

of people and all age groups. He became a favorite of children, who felt they could trust his "homespun, cherubic, little-boy face" (as Minta described it), and proved popular among adults, who enjoyed his stunts and devilish pranks. He quickly became a major Keystone money-maker. But he still was astonished that he actually had a following and fans.

When the first fan letters arrived at Keystone, Arbuckle was flabbergasted. Most were addressed simply to "The Fat Boy" or "Fatty" in care of Keystone Studios. He went quietly off to the side of the dressing rooms and read the letters several times. He had disappeared for about an hour and Minta became concerned. When she found him, he had tears in his eyes and was silent. He later said he was shocked that people would take time out from their lives to write such nice letters. Up until his death he failed to comprehend either his popularity or the fickle moods of film audiences. He was as confused by this outpouring of affection as he later was by the outcry of hate. He believed he had done nothing to warrant either emotion.

No one in Arbuckle's day, from the press to his fans to his friends, seemed to agree on exactly what it was that made him so popular. Some believed that his tremendous size instantly set him apart from every other screen actor, making him noticeable and recognizable to movie audiences, who soon began to look for him in films. Others claimed that it was Arbuckle's athletic ability and agility that put him several notches above other comedians. He could perform any stunt with grace and ease, appearing lighter on his feet and more limber than someone less than half his weight. Still others insisted it was Roscoe's innocence, his baby face, and the general manner in which he acted, even during chases and while pulling outlandish pranks.

In any event, everyone agreed that Roscoe was becoming a household name and a solid draw for Keystone. At twenty-six years old, he was a STAR, an "overnight success" who had worked at odd jobs and on vaudeville stages for nearly twenty years before he was "discovered" by Mack Sennett, who accepted full credit.

Keystone used Roscoe's name and photograph in its newspaper ads and press releases, though many actors were still not given credit in the films or on the posters displayed in the theaters. One of the first publicity interviews with Roscoe, published in July of 1913, offers an idea of how the comedian was being promoted. It gave Arbuckle's weight at 300 pounds (he actually weighed 275 at this time) and claimed he scarfed down three steaks and all the trimmings, from baked potatoes to two loaves of bread, at one sitting. (The truth is that Roscoe usually nibbled at meals and rarely ate more than the average man. No matter how he ate, his weight usually hovered between 250 and 275 pounds.) It labeled him a prime athlete, the most capable athlete on the Keystone lot, which was probably true. In fact, he was the only member of the Keystone Cops who was never injured performing any stunts.

One account told of Roscoe entering a 100-yard dash against college track-team sprinters and winning. Another said he could leap straight out of the water "like a porpoise" (a stunt he performed in many films, learned during his routine swims at Santa Monica). Still another article claimed he could take a fall from ten to fifteen feet, land on cement, and be "up and running in a flash." Roscoe was an excellent diver and trained well for his stunts. He swam in the ocean several miles each day, practiced high dives from any number of dangerous locations, and ran each day to keep up his lung capacity and thus avoid looking tired in his films.

Other reports commented on "Roscoe the Movie Star" who was wealthy (his salary was slowly being increased from $18 to $25 a week to $175 a week while the average wage was still close to $5 a week). Pictures showed him as a fancy dresser in silk shirts and spats, failing to mention that appearance had always been of prime concern to Arbuckle, who dressed as if he had money even when he was broke. One account told of his penchant for dice and gambling and how he "customarily engaged a boy to pick up his dice for him during crap games on the Keystone lot." Highly unlikely, because Roscoe abhorred gambling and worked too long and hard for his money to throw it away on any game of chance.

By the end of his first year at Keystone, Roscoe had appeared in at least thirty half-reel and one-reel comedies. The exact number will probably never be known because it is assumed he appeared in some films without credit, and titles to the comedies were often changed during production and after they were released.

In December 1913, the Keystone Studios were on the verge of a major upheaval. Ford Sterling, who drew the top salary at Keystone of $200 a week, was openly discontented and demanded more money and star billing in his comedies—two demands that Sennett flatly refused to meet. It was common knowledge throughout the industry that Sterling was looking to move to another studio. He set about making life miserable for many of his co-workers by showing up late to shoots and missing staging cues. It was also no secret that Mack Sennett was looking for someone to fill Sterling's shoes (which literally happened). Roscoe appeared to be the heir-apparent and no one on the lot (which had seen some of comedy's brightest stars such as Charley Chase, Edgar Kennedy, Charlie Murray, Hank Mann, Slim Summerville, Chester Conklin, Mack Swain, and Al St. John) contested Arbuckle's bid for the top spot. Roscoe's salary was raised to $200 a week and he seemed assured of being the country's most popular comedian. But he had not counted on a young upstart, an unknown stage comic from England.

According to Kevin Brownlow's book, *The Parade's Gone By* . . . , Charlie Chaplin came under serious consideration as a Keystone contract player during a dinner/theater party attended by Mack Sennett, Minta Durfee, and some others from the studio. The group ended its evening at the local Sullivan and Considine Theater where Chaplin was performing. Sennett had been well aware of Chaplin for quite some time, had seen his stage work, and offered him a contract, though he sensed Chaplin's slower, more subtly paced manner would clash with the brash, bawdy Keystone style. His instincts were correct.

Chaplin signed a one-year contract, worth $150 a week the first three months, $175 to $200 by the contract's end, slightly less than Arbuckle's deal. He was to prepare four one-reel comedies per month, which were to be released approximately one per week though the dates varied slightly.

Chaplin was received coolly by the Keystone players. They resented his manner of dress, which was disheveled and rumpled, often making Sennett himself look like a dandy. He spoke slowly in a precise English accent that many interpreted as pretentious. He was quiet and analytical. In short, he was considered someone not to be trusted.

"He was an odd duck, that Chaplin," Minta remembered. "He just walked around staring at everyone. Poor Mabel. Sennett put her in Chaplin's first film as his leading lady. She just hated him . . . called him an 'English so-and-so.' She had a big fight with Mack Sennett over working with Chaplin. She just refused to do it. I think she took a stand against Charlie out of concern for Roscoe. She felt Chaplin was up-staging Roscoe and Roscoe might be left in the dust. In some ways she was right, I guess. Well anyway, Sennett put me in the picture instead of Mabel. That's how I got to be Charlie Chaplin's first leading lady."

In truth, Virginia Kirtley was cast opposite Chaplin and Minta appeared in a supporting role.

Making a Living was released February 2, 1914, with Chaplin playing the lead (but not as Charlie the Tramp, a character he had yet to invent), Minta Durfee, Alice Davenport, and Chester Conklin. The short was directed by Henry Lehrman, who also worked himself into the cast. The working situation between Chaplin and Lehrman was even more explosive than the clashes the director had with Arbuckle—he detested Chaplin's style of slow, deliberate pantomime and tried to boss and intimidate the young Englishman.

The battles were not entirely Lehrman's fault. Chaplin had no concept of film pacing and timing and the relationship between reality and camera shooting. He could not understand how he was supposed to be reacting to something he could not see, and yet the scenes would blend perfectly when several shots were spliced together. That is, he could not understand shooting scenes out of sequence.

Lehrman had control over the final editing of the first series of Chaplin shorts, and sliced out every original gag contributed by Chaplin and cut Chaplin's screen time considerably. There was an obvious jealousy of Chaplin's knowledge and Chaplin had no respect for Lehrman. He complained bitterly to Sennett, who either refused to take sides or accurately suspected he had a serious problem on his hands.

Sennett was so fearful that he had tied a millstone to the company that he wired the studio's owners, Kessell and Bauman, to explain his position before the first comedy was released, which he predicted would be a flop.

Moving Picture World reviewed the film *Making a Living* (which was released without a listing of the cast), noting that " . . . the clever player who takes the part of the nervy and very nifty sharper . . . is a comedian of the first water." It surprised many people, most of all Mack Sennett. The glowing reviews also helped affirm Chaplin's position against Lehrman.

As was the custom at Keystone, Sennett sent his crews out to take stock and background shots during real events. An auto race, which was more of a children's Soap Box Derby, was being held on the streets in the beach city of Venice, California. It was during this film that Chaplin stumbled onto his signature "Tramp" costume.

There are several popular stories about how Chaplin developed the Tramp character, whom Chaplin called "The Little Fellow." One version has it that Sennett, tired of his star's ragged dress, ordered Chaplin to buy a new suit of clothes. Chaplin was born in the slums of England and throughout his life was quite reluctant to part with a dime. He allegedly coerced Sennett into giving him twenty-five dollars for a new suit of clothes, pocketed the money, then headed straight to a trash barrel and pulled out a mismatched suit of torn and discarded clothes.

The true story owes much to Minta Durfee, Roscoe Arbuckle, and the Keystone company. Sennett thought the auto race would look better if Chaplin played his part in a costume. Desperately in need of an outfit, Chaplin rummaged through the dressing rooms (or studio wardrobe) at Keystone. He grabbed what he found stashed in drawers or tossed on chairs. His famous baggy pants were Arbuckle's held up by a rope, the too-small derby hat belonged to Minta's father, the oversized shoes were Ford Sterling's size-14 Keystone Cop shoes (featured in many earlier scenes in which Sterling was asleep with those gargantuan shoes propped up on the desk), which Chaplin wore on the wrong feet to keep them from falling off, the coat is believed to be a prop coat of Mabel Normand's, the toothbrush moustache was cut down from one of Mack Swain's walrus moustaches and held on with spirit glue, and the bamboo cane was leaning in a corner. The costume was a smashing success with audiences and from that day forward established Charlie Chaplin as a box-office draw and an instantly recognizable screen character.

Now Normand was willing to work with Chaplin and they co-starred in *Mabel's Strange Predicament*, which became Chaplin's third Keystone comedy. Again, Lehrman directed and again the two clashed. This time Sennett had no choice but to take Chaplin's side inasmuch as he was now a proven box-office success. Lehrman stormed off during production of his next short, *A Rural Demon*, to join Ford Sterling in the Sterling Film Company. Later Lehrman started his own production company, L-KO, (Lehrman-Knock-Out), which released its films through Universal.

With Lehrman gone, Arbuckle seized an opportunity he had been waiting for since shortly after his arrival at Keystone. He approached Sennett about directing his own comedies. He knew it would be rough going because the boss rarely trusted anyone in any position of control. But Arbuckle had proved himself a capable comedian and solid gag writer and Sennett very reluctantly gave him a chance. He agreed to let Roscoe head his own comedy unit with one proviso—if the output slackened or the quality faltered, Arbuckle would be held solely responsible. The two agreed. Roscoe was well prepared for the job.

When he first arrived at Sennett and had the series of blowouts with Lehrman, Roscoe listened, studied, and learned how to perform before a camera. But he also did something that no other comedian or director on the lot had done. Fascinated by the workings of the camera and the process of imprinting images on celluloid, Arbuckle borrowed a studio camera after the lot was closed for the night. He locked himself in the dressing room and completely dismantled the camera, analyzing every part, physically putting the film stock through the camera, studying how the lenses reacted to different lights. By the time he accepted his first directing job, he knew the camera inside and out and completely understood the process of filmmaking. Though many critics claim he was not an innovator, as was Chaplin, he was able to find new twists on old gags by using natural light and shadows to enhance scenes, and by placing the camera at unusual angles, something few other directors even considered.

Arbuckle's comedies were not strictly slapstick; they were a mixture of low comedy and high drama with highly charged action and tender love scenes. Though they failed to evolve to the sophisticated level of the later Chaplin comedies, they had their own look and feel, and stood above and apart from the majority of comedies the studios were churning out in the early teens. *Barnyard Flirtations* was cranked out, from inception to final edit, in five days. Arbuckle proved himself and was allowed on occasion to expand his shorts to two reels when the story merited the additional length. Sennett was pleased. The studio seemed to be back on course.

Things were going so well, in fact, that Sennett put his job on the line to do a comedy feature—something unheard of by anyone at Keystone or in the front offices of Kessell and Bauman. Against the wishes of his superiors, Sennett bought the rights to the stage play called *Tillie's Nightmare*, in which character actress Marie Dressler starred. Dressler was part of the package. The movie, later titled *Tillie's Punctured Romance*, was to be six reels long, a length considered absurd by almost everyone, because the standard for comedy was still one reel, two reels for rare exceptions. Nearly the entire Sennett roster was set to appear in the feature and it promised to be a great success. There was only one fly in the ointment —Roscoe "Fatty" Arbuckle.

Minta claimed Dressler was a very determined, confident woman who commanded great control over her work. She had an immediate understanding of where to place actors and displayed a sixth sense about anyone who would potentially prove a threat by upstaging her. Roscoe was such a threat. Because of his bulk, he stood out from the rest of the group no matter how well he was dressed or hidden in the back. Dressler insisted Roscoe be barred from the picture. Minta and Al St. John threatened to walk out if Roscoe was to be ostracized, but were ordered by Sennett to remain in the cast.

Roscoe took the rejection personally. He never expressed his resentment to anyone on the lot, but took his anger out on Minta at home. The more Minta tried to draw him out, the more he withdrew from her, usually lapsing into total silence after a brief argument. The pattern was beginning to become a regular routine and the marriage seemed headed for trouble.

To prove to himself that being ostracized by Dressler was unimportant, Arbuckle threw himself more deeply into his work; he stayed up most nights sketching out plots and comedy routines, camera angles and stunts for upcoming films. When he stayed up working, he curled up with a notebook, a pencil, and a bottle of whiskey. But he appeared to be handling the alcohol and lack of sleep. By morning there was no trace of whiskey on his breath, he never drank at work nor arrived at work showing the effects of alcohol, and he seemed alert and refreshed. He drew energy from work—he handled every aspect of his unit's production. The more work he took on, the better his spirits. He was turning into a workaholic as well as fighting the first signs of alcoholism.

8

By the end of 1914, Mack Sennett's armor was beginning to crack. Though making hundreds of thousands of dollars' profit for Keystone, Sennett kept his stars at the lowest possible salaries (though most of the salaries were handsome by average standards). He hated parceling out authority even more than he loathed handing out raises. It was only a matter of time before Sennett would face a showdown with Charlie Chaplin—now a popular and highly recognizable star.

Chaplin did not ask for control—he demanded it and never questioned that his demand would be met. He did not ask for more money—he insisted upon it. Chaplin's ego matched his popularity, and in December 1914 he announced that he intended to renegotiate his contract with Keystone for a significant raise. Sennett offered $400 a week, making him the highest-paid star on the lot. Chaplin countered with $570, as well as a push for total and unsupervised control over his unit, which was turned down.

Sennett believed he could wear Chaplin down and convince him he would be unable to find work at another studio if he turned down the deal at Keystone. To make Chaplin believe there were no other offers, Sennett posted a guard around the studio to keep agents from rival companies away. But the plan was not foolproof. Keystone was casting day extras for a cowboy spoof and hired a number of strangers to fill in the background shots. One of the "extras" was in fact an agent from rival studio Essanay, who cornered Chaplin with a

$1,250 a week offer and complete control over his production. Chaplin accepted on the spot and walked off the lot that day with the "cowboy" agent. Sennett later admitted that letting Chaplin go was the most serious mistake he had ever made.

Sennett also made another grave error, this one far more tragic, which ultimately destroyed the one woman he loved above all else. The on-again off-again love affair between Mack and Mabel was well known throughout the motion-picture industry. In fact, it was such old news that it was no longer the subject of gossip by 1915. After seven years of companionship, Mabel admitted she had just about given up on any prospects of marrying Sennett.

Toward the middle of the year, Sennett's mother came to Southern California for a vacation and for a long-overdue visit with her son. Mack and Mabel played their relationship down, not knowing that Mrs. Sinnott (which was Sennett's real name) knew full well of her son's affair and thought it was shameful.

According to Minta, Mrs. Sinnott saw Mabel as a hussy, chasing after and trying to tie down her son. Hoping to break up the romance, she ordered Mabel to steer clear of Mack, insinuating that he had no intention of marrying her.

In a rage, Mabel stormed into Sennett's office, fired the question of marriage point-blank and demanded to know his intentions. Backed into a corner, Sennett proposed and a July date was set.

One afternoon, Mabel, Minta, and two actress friends, Ann Luther and Mae Busch (Busch is best remembered today as "the ever-popular Mae Busch" for her recurring role as the rolling-pin wielding, shrewish wife in scores of Laurel and Hardy comedies), spent the afternoon together at Santa Monica beach, playing in the water and sunning themselves. At the end of the day, Sennett picked the group up and drove each one home. Mabel was the first, Busch the last to be dropped off.

Several hours later, Mabel received a puzzling phone call, probably from Luther, telling her to get over to Mack's home "quick as you can." When she rang the doorbell, Sennett answered wearing only his shorts. Mabel said she remembered seeing a woman running into another room behind him. She said that woman was Mae Busch whom, up until that point, she had considered one of her best friends. Then, suddenly, from out of nowhere, a vase caught Mabel on the forehead, knocking her cold. She woke up in her home several hours later.

According to Minta, Mabel went to Mack's house with another woman, who waited by the car. When she saw Mabel stagger out of the house, blood gushing from her forehead, she helped Mabel to the car, drove her home, and called Minta and Roscoe, who arrived within the hour. Mabel had a petrifying fear of hospitals and refused to go for treatment. Roscoe phoned for a doctor, who bandaged the actress and found the head wound to be serious. He insisted that, if necessary, Roscoe carry Normand to the hospital to save her life. Arbuckle did just that.

Normand lapsed in and out of consciousness and a detailed examination revealed a massive blood clot in her head. There was no choice but to operate—an operation that doctors feared she might not survive.

When word of the accident spread through the studio, the hospital waiting room quickly filled with Mabel's friends and co-workers. Two people were conspicuous by their absence—Mack Sennett and Mae Busch.

Adela Rogers St. John claims that within days of her release, Mabel attempted suicide by drowning. The seven-year love affair was over. And, for all intents and purposes, Mabel Normand's life was destroyed.

Mabel returned to Keystone after a three-month absence. When she arrived she was cool and distant with everyone, even the Arbuckles; she said strange things as if she had caught herself midstream and was verbalizing the fragments of a thought; her actions were erratic and disjointed. The head injury had apparently affected her mind. She avoided any contact with Sennett except what was necessary to the production. As an act of contrition, Sennett eventually cast Normand in a feature, *Mickey*, in which Minta supported. Mabel's attitude toward her former lover did not soften, but the feature was considered successful.

Roscoe said he believed that Sennett never felt any remorse

over the clandestine affair with Mae Busch and the accident that nearly killed Mabel that night in his home. In fact, when the newspapers started asking questions about the sudden lack of "Fatty and Mabel" comedies and the disappearance of Mabel Normand from the screen, Sennett explained that Normand had gotten hurt doing a stunt with Arbuckle. When she returned to the studio, Sennett set up a press session and ordered the pair to go along with the lie.

An article oddly titled "Why Aren't We Killed?" appeared in *Photoplay* magazine in April 1916. It explains how the hefty Arbuckle missed his mark on several stunts calling for death-defying retakes, how his girth broke props and the only reason he was not injured was because of his unusual athletic prowess.

Arbuckle said, "I am the only man my size and weight the New York Life Insurance Company will issue a policy to. I am five feet, seven inches tall and weigh three hundred and eighty-five pounds which is forty percent more than the law allows. But I passed every physical test they put up to me . . . when you're in shape you won't get hurt."

Mabel had a different answer when asked why she had never been killed doing stunt work, especially with Arbuckle. She told the interviewer, "Why haven't I been killed? Why— I have! I guess you don't read the Los Angeles papers . . . but it wasn't permanent . . . but that didn't make it any better while it lasted." She was obviously referring to the brush with death from the accident at Sennett's home.

"How did it happen?"

'Roscoe sat on my head by mistake. I was unconscious for twelve days and laid up for three months. Don't talk to me about being killed. I've been through it."

"Was that your only serious [brush with] death in all your adventures?"

"Yes. But I just live along from day to day. I never make any plans."

The interviewer pointed out the different attitudes for survival between the stars—Roscoe pinning everything on strength, speed, and agility, Mabel anticipating the worst. He prophetically said there was "not perfect harmony on the Keystone lot." Though he was referring to the contrasting attitudes between Roscoe and Mabel, he had no idea how close to the truth his remark actually was.

Shortly after *Mickey* was completed, Mabel signed a five-year contract with Samuel Goldwyn, but her behavior after the accident continued to become more bizarre with each passing day. She disappeared in the middle of a production, leaving no note, turning up in Paris. She spent money wildly, much of it on a ravenous cocaine habit that devoured her energy, destroyed her beauty, and consumed her senses. She was pursued by Goldwyn and still chased by Sennett, but she eventually rebuffed both advances. She had no conception of what was happening in her life.

Then, in 1922, she was implicated as a prime suspect in the murder of director William Desmond Taylor. Though she was innocent, it demolished what was left of her career. She contracted tuberculosis, and her health rapidly declined. Mack reportedly continued to send her money to help pay her bills. She died in 1930 at age thirty-five, leaving all of her money to various Los Angeles area orphanages.

While the ordeal with Mabel was still unfolding, life at Keystone continued at a hectic pace. With Chaplin's abrupt departure, Arbuckle finally won the much-sought-after position as top comedian on the lot. His salary was increased once more, bringing him $450 a week and control over his unit (the only person granted such control by Sennett). Sennett openly called Roscoe his "number one, right-hand man" and even consulted him on creative decisions. Roscoe shared his energy, talent, and enthusiasm with other units and often stepped in to help with other productions as well as his own.

By 1916, the "Fatty" comedies hit their stride. They had been expanded to two-reelers and were enormously successful. They were evenly paced, usually evolving around "boy meets girl, boy loses girl, boy gets girl" plots with acrobatics and tender "romantic" endings. Arbuckle even worked his old vaudeville routine of dressing as a woman into many of the shorts. The routine quickly became an Arbuckle trademark and was greeted with howls of laughter by audiences who came to expect the gag.

Minta appeared in many of the comedies, along with a

ninety-pound English pit bull named Luke, named after Keystone director Wilfred Lucas, who gave Minta the dog as a bribe to perform a dangerous stunt. Luke was officially placed on the Keystone payroll at $150 a week. He was an unusual dog in that he took commands on the first order and was quite atheltic and fearless when performing stunts.

The newspapers and fan magazines clamored for interviews with Roscoe. He made personal appearances at local Los Angeles area theaters to promote his comedies; the appearances usually included a few pratfalls, somersaults, and a song or two that usually left audiences standing for an ovation.

To meet the insatiable demand for information on the star, the front offices of Kessell and Bauman drummed up an official studio press release, giving Roscoe the complete rundown on his "background," or at least his background as the studio wanted it to be. Arbuckle was ordered to memorize it and not vary from it when granting interviews.

According to the release, dated March 1916, Arbuckle was "born in Kansas to an average, middle class working family of five. At the age of one he learned the state had gone dry and emigrated to California, where he has since resided. He is a graduate of Santa Clara college, where he was a football star and glee club feature. At the tender age of 18 and weight of 230, he began his theatrical career singing illustrated songs . . . [He eventually] followed the procession to the big tent and has been in movies ever since. During that time he has fallen down stairs, been pounded, knocked and slammed, dived off high piers into the ocean and thrown off boats."

Arbuckle was also told to give the following as the secret to his success—"arise before 9AM. Dress and lace your own shoes. This develops the abdominal muscles. Brush your teeth. If right-handed, comb your hair with the left hand as the toothbrush has already provided sufficient exercise for the right. Then eat a light breakfast to wit:

"Strawberries and cream, a nice 'T'-bone steak with a side order of fried potatoes and not more than four fried eggs, several pieces of toast and coffee. Do not drink more than three cups. If you feel you've eaten too much, take a little exercise such as rolling a few cigarettes. If this proves insufficient, join an athletic club where the bar opens early. By this time you will be ready for lunch . . ."

Arbuckle's drinking was now well-known at the studios among his movie cronies and was now being highly-touted in the newspapers and magazines as "funny", sadly encouraging his alcoholism. He was a company man who toed the company line. When the studio played up his drinking, he played right along with it in the false belief that it gave him "character". Before long it was rare to see him relaxing between takes without a drink, and there were even reports of his taking a swig or two off-camera during production.

Drinking was common in most American homes and predominant on every movie lot in the country, along with a growing increase in drug use among the stars. Town drunks were the village clowns, for men drinking was to be expected. Alcoholics were portrayed in almost every comedy—the drunk teetering on the edge of a cliff or wire or directing traffic, the man with the double-vision who saw pink "elephants". The more Arbuckle told jokes about drinking, the more the press swallowed it.

Arbuckle told Minta he needed whiskey to calm him down, to ease the stress of writing, directing and acting at the studio and to take the pressure off "being a star". He said it was the social thing to do. He failed to convince her, and was probably trying to convince himself. What he could not see was that alcohol brought out another side to the usually gentle, easy-going, innocent Roscoe, a side Minta had already seen and feared.

When he drank with friends he was jovial, fun, the "life of the party", the first to dance, incite everyone else into a good time. But when he drank alone, at home, he was mean, petty and hostile.

Roscoe withdrew physically from Minta during the Dressler incident and sexual relations since that time had been virtually non-existent. He spent so much time away from home (opting to sleep in his Keystone dressing room on many nights) that when he did return home he was treated more as a guest than one of the family. Over Minta's objections, Flora (Minta's mother) went out of her way to cook Roscoe's favorite foods and pamper her son-in-law hoping to encourage him to stay home. Worse, she continually took Roscoe's side against Minta, believing her daughter had to be responsible for driving Roscoe out of the house. Minta became cool toward her husband and stopped trying to win him over. By the end of January 1916, they were man and wife in name only, though they continued to work together and neither strayed from their wedding vows.

Unbeknown to them, the final, driving wedge in their union awaited three-thousand miles east. Triangle Film Corporation (a major distributor) had recently taken over distribution of the Keystone films. Arbuckle received orders from the front offices to pack his bags and move his troupe to the Triangle/Keystone studios in Fort Lee, New Jersey. Minta and Roscoe travelled East together as man and wife, but Roscoe would return to Los Angeles six months later—alone.

9

Triangle/Keystone "leaked" to the press the time and date of the departure of Arbuckle's entourage, which included Roscoe, Minta, Al St. John and Luke the Dog. Mabel Normand stayed in Los Angeles "recovering" from that trumped-up accident in which Roscoe purportedly sat on her head. As the group, they were greeted by a crush of reporters and a mob of fans snapping photos, waving pieces of paper for autographs, pushing and fighting in an attempt to touch the stars. If Roscoe had any doubts about his popularity, they must certainly have vanished by this reception. His once misty-eyed astonishment over fan mail was replaced by an outward air of confidence, and delight in the outpouring of affection which he was now receiving and absorbing from the crowd.

As he boarded the train in downtown Los Angeles, he made a brief statement which, once again, had the ear-marks of a front office statement.

"We're leaving to make some pictures on the East Coast. We love California, but with all the movie companies out here lately we thought a change of scenery would give our pictures a fresh look. We will be back in a few months. Don't forget us!"

Mabel had wanted to go back East to be with her family and sorely needed a vacation, which she had not had in four years. She was determined to go and eventually did. As for Roscoe, he thought the trip out would be fun and nothing more.

Arbuckle answered one question about sleeping conditions, which focused on his compartment—what it looked like, what size his bed was, if it was a deluxe room, etc. He answered briefly and jokingly, "My compartment will be the dining car, boys!" And they were off.

The trip was uneventful; most of the time Roscoe stayed up nights playing cards, drinking and joking with St. John and others on board. Minta kept to herself, reading or just thinking. They slept in separate compartments.

Arbuckle's arrival in New Jersey was headline news; the papers carried many of the now usual stories about what he allegedly ate (each one a greater exaggeration than the next), his athletic abilities, his charming manners and well-polished looks. Roscoe was a gracious host to the newspaper and magazine reporters who now made the Fort Lee studio a daily beat. He acted as tour guide, got to know many of them on a first name basis and was free and open with questions and answers, rattled off quips, easily laughed, and in what may have been his best performance, made them believe that his marriage was one of those rare "ideal" Hollywood unions. Minta was ordered to stay away from reporters.

Arbuckle was caught off-guard when several reporters printed stories about the violence and serious injuries that occurred "on a daily basis" on the Arbuckle sets. Sprains, cuts, broken noses and arms during stunt attempts were considered part of the day's work by those in the movie business at that time. But film audiences experienced only the thrills and laughs of wild and perilous stunts, probably assuming that it was all "make believe". When reporters wrote in horror of the real-life injuries, Arbuckle was ordered to smooth things. Triangle/Keystone was afraid that if audiences learned of the real danger in many stunts, they would not find them funny. That, it feared, would hit the studios square in the bank account.

Roscoe played down the injuries in his now-famous, joking affable manner. He also promised the new "Fatty" pictures would play down the violent slapstick and concentrate on story, which was a definite break from the usual Keystone style.

The studio gates were usually lined with fans who arrived

early and stayed late hoping to get a glimpse of "Fatty" Arbuckle, now considered one of the most popular comedians in film, second only to Charlie Chaplin, who was still coming in to his own. Though Roscoe was still shy, he said he enjoyed the idea that people were actually coming out to see him. It was the closest he was able to get to a live audience that he so enjoyed during his time in vaudeville.

One thing he could not get accustomed to was the nickname "Fatty". Although it was used in the title of his pictures and in advertising, he grimaced when someone shouted that name in public. When in a good mood, he would politely remind the person of his real name. When rushed or angry, he would simply snap back, "I have a name, you know."

There were only occasional sparks of affection between Roscoe and Minta. Roscoe knew he was becoming obsessed with his work. He drove himself harder than anyone else at Keystone; almost as if he set some unreachable goal of perfection which he was determined to surpass. One night he confessed to Minta that he felt there was always someone waiting for him to slip, to prove he was no good. Minta believed his paranoia stemmed from his father, who drummed an inferiority complex into his son.

"Sometimes when I see the people lined at the gates they frighten me. I see them grabbing at me, but not wanting to touch me, but to tear at me. I don't know why, Minty. It's like they'll turn on me any minute. It's all I can do not to run. Silly, huh?"

Minta said Roscoe had nightmares, usually brought on by the strain of working at the studio, and probably touched off in part by his drinking. The nightmares echoed his vision of the crowd at the gates. He said he dreamed that the crowds had turned against him and were coming after him, maybe to kill him. He never finished that recurring nightmare, each time waking up just as the mob surrounded him. An odd premonition?

By May Roscoe began to feel more comfortable with the East. His obsessive push for perfection was beginning to find its own, less frantic, pace. He became more used to the commotion at the gates, the continual barrage of press people and fans stopping him on the streets. He relaxed and paid more attention to Minta, though they still failed to actually live as man and wife.

"We're going to the opera tonight, Minty. I have tickets for the Met."

'You hate the opera. You always said those screeching prima donnas give you a headache."

"Caruso's performing."

The lobby of the Metropolitan Opera House was a sea of glittering diamonds, crystal, and sequins—women in shimmering ball gowns, men in silk top hats and tails. For the first time since he became a recognizable star, Roscoe blended with the crowd, unnoticed. He enjoyed the anonymity.

Arbuckle squirmed and shifted in his seat during the first act. During the second act, he slipped away, creating a slight disturbance climbing over other patrons as he made his way to the aisle. Minta assumed her husband had stepped out into the lobby to get away from the "screeching prima donna." He stayed away until Caruso returned, then he reappeared, climbing over laps and stepping on feet to get back to his seat. It soon became a pattern—Caruso exited the stage, Roscoe left his seat. Caruso returned, Roscoe returned.

During intermission, Minta was furious and dressed down her husband in front of the crowd. Embarrassed, he took Minta backstage to explain.

"Roscoe, you only go backstage after a vaudeville show, not the grand opera!"

The reason for Arbuckle's peculiar behavior became clear. A man of his word, when he said he wanted to see Caruso he meant it. He came to see Caruso and only Caruso. He never said he wanted to see the opera. Roscoe had been meeting Caruso backstage and talking between his cues. Arbuckle had secretly been a fan of Caruso's for many years but had never had the opportunity to meet him. His stay in New York provided the first opportunity and Arbuckle had no intention of wasting it.

The two men immediately hit it off. Much to Roscoe's amazement, Caruso was also a fan of Arbuckle's, had heard about his smooth tenor voice and ordered a command performance. The opera star was so impressed that he nearly convinced Arbuckle to leave films to pursue a career as a professional singer!

"With training you can become the second greatest singer in the world. I strongly encourage you to give up this film business and perfect your God-given talent."

Roscoe seriously considered the notion. He had been losing an ongoing battle for a raise from Triangle/Keystone. He felt stymied by front-office politics and control. His films grossed hundreds of thousands of dollars for the studio, yet he was continually told it could not afford to increase his salary, which was about five hundred dollars a week, adequate but still one third that of Chaplin, with whom Roscoe felt competitive.

It was this competitiveness that motivated Arbuckle, not greed. He was generous with Minta even though their relationship was severely strained. He bought her diamonds and expensive jewelry and perfume, and he sent presents home to the Durfees. He loaned money to studio friends, who rarely repaid their debts. Roscoe never asked for payment either. "If they had the money, they'd pay," he believed. "If they don't have it, there's not much point in asking for it." He also donated heavily to charities and was known as a soft touch for strangers and panhandlers. Roscoe simply believed his comedies were as successful financially as Chaplin's and he was at least as popular; therefore he should be adequately compensated. He needed help and advice.

He also needed someone to intervene in the bombardment of offers and counteroffers from every movie studio and film company in America, some offering a raise in pay and for more control and others promising neither, only the "prestige" of a partnership in a fledgling company.

Agents had been commonplace in the theater for many years, used for everything from booking tours to securing clients jobs with circuits and negotiating pay raises to playing nursemaid to troublesome but popular comedians and actors. But in 1916, most film actors did their own negotiating.

There were few "stars" in films. Mary Pickford and Florence Lawrence were two of the first actually to become stars with recognizable names and audience drawing power. But even then their fight was long and hard. Early studios billed their actions with nicknames such as "The Biograph Girl" or "The Girl with the Curls," to prevent audiences from demanding a "Mary Pickford" film. Studio bosses correctly believed that once the actors got an inkling of their draw, they would make demands on the studios for power and money, and would also be sought after by rival companies.

By 1916 only a handful of actors had such "star power"— Mary Pickford, Douglas Fairbanks, Charlie Chaplin, and Roscoe Arbuckle. Arbuckle received the lowest salary of the group by at least two thirds. Pickford's mother (along with Mary herself) served as her agent and they made a formidable pair. Chaplin's brother Syd did Charlie's negotiating and was very shrewd, and Fairbanks did his own wheeling and dealing. But Arbuckle was neither tough-willed nor cunning. He was a pushover.

Max Hart was a popular theatrical agent who was beginning to woo clients in motion pictures. Arbuckle was a major catch.

"I feel funny going to an agent. Like I'm stabbing Mack Sennett in the back. I feel a loyalty to Mack, and having someone else go in to air my demands makes me feel like a troublemaker."

"Remember, Roscoe," Hart said as they shook hands on the deal, "there's no such thing as loyalty in this or any other business. When they need you, you hold the aces. When they don't, there's nothing you can do. You have to make the best deal when you're holding the aces."

Hart said he could quadruple Arbuckle's deal at Sennett, getting him at least two thousand a week. But he had to have Minta and Al St. John as part of the package. Roscoe agreed in Hart's office, and subsequently informed Minta and St. John that they now had professional representation. The two went along with the plan without question or discussion. Being included in a deal with one of the biggest stars in America was not something to be upset about. Roscoe's new contract with Triangle/Keystone was set to begin as soon as the two inked their deal.

Word of the pending agreement was news in every fan magazine, newspaper entertainment section, and motion-picture-studio front office in America. Within days Roscoe was besieged with bigger and better offers from studios and managers alike. Among those men offering to outdo any deal of Hart's was former actor Lou Anger, who enticed Roscoe with a plan to make him the highest-paid and most powerful film comedian in America. It was an offer that seemed too good not to hear. Arbuckle agreed to a clandestine rendezvous in Atlantic City—away from Hart, away from Triangle/Keystone, and away from Minta.

Before long Anger was a frequent visitor on the Fort Lee lot. He hovered around Roscoe, who continually looked over at Anger for approval. Roscoe still had not introduced Anger to Minta, nor had he mentioned anything about their meeting in Atlantic City. Minta and others on the lot became suspicious but kept their curiosity to themselves, hoping Roscoe would explain in due time.

Mabel Normand had been ordered to the New Jersey lot in a front-office maneuver to rekindle the "Fatty and Mabel" movie magic. It also hoped that putting the two stars, and two friends, back together would compel Roscoe to stay with Triangle/Keystone. Roscoe was overjoyed to be back with Mabel, but after one film Normand went on to her feature, *Mickey*, in which Minta co-starred, and Roscoe said he needed a well-deserved rest and wanted to travel. He booked himself and Minta on a one-month return tour of the Orient. Minta would then return to Keystone to begin work on the Normand film.

The tour was a professional triumph but a personal disaster. Roscoe had been away from the stage for nearly three years and had completely acclimated himself to the schedule, conditions, and pacing of film. Now live audiences made him edgy; he detested living out of suitcases and was continually irritable on the road. He and Minta fought bitterly. But his eyes were opened to something he had never imagined. He had never suspected he was an international star.

He was fawned over in China and Japan. Crowds followed him on the streets shouting various versions of his name. Four years ago he had toured the Orient as a part of a vaudeville show—this time out he was a star in his own right! Silent

"N THE CLUTCHES OF THE GANG" – Jan. 1914. Considered one of the best Keystone Cop comedies. Nine months before Roscoe starred in his own "FATTY" series. *Author's Collection*

"FATTY'S CHANCE ACQUAINTANCE" – March 1915. Arbuckle replaced Charlie Chaplin as Keystone's big star. *Author's Collection*

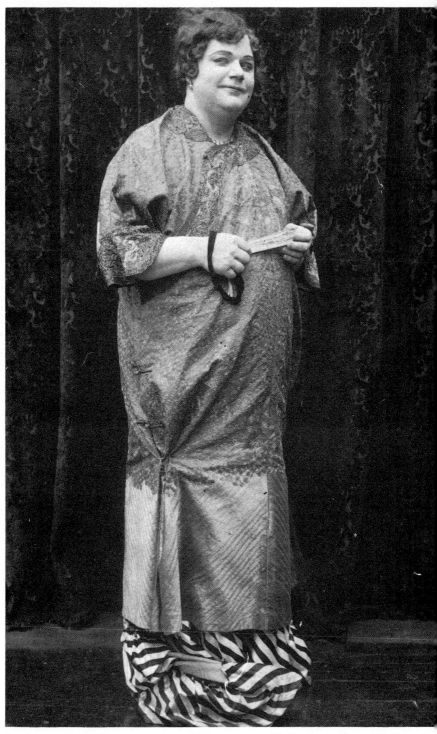

Roscoe as an international star, after a return engagement in the Orient, circa 1916. One of his infamous appearances as a female impersonator.

Author's Collection from Minta Durfee Arbuckle

Minta Durfee, Age 18

ROSCOE ARBUCKLE
KEYSTONE COMEDIES

103 H.P.P.

Roscoe's actor's composite. Minta in the upper right corner, Luke the dog at Roscoe's feet.
circa 1916.   *Author's Collection*

An arduous 23-city tour has ended. Roscoe had no idea he was made the fall guy for Zukor's Boston orgy. Zukor is on Roscoe's right, Minta on his left (Roscoe's cane can be seen in front of Minta's skirt). Lou Anger is on the car. Circa March 1917.

Author's Collection from Minta Durfee Arbuckle

Arbuckle's "Comique" Troupe. Lou Anger on left in cap and tie, Buster Keaton stands next to Anger, Alice Lake is between Keaton and Arbuckle. Al St. John squats under the camera. Circa 1917.

Author's Collection from Minta Durfee Arbuckle

Best friends – Roscoe and Buster Keaton. The film – "GOOD NIGHT NURSE" – 1918.
Author's Collection

Roscoe had everything from popular songs to household products named after him . . . an indication of his popularity.

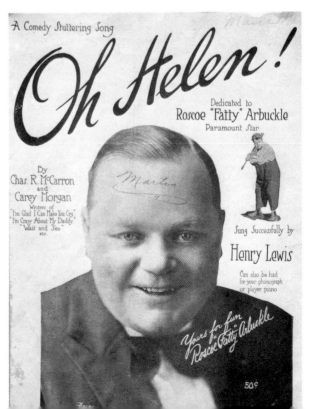

A Comedy Stuttering Song

Oh Helen!

Dedicated to
Roscoe "Fatty" Arbuckle
Paramount Star

By
Chas. R. McCarron
and
Carey Morgan
Writers of
"I'm Glad I Can Make You Cry"
"I'm Crazy About My Daddy"
"Wait and See"
etc.

Sung Successfully by
Henry Lewis

Can also be had
for your phonograph
or player piano

Yours for fun
Roscoe Fatty Arbuckle

50¢

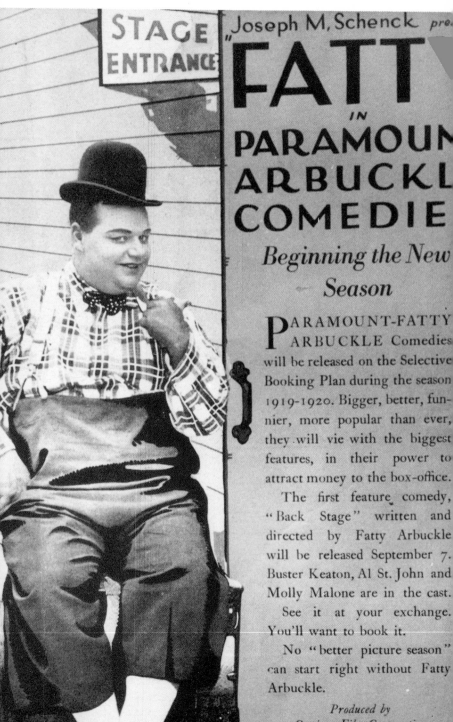

A massive publicity campaign was launched to kick off a new season of successful Arbuckle comedies.

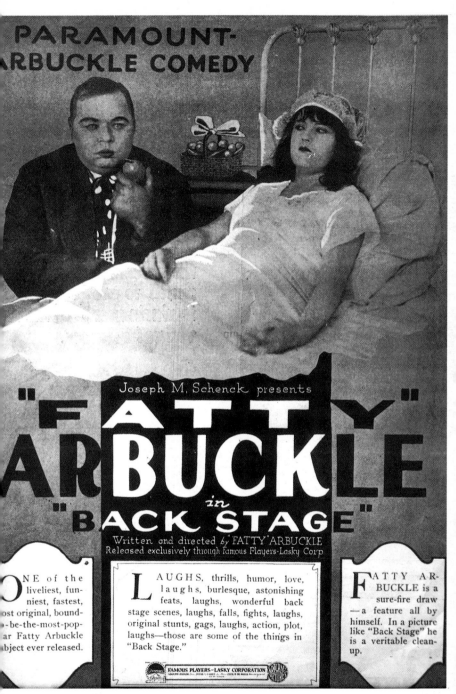

'BACK STAGE" was a two-reeler, the first ever done in colour (tinting).

The last known photo of Virginia Rappé. Though portrayed by the prosecution as an innocent starlet, she was anything but.

films had shattered the language barrier and Roscoe discovered he was loved and his comedies enjoyed by children
and adults in countries and cities he had never heard of. He
saw his two-reelers with titles in Chinese, Japanese, and every
foreign language imaginable. Now he was certain Triangle/
Keystone had played him for a chump. He told Minta Max
Hart was correct—there was no such thing as loyalty. He said
he had to watch out for himself from now on.

Minta disliked traveling only slightly less than Roscoe and
the two began to get on each other's nerves. Roscoe usually
drank every night to unwind and block out what he considered Minta's continual nagging about the tour and his
drinking. They slept apart and barely spoke to one another
during the day. At times, Roscoe stayed out all night, walking
out after an argument. Minta never questioned where he had
been, assuming only that he'd found a bar and made some
new friends. If nothing else was left in their marriage, there
was still trust. She knew Roscoe never strayed; he was too shy
about his size and too honorable a gentleman to cheat on his
wife.

When they returned to New York, something was different. Arbuckle spent an increasing time away from the lot and
in meetings with Anger. Finally the truth came out.

Adolph Zukor was the country's biggest "raider" of stars
in the motion-picture business. Zukor controlled the reins on
the East Coast; his partner, Jesse Lasky, oversaw production
on the West Coast. Under his Paramount banner (a
subsidiary company of Famous Players-Lasky Corporation),
Zukor's studio became one of the nation's most prolific,
cranking out three features per week. His slogan—"If It's a
Paramount Picture It's the Best Show in Town"—was a
household phrase by 1917. He perfected the block-booking
technique in which theater owners and distributors took a
mass of titles, sight unseen, in order to secure the rights to the
bigger shows that would guarantee packed houses. Zukor's
block-booking gave his lesser stars a chance at screen time
and helped turn a tidy profit for films considered losers. It
also turned a tidy profit for Zukor, who quickly upped the
ante on block-booking packages that offered titles for his
biggest stars.

Zukor was ruthless; if he could not buy out the competition he destroyed them. When rival Harry Aitken teamed with D.W. Griffith, Thomas Ince, and Mack Sennett to form Triangle Film Corporation as a direct assault against Zukor's machine, Zukor set the wheels in motion to break the syndicate apart. He barraged the group with lucrative individual offers to produce for Paramount and he immediately succeeded in winning Griffith and Ince over to his stable.

(Sennett remained the last holdout but he finally went to Paramount in 1917. With Arbuckle, his biggest money maker, gone, Normand's career just about finished, and his partnership dismantled, Sennett saw the move to Zukor's studio as an opportunity to make a fresh start. He eventually left to form his own company, Mack Sennett Productions, which made stars of such comedians as Harry Langdon, Larry Semon, Raymond Griffith, and others, and enlisted the services of the French film distributor Pathé, by now the world's largest.)

Zukor was the most feared and most hated studio chief in the film business, and he was also the richest and most powerful. When some exhibitors boycotted Zukor's films because of his tyrannical booking methods, he simply built his own theaters, placing movie palaces in key cities to trounce the competition. Soon, other producer/distributors followed his lead.

He lured top stars with promises of untold riches and control. He signed Mary Pickford, Douglas Fairbanks, William S. Hart, Dorothy and Lillian Gish, Marguerite Clark, Arbuckle's friend Hobart Bosworth, and the boy who would soon soar to the heights of stardom only to crash at Zukor's hands—Wallace Reid. Zukor had made a bid at Chaplin but refused to pay his demand of $1 million a year. (Pickford eventually left when lured away by the newly formed First National Pictures, which took direct aim at Zukor's Paramount. It paid Chaplin $1.75 million a year and offered Pickford even more.) Zukor was now gunning after Roscoe Arbuckle. Lou Anger was sent out as front man to test the waters.

"I never trusted that man. He was secretive and seemed

always to have some sort of hidden agenda . . . you know, like you weren't getting the whole story. Roscoe always told me that the toughest thing to keep in this business was your integrity. He said, 'Minty, once you compromise your integrity, then you've compromised everything, then they've got you.' Well, let me tell you, this man was the trap that snared Roscoe. With Lou Anger . . . they got Roscoe. It was the beginning of the end.''

Anger was hired as an agent for film producer Joseph Schenck, who was making a significant mark on the motion-picture industry. (He later headed United Artists. His brother, Nicholas, was president of Loew's Incorporated, the parent company of Metro-Goldwyn-Mayer.) Schenck had a producing deal with Paramount and Zukor, and bringing Roscoe Arbuckle into the fold would be a significant boost in power and prestige for Schenck. Through Schenck, Anger offered Arbuckle what few other stars in the industry had—complete artistic control of his films, as well as a paid salary of $250,000 a year with unspecified perks and bonuses based on gross earnings of the films. Those perks and bonuses could bring in as much as $1 million a year, making him the second-highest-paid comedian in the motion-picture business. The front man was his rival, Charlie Chaplin, a point not lost on Roscoe.

There was another point not lost on Roscoe either—a Catch-22 in the deal. Of his $5,000 a week salary, $1,000 of it had to be turned over to Schenck, to whom Arbuckle would technically be signed. (Schenck would ''lease'' Arbuckle's services to Famous Players-Lasky and Paramount.) Ten percent of the remaining $4,000 a week would go to Anger as Arbuckle's agent. That left Roscoe with $3,500 a week, a significant comedown from the initial offer, but a major boost from his current salary at Keystone and better than what Max Hart could negotiate for him.

Anger and Schenck leveled tremendous pressure on Arbuckle not only to sign but to make a speedy decision so as to avoid any second thoughts about breaking his contract with Hart. Arbuckle caved in to the pressure and enticement of the offer and signed with Anger. He never consulted Minta, St. John, or Max Hart until after the deal was sealed.

If Hart was angry at the double-dealing, he never said so in public. He graciously wished Roscoe well. Hart understood the business and realized he could not afford to fight a court battle over the contract.

Minta was less magnanimous. Her anger was aimed in two directions—one at not being consulted about the Anger/Schenck offer, the other at not being included in the lucrative package. The last bastion of their marriage had been shattered—any trust was gone.

10

"Minty, I'm a star now. I don't need anyone. My name is in lights, not yours."

"But Roscoe, we've always worked as a team. Your agreement with Anger leaves me out in the cold. Please stay with Max Hart. You had an agreement. You must honor it."

"Business is business. This is nothing personal with Hart or you, Minty. I have to watch out for myself. I've worked too hard to pass this by."

The conversation erupted into a violent argument.

"I've worked hard, too, Roscoe. And I've been overshadowed by you. I've made concessions and career changes for you. I've given you eight years of my life, helping you, encouraging you, playing second fiddle to Mabel Normand. I thought we had a commitment to one another."

"I've carried you since we got married. I got you work at Sennett. I got you set up with Hart. He only wanted me but I worked the deal to sign you and Al. What else do you want? Quit riding my coattails!"

With those words, Roscoe professionally separated from his wife. The emotional separation had been building for months, but they still lived together under one roof. Minta believed it was not fame that went to her husband's head, but Lou Anger. She believed Anger had put Roscoe up to distancing himself from her, that Anger had been goading Roscoe into a divorce.

Arbuckle's aligning with Famous Players-Lasky and Paramount was heralded with major fanfare and significant press coverage. *Moving Picture World* echoed similar newspaper articles on the precedent-setting deal.

> Celebrated comedian to begin work on production of two-reelers in March. "Fatty" Arbuckle, the funniest man on the screen, who has long abandoned his first name of Roscoe . . . has entered into a contract with Paramount Pictures Corporation. These pictures will be distributed by Paramount, but not on the "Paramount Program" which includes pictures only by the Famous Players, Lasky, and Morosco Companies . . . Arbuckle to form his own unit, Comique.
>
> "Fatty" Arbuckle has capitalized his huge size so successfully that he stands today acknowledged to be worth his weight in laughs and is admittedly "the" fat comedian of the screen. The secret of Arbuckle's great popularity is the fact that he makes his audience laugh at him as well as with him, never fearing to be made the victim of a joke . . . instead of insisting to be the one who always plays the jokes on others.
>
> The fact that Arbuckle directs his own pictures is important because he will set tasks for himself to do what no other director would have the moral courage to ask him to perform.
>
> "One of the most important factors in screen comedy is speed," declared the Rotund One. "By that I do not refer to speed in the slang sense of the word as applied to vulgarity, but to speed of plot and action. Keep things jumping and your audience will be with you every moment."

With that announcement, Arbuckle was Joe Schenck's property for five years. The new production company was to be called Comique, patterned after the French word for "comic," with Arbuckle as star and director, Herbert Warren as scenario editor, Schenck as producer, and Anger as business manager. They would begin work January 15, 1917.

An unusual article in *Moving Picture World* indicates that Famous Players-Lasky was probably not Schenck's first choice as a studio to release the Arbuckle comedies. It says that Lewis Selznick had some sort of distribution arrangement with Schenck to produce the two-reelers in New York. In late December of 1917, Schenck, his wife, Norma, Marcus Loew, and producer Lewis Selznick traveled to Los Angeles to consider several studios that had been part of the Selznick Studios interest. It also hints at the reason why Al St. John abruptly left Keystone to follow his uncle to Comique.

> . . . As previously announced in this paper Roscoe Arbuckle, the rotund Keystone comedian, has been signed up by Mr. Schenck to head a company of his own to produce comedies for the Selznick program . . . His assistant director will be Al. St. John, also of Keystone. St. John will be given a company of his own under Arbuckle's supervision . . . They have decided that after a conference with Arbuckle, all the pictures for the Selznick program will, for the present, be produced in New York.

St. John eventually did receive his own unit, released through Paramount. As for Comique, the initial series of Arbuckle shorts was shot in New York. This may be due in part to the split between Schenck and Selznick, and the subsequent signing with Famous Players-Lasky which encouraged New York production.

But a personal complication set in several months before the new company was to get under way, one that would give Arbuckle an inkling of the ruthless and coldhearted attitude of his new boss, Adolph Zukor.

In August of 1916, Roscoe developed a carbuncle on the inside of his left thigh. The carbuncle began as a small boil, of which Roscoe thought nothing. But within days it became infected and grew, causing Roscoe tremendous pain. By the Labor Day weekend he was unable to walk. He kept screaming, "My leg's on fire, Minty! My leg's burning up!" Minta phoned a doctor, who lanced the carbuncle and drained it, ordering Roscoe to recuperate at home. Roscoe screamed with pain. To quiet him down, the doctor gave him an injection of morphine, which was considered a common painkiller in the 'teens. He also handed Minta a packet containing enough of the drug to keep Roscoe out of pain for at least two weeks with a daily dose. Following orders, Minta adminstered the deadly prescription each morning. Within days, Arbuckle was hooked on the drug.

Unfortunately, the doctor's work was not effective. The carbuncle became reinfected; this time the infection spread across the entire thigh, which was swollen and bright red. Roscoe was now bedridden and demanded greater doses of morphine to alleviate the unbearable agony. Several times he erupted into hysterical, uncontrollable screaming fits, then passed out from the pain. When the doctor returned, he immediately sliced the entire thigh open lengthwise to drain the infection. He also told Minta that the leg would have to be amputated.

Roscoe's career in movies would be finished. Panicked, Minta phoned two people—her mother, and Roscoe's friend and neighbor Hobart Bosworth, who immediately summoned other doctors. Since it was the Labor Day weekend, most doctors were not home or were not answering calls. Eventually several doctors were reached and Roscoe was rushed to the hospital, where his leg was treated and saved.

Once the infection was reduced, Roscoe had to endure a second problem, his morphine addiction. He was given two choices: one was to be weaned off the morphine with other, less-addictive drugs, then weaned off those drugs until he was clean. The process would take months. Or he could undergo abrupt withdrawal, which was a terrifying ordeal; the pain of that would be far worse than what he had already suffered. This method would take several weeks. Roscoe argued that abrupt withdrawal would be best all around. He believed several weeks' pain would be better, careerwise, than an extended ordeal over several months.

Roscoe was locked in a padded room with only a bed. He would not be allowed any visitors and his screams of pain would not be answered. Minta remained outside the room for several hours, but finally left when the screaming started. It was more than she could stand. She said she could not bear to hear her husband screaming in pain, knowing she could not step in to help him. She returned to work to complete her work on the Mabel Normand film *Mickey*, and phoned the hospital daily for word of Roscoe's recovery. Within two weeks, he was released, clean from the drugs, but a much changed man.

While recuperating at home, Roscoe was visited daily by friends from the Keystone lot. He received phone calls and letters from friends. His fan mail was forwarded to him at home. News of Roscoe's illness was kept to a minimum, with the press knowing only something about a "sore leg injured during a stunt" or "taking time off to relax before beginning work at Paramount." News of the morphine problem was kept quiet.

Roscoe also received flowers from Joe Schenck with wishes for a speedy recovery. Nothing at all from Adolph Zukor. He was visited only once by Lou Anger, who informed him that Paramount had booked him on a twenty-three-city promotional tour set to begin February 17. Anger told Roscoe that Paramount expected him to be fully recovered by that time, that Paramount was banking heavily on the tour as a promotion to launch Comique. One look at Roscoe indicated serious doubt about his future in films.

During his ordeal, Roscoe's weight dropped from 275 pounds to 193—his lowest weight as an adult. He looked emaciated, his pajamas hung on him, his once-tight skin sagged, and he had dark circles around his eyes. And he still could not walk. The tour was five months off, but it was apparent Roscoe's recovery would be long and slow. He was also terrified that he would be crippled for the rest of his life.

Anger reported back to Schenck, who tried to get the tour canceled or postponed. He received a cryptic telegram back from Zukor's office. The "R" in the memo refers to Roscoe. Apparently Zukor was beginning to have his doubts about the deal with Schenck.

"R a mistake? Advise. Too much at stake. Tour on."

Zukor saw Arbuckle as a commodity and hoped he had not bargained for damaged goods.

By February 1917, Arbuckle had put some of the weight back on, but he still looked sickly and too weak to walk under his own power. He used a crutch to hold himself up at home, and often leaned on Minta's arm for support in public. Hoping he would continue to regain his health and weight, Schenck ordered three suits of clothes for Arbuckle—his current size, a size larger, and the 275-pound size the public expected to see. But when the comedian failed to put on enough bulk by the time the tour was ready to begin, Schenck ordered Arbuckle to "pad up" his suits with foam rubber. The foam rubber was taped to his legs, arms, and stomach. Though his face was still drawn, the rest of his body appeared more "normal" for "Fatty" Arbuckle, Paramount star.

The tour was formally launched with a dinner at the Alexandria Hotel in Los Angeles. Los Angeles District Attorney Thomas Woolwine (who was later to scuttle the investigation of the murder of Paramount director William Desmond Taylor, allegedly under Zukor's orders), Hobart Bosworth, Jesse Lasky, Adolph Zukor, Joe Schenck, and Lou Anger were assigned to sit at the "celebrity" table with Roscoe and Minta. Roscoe was to make a grand entrance as a guest of honor.

While he was waiting in the hall for his cue, Roscoe's legs buckled and he could not walk. Minta signaled Anger, who excused himself from the table. Over Minta's objections, Anger had insisted Roscoe walk into the hall without crutches, continuing his facade that everything was well with the comedian. When Roscoe fell, Anger agreed to help escort him into the hall. He held Roscoe by one arm, Minta held the other, and the illusion never betrayed the truth. Zukor seemed pleased and said a few complimentary words after Roscoe's speech of gratitude to Zukor, Schenck and Paramount.

And the tour began. The group traveled by railroad in a private car donated by society matron Evalyn Walsh McLean, who was a prominent newspaperwoman in Washington.

The first stop was Kansas City, where Roscoe was mobbed by crowds and lectured at boys' clubs and teachers' societies, women's groups and community meetings. Anger booked him to appear before every local theater owners' group who asked for an audience with the comedian. Though Roscoe was still weak, Anger continued to push. "These are the people who are paying you that salary, Arbuckle. Don't bite the hand that feeds you, sick or not."

The tour pulled in and out of every major city across America, finally winding up in New York in March. Roscoe was tired and still in pain. Doctors who traveled with the tour had been pumping him with painkillers, which often dulled his senses or left him confused or hostile. He and Minta fought and bickered constantly. Each fight ended with Roscoe going off on a drinking binge and Minta locking herself in a room and refusing to speak to her husband.

"It was a pattern. We'd fight, Roscoe would drink, I'd go off in anger. Sometimes it was over something silly. But a lot of the time it was over Lou Anger. He controlled Roscoe like a puppet. Anger snapped his fingers and Roscoe jumped. Anger was clearly pulling the strings. I know he was also filling Roscoe's head with all sorts of ideas about me. I knew he was openly trying to break us up."

Once after a particularly violent battle, Roscoe saw a display bottle of perfume in a drugstore window. When he found out it was filled with colored water, he asked the salesclerk to dump out the water and fill it with the real thing—an expensive French perfume. By the time the salesclerk was through, it cost a small fortune. Roscoe sent the huge bottle to Minta, no note. He thought it was funny, but Minta did not laugh. What she really wanted was an apology.

The fights usually ended with Roscoe sending flowers, or perfume, or diamonds to Minta. But never did he apologize. Minta said that was all she wished for, an apology, instead of expensive gifts. "He never knew how to say that one word—'sorry.' That's all it would have taken."

Before the tour was formally to end, the entourage was to drop the railroad car off in Boston, then return to New York on the public train. The big finish was a banquet, hosted by Paramount for the New England theater exhibitors, with Roscoe as the guest speaker. After a brief speech, an exhausted Roscoe Arbuckle went back to his hotel, and to bed.

Roscoe did not know it, but he was about to become the

scapegoat for a party filled with debauchery, sex orgies, and bribes.

Brownie Kennedy was a madam with a long string of aliases, a long police record, and a brothel called Mishawum Manor in Woburn, Massachusetts. The brothel offered clients sumptuous food, champagne, and women. According to popular belief, Arbuckle, Zukor, Paramount presidents Hiram Abrams and Walter Greene, Jesse Lasky, and others left the Boston reception and made a beeline for Brownie's place. The group guzzled champagne, enjoyed the women, and paid a hefty bill of more than one thousand dollars.

Several days later Abrams received a phone call from Mayor Curley of Boston, who said the girls at the orgy were talking around town, were naming names and garnering an increasing amount of publicity. Though the girls were prostitutes, they were minors. The police had raided Kennedy's place and were hauling her in on charges. (She eventually got off with a fine and a slap on the wrist.) It would be only a matter of time before the scandal hit the national papers. Paramount's reputation would be sullied and several prominent people (in particular Arbuckle, Lasky, and Zukor) destroyed by the gossip.

According to David Yallo's *The Day the Laughter Stopped*, Boston lawyer David Coakley said he could clear the matter with $100,000 in bribes handed out to the right people. Zukor balked, but eventually he, Lasky, and the other two Paramount executives ponied up and the matter was quashed.

There was only one major error in the story—Arbuckle was not present. In fact, he had not even known about the orgy and the eventual hush money until he read the details in exaggerated form during his own trial five years later. But nevertheless, the story of Brownie Kennedy and her roadhouse sex party with Paramount executives stigmatized Arbuckle during his later struggle to find work in films. Adolph Zukor openly denied any involvement in the Kennedy affair. When Arbuckle's name was erroneously attached to the scandal, Zukor never spoke out to clear Roscoe's name, furthering the belief that Arbuckle had a penchant for such sex orgies.

By the time the tour was formally ended, Roscoe was incapable of any sex life at all. In fact, most likely because of his illness and the problems with his leg, he had become impotent, at least with Minta.

"It was to be one of the last times we tried. Roscoe took me in his arms and cuddled me. We had been fighting quite a lot by then, but Roscoe and I did try to make one last go of things. We kissed for a while, and caressed, you know. Then he started crying. He said he couldn't make love to me, it had been so long and he just wasn't able to. I think because of his leg. Roscoe cried like a baby that night. I cried, too, for him."

Two weeks later, the marriage was officially on the rocks. Roscoe had been spending an increasing amount of time at the Friars Club, a fraternity of sorts for men in theater or films, which Roscoe had recently joined. At first he said he needed to go there to relax with his cronies and to take sorely needed massages and baths for his legs and to regain his health. But by the end of March, Minta learned the real reason for his extended visits.

In a very distant and somewhat nervous phone call, Lou Anger asked Minta to ship Roscoe's clothes to the club. Anger apparently had been setting the stage for the next step of his master plan—to drive the final wedge between Roscoe and Minta, thereby eliminating Minta's influence on Roscoe, who would now be completely under Anger's control. Roscoe was too trusting, too innocent, and too blind to see it coming.

11

Roscoe was getting his health back. By the end of March he had regained most of his weight and had finally been able to appear in public without the padding. Though he still looked tired, his old spark was beginning to come back. He was ready to get back to work. Minta still had hopes that she would appear with him in his new series of comedies. But those hopes were very short-lived.

"Roscoe left me, just like that. I think the excitement of the tour, all those people making such a fuss over him, the money he was going to receive . . . it all went to his head. I was part of his old life, the part that meant a struggle. He saw himself headed into a new life and I just wasn't part of it. I didn't fit in. At least that's what Lou Anger made him believe. So he moved into the Friars Club and our marriage was over."

When Roscoe arrived at the hotel to pick up his clothes, he and Minta had another knock-down, drag-out battle. This time, Roscoe started throwing anything he could lift, smashing vases and mirrors. He accused Minta of trying to destroy him by holding him back. Though he was normally a calm and easygoing man, Roscoe's rage was out of control.

He sent no telegrams and made no calls to Minta for three days. He holed himself up in a room at the Friars Club to sort out his thoughts and collect himself. When he finally did call Minta, the conversation was strained. She asked to see him, but he said they could not meet. He had a prior commitment with Anger and Schenck. Women were not allowed in the Friars Club, so Minta had no choice but to wait. She later

110

learned that Roscoe had not been staying at the Friars as he indicated, but in an area called Sheepshead Bay. His hosts were Lou Anger and Joe Schenck, who were coaching him on how to negotiate a "proper" separation, and eventual divorce, from his wife.

When he returned he arranged a quiet meeting with Minta. He calmly laid out his offer—five hundred dollars a week support while they lived separately as man and wife; Minta was not to interfere in any plans for the new company. Reluctantly, Minta agreed. Anger's plan had succeeded. Arbuckle's first two-reeler under the new Comique banner was set to begin scripting and preproduction.

Joe Schenck's wife, actress Norma Talmadge, was the eldest of three sisters and had had great success in motion pictures and stage. One sister, Constance, was also a star. The other sister, Natalie, was working as a secretary and script girl and later married Buster Keaton. Norma had also established her own studio, the Colony Studio, in a loft building on East Forty-eighth Street in New York. Part of the Colony Studio was leased by Comique in a deal negotiated by Schenck and the Talmadge sisters used other sections of the studio for their own productions. Rehearsals on *The Butcher Boy* were to begin immediately.

It was one big happy family. With the activity of work taking his mind off his personal problems, Roscoe's dour mood lifted and he seemed back in good spirits. Work, both creative and physical, was the one antidote to Roscoe's worries, and he was jubilant over the prospect of beginning a new phase of his already illustrious career. He sat in on every script meeting with newly hired writers Joe Roach and Merberwarren, who were later joined by Vincent Bryan and Jean Havez—all top writers. He worked closely with the cameraman and carefully coached his stock company. He was free to call the shots and make decisions without the usual interference from the front offices that he had experienced at Keystone. He was exhilarated and filled with life once again.

Roscoe later told friends that this new beginning was the best thing that had ever happened to him. "I knew I stepped on a lot of toes, and I knew that Minta got caught in a lot of it. I hated to think that anyone got hurt, but the struggle for me was worth it. I paid for this for many years. This was the plum I waited for." He also told film stunt man/comedian/producer Joe Rock that "for once the Gods, whoever they might be, smiled on me. After all the bad years I had trying to get here, I finally found my niche."

He was also to find a young stage comedian who would become his lifelong friend, ally, and confidant. His name was Buster Keaton.

Keaton was a client of Max Hart, who had been handling Keaton's whole family when they toured in vaudeville. He booked Buster into what was to be his first show as a solo performer, away from the rest of the Keatons. Titled *The Passing Show*, it was produced by J.J. Shubert and was slated for a big run in New York before a road tour.

Several days before the show was to begin rehearsals, Keaton bumped into Lou Anger on the street. Anger was walking with Roscoe, who was well known to Keaton. Arbuckle had also seen Keaton on the stage. Both were admirers of the other's work. Arbuckle and Anger told Keaton of the new production company they had started and asked him to stop by for a visit. Until this time, Buster had not seriously considered life in motion pictures. For him, vaudeville had been quite lucrative. He was earning $250 a week on stage. He assumed film work would be comparable and was shocked when he received his first paycheck—$40 for the week. He was rapidly increased to $75, then $125 dollars a week as a member of the Comique stock company. But this gamble paid off in the long run. He eventually proved so popular that within two years he was given his own company and became an international star.

Keaton had never seen a movie being filmed before and Roscoe invited him to the set to see the zaniness firsthand. The moment Roscoe saw Keaton standing offstage, he waved him over to perform on camera. The scene was shot in one take. Buster's film debut ended up in the final cut. He became an integral part of the cast and of the Comique company. At the core of the company were Arbuckle, Al St. John, Alice Lake, Luke the Dog, and Joe Bordeau (once Roscoe's chauffeur), joined in different comedies by various extras and supporting players. Though Luke the Dog was actually Minta's pet, he became so closely associated with the "Fatty" comedies that Roscoe kept him, and featured him in the series, with no objection from Minta.

The two-reeler that launched both Keaton's film career and the Comique company was *The Butcher Boy*, which is still shown today in revival houses, and still stands as one of the best silent comedies ever produced.

The story revolves around two locations—a country store followed by a girl's boarding school. The film opens at the store with St. John working as a clerk, Roscoe Arbuckle as the bewildered butcher boy, and Josephine Stevens (who appeared only in this film for Roscoe) as the "love interest." Buster Keaton strolls in as a customer looking to buy molasses. Hoping to cheat the store out of a quarter, he drops the coin into his bucket, then asks Roscoe to fill the pail with molasses, assuming Arbuckle would rather forego the quarter than fish through the goo. Roscoe obliges, but outfoxes Keaton by pouring the gooey sweetener into Buster's porkpie hat, which subsequently sticks to Keaton's head. Eventually molasses is everywhere, a fight erupts, pies are thrown, and sacks of flour fly among Roscoe, St. John, and Keaton. The store is a disaster. Stevens is whisked off to boarding school by her uncle to escape the influence of the lunatics.

In order to sneak into the school to see his love, Roscoe dons his now-famous dress and curls. He flirts, winks, dances, and plays coy, doing an outstanding and convincing act as a young girl. St. John tries the same ruse to get in, but is eventually uncovered. A fight ensues, Keaton is called in to help St. John, but Luke the Dog keeps them at bay in front of the schoomarm. Finally Roscoe gets the girl.

The Butcher Boy relied on sight gags and the building of gags into routines (such as the molasses gag building into a major battle). Roscoe steered clear of car chases, physical violence (the fight scenes were more acrobatics than fisticuffs), and concentrated more on story. His freedom from the confines of the Sennett/Keystone days was clearly evident, and the style and subtleties of the film show why Arbuckle stood far above the mainstream screen comedians of his day.

His comedies distinguished themselves from Chaplin's

early two-reelers in that they were gentler, and Roscoe played more to the camera than did Chaplin, who often relied on his obvious athletic prowess and physical violence. Arbuckle had several costumes (his baggy pants and too-small derby being trademark and his dresses being an anticipated gag) while Chaplin now wore only his famous Tramp costume. It is clear why Roscoe was a favorite of middle-class adults and children of every social class, while the core of Chaplin's early audience was upper-class adults and children.

The Butcher Boy was hailed as a great success in almost every newspaper and movie magazine. "A rollicking two reels of round-house and romance," "Fatty's latest will set audiences to uncontrollable laughter," "Newcomer Keaton can take a fall and still come up swinging for laughs." Exhibitors clamored for the new Arbuckle series and within days of the first release Famous Players-Lasky doubled its rental of prints of the new comedy.

The film immediately showed a tidy profit, good news for Arbuckle, Schenck, and Anger, who each garnered a share of the take. (Schenck received the most, 25 percent of the net.) They also held privately-owned stock in Comique, each owning 25 percent of the company with the remaining 10 percent parceled out among several executives at Paramount (Zukor among them). With the profits from the distribution, the salary, perks, and subsequent increase in stock value, Arbuckle stood to make $1 million his first year with Comique!

The world was clearly in Roscoe's pocket; he had it all—fame, fortune, and the prospect of everything getting better every day. But through the haze of the glory and the confusion of his sudden riches, Roscoe made a serious mistake that would haunt him for most of his life. He tried to bury his income from the Internal Revenue Service.

Whether he fudged the facts on his taxes deliberately or unknowingly will never be clear. But records uncovered for the years 1918 through 1920 show Arbuckle declared his total income at $250,000: the salary he received from Famous Players-Lasky. There is no indication of the additional income from Comique stock or profits on his films which skyrocketed his income to four times that amount. He listed deductions for those three years as the amounts paid to Schenck and Anger in commissions, with, in 1919, a five hundred dollar per week deduction for "support" of Minta Durfee.

Roscoe also listed several other debts and deductions, specifically from other stock investments (Famous Players-Lasky stock among them) and two real-estate investments in New York which Roscoe took as a loss.

Roscoe later admitted to authorities during a 1922 IRS probe that Anger was the mastermind behind the real-estate and stock deals (which were legitimate) and that he usually managed Roscoe's finances. But to name him as the culprit behind the alleged fraud would be speculation. In any event, Roscoe started laying the groundwork for the first of a barrage of accusations, real and trumped up, that would soon taint his reputation and destroy his career.

As far as Roscoe was concerned, 1917 was proving to be a banner year. His new company was enormously successful, and he had more money than he ever imagined, a widening circle of friends, and adulation from a very receptive public in America and around the world. Roscoe's picture appeared in advertisements for a range of products from chewing gum to soap to cigarettes. There was rarely a day when his name was not mentioned in a newspaper or movie fan magazine. He was generous to a fault with friends and spent enormous amounts of money on gifts for co-workers and crews. He never turned down anyone who needed a handout.

In *My Wonderful World of Slapstick*, Buster Keaton recalls his early years with Roscoe. "The longer I worked with Roscoe the more I liked him . . . He took falls no other man his weight ever attempted, had a wonderful mind for action gags, which he could devise on the spot . . . Arbuckle was a rarity, a truly jolly fat man. He had no meanness, malice or jealousy in him. Everything seemed to amuse and delight him. He was free with advice and too free in spending and lending money. I could not have found a better-natured man to teach me the movie business, or a more knowledgeable one. We never had an argument."

In fact Roscoe and Buster became the best of friends and quickly earned a reputation in New York (and later in Los

Angeles) as a devilish pair of practical jokers. One of their earliest gags happened during the filming of *The Butcher Boy*, during a sequence in which Roscoe throws a blackberry pie at Al St. John.

Buster, Roscoe, and Al had become extremely annoyed at a young man who was continually playing up to an actress named Anita King (who was working with another company on the Talmadge lot). The man was knocking himself out kissing her hand, holding doors open, making a complete fool of himself (in their eyes) over this girl. Buster, Roscoe, and Al staged their pie-throwing scene so that when Roscoe hurled a pie, St. John ducked, sailing the pie smack into the young Lothario's face.

When the pie hit the man, the trio reached over to apologize, claiming it was an accident. But under the guise of brushing off the mess, Buster, Roscoe, and Al smeared the blackberry further. The man was never quite sure if he was set up or not.

In addition to being a co-conspirator, Keaton also became a trusted gagman and writer, bringing over many of the routines and jokes he had developed from his life in vaudeville. Often, Roscoe just let Buster loose on the set to improvise, instructing the cameramen to roll and the actors to play off Keaton. He proved to be an invaluable companion, both personally and professionally, to Arbuckle. He called Roscoe his greatest influence and his greatest friend. The two men were inseparable, making the rounds of clubs at night, working and perfecting stunts and jokes during the day.

The Comique company had no specific lot of its own, bouncing from studio to studio in and around New York to save money and to avoid complaints from neighbors about the noise they made during late-night shooting. It seemed that from the beginning of their time in New York, Schenck had been scouting out a more permanent home for the Comique company.

In October of 1917, Schenck ordered the group to pack up and head west, to permanently relocate in Southern California.

The Hollywood Roscoe left in 1916 was quite different from the town to which he returned. The population had skyrocketed nearly 150 percent. Movie stars now ruled the town, earning thousands of dollars a week while the rest of the country struggled to survive the effects of the Great War and wages of ten dollars a week. Where they were once treated as second-class citizens (no dogs or actors allowed in boardinghouses), they were now welcomed as royalty, hounded by fans for autographs, chased by photographers for pictures.

Forty million Americans spent thousands of nickels and dimes at movie theaters each week to see Chaplin, Fairbanks, Pickford, Mary Miles Minter, William S. Hart, Harold Lloyd, Wally Reid, Lillian and Dorothy Gish, and Roscoe "Fatty" Arbuckle. The motion-picture business raked in more than $25 million per year in profits from hourlong features and fifteen-minute two-reelers. Theaters sprang up all over the country, gobbling up films as fast as producers could churn them out.

Many of the stars were just kids, barely out of their teens at most. Many were from poor families; Arbuckle's background was typical. But once they caught the nod from a producer and the eye of a camera they were catapulted into the high life, a life of decadent parties filled with booze and drugs, money beyond their imagination, mansions, sports cars and unheard-of luxuries. They spent money as fast as they earned it.

The movie business was no longer the bottom of the barrel of the entertainment industry. Stage actors who once turned up their noses at motion pictures, or who accepted work under a cloak of secrecy and anonymity, now lined up for supporting parts and starring roles.

Hollywood was still an oddly rural cowboy town with dirt roads, few night spots, and little in the way of social life. But it had a certain innocence, a wide-eyed naïveté where anyone with a good idea and a bit of gumption could talk his way onto a studio lot and get in on the action. It was all too new for any snobbishness.

Roscoe, who always favored California, was thrilled at the idea of returning and immediately began thinking of a plot with a solid western theme. His second two-reeler, shot in Long Beach, California, was titled *Out West*, a spoof on the

Old West, complete with a saloon, show girls, and outlaws. It also proved to be one of his biggest successes to date.

When Roscoe, Buster, Al St. John, Alice Lake, and company headed west, one person remained behind. Minta chose to stay in New York, where she would seek work in films and onstage. Her marriage was over, and a final decree was pending through the persistence of Lou Anger.

Without the emotional and physical ties of a wife, Roscoe was completely free. He later told Joe Rock that he "felt like a tremendous burden had been lifted again. There were no ties, no more arguments, just complete freedom to work as hard as he wanted and play when he needed. He felt like a kid again. Only this time he was living the childhood he never really had before. He said it was great fun!"

That fun manifested itself in a number of ways—usually in the form of gags and practical jokes with Keaton.

The two played baseball, cards and went fishing. They also had a secret code for their jokes; they called them "Special Operations." One prank was played on actress Pauline Frederick, who had an enormous mansion in Beverly Hills. In the late teens, actors spent money wildly, and usually to impress fellow actors. One of the popular status symbols among the nouveaux riches of Hollywood was to import grass lawns from England. Frederick had done just that, planting an enormous imported lawn in front of her mansion.

One day, just after dawn, Keaton, Arbuckle, and St. John arrived at Frederick's posing as water-company workers (complete with a rented water-company truck), informing the butler that there was a water leak reported to the company. To track down the "leak," they rolled up the entire lawn and carted it away! They, of course, returned it after Frederick woke up to find a field of dirt where her newly planted lawn had rested the day before.

There was also a get-rich-quick scheme of Roscoe's. He saw horse-drawn trucks hauling gravel away for five dollars a load. He believed that if he bought the gravel pit, hired the drivers and wagons, and sold the gravel to construction companies, he could make at least one hundred dollars a day profit. The scheme was turned down by Anger who saw no future in the gravel business. He told Roscoe to stick to more secure investments such as the stock market. A short time after Roscoe turned the gravel deal down, oil was discovered in the pit.

The core group of Arbuckle, Keaton, St. John, and Alice Lake turned out a highly successful two-reeler for Famous Players-Lasky every other month, each bringing in unprecedented profits for Zukor's Paramount and the Comique company stockholders. Arbuckle was threatening Chaplin's position as the most popular comedian in the world. He openly admitted that his "core" company helped put him there. Roscoe was on a roll; he was mobbed on the streets, he was noted for his free spending. (One interview claimed Roscoe spent nearly half a million dollars per year on clothes, toiletries, cars, and presents—which presented a curious financial problem in light of his income-tax declarations of $250,000 per year.) There was no stopping him.

But in November of 1918, America entered the "War to End All Wars" and the man whom Roscoe called "my right hand" was called to serve his country. When Buster Keaton was drafted into the army, Roscoe wept. He said he felt as if his world was coming to an end.

12

While Buster Keaton was serving his time with the 40th Infantry (as a private earning thirty dollars a month), the Hollywood studios were undergoing a major upheaval, with a power struggle under way by several top moguls. At the forefront of the struggle was Adolph Zukor, who made several unscrupulous moves to seize control of the motion-picture industry. What Zukor saw was the threat of too many studios competing for too little theater space. Small studios were cropping up twice as fast as others went out of business. Anyone with a few hundred dollars, an idea, and a camera headed west to take a shot at moving pictures and openly peddled their wares to anyone who would give them time and space. Any stars who turned a profit were quickly raided by the larger, more profitable studios, lured into breaking contracts with offers of bigger money and better films. Producers battled producers for writers, directors, and actors. Studio presidents battled one another for control of production companies and theaters. The entire town seemed to be one massive board game in which the players were the would-be moguls, the pawns the actors.

Louis B. Mayer, a major producer, left Metro Pictures to form his own production company which would eventually be absorbed into M-G-M. Loew's the reigning exhibitor chain, was swallowing up minor movie houses in its push for domination of the theaters across America, and eventually won control of Metro Pictures and Goldwyn Pictures in a take-over bid.

The shrewd Adolph Zukor was laying the groundwork to buy up theaters and expand his empire into exhibition as well as production, enhancing the clout of the powerful film-making empire. While planning his move, he continued to release expensive feaures under his Artcraft label, the lower-budget films under the newly created Realart. He was in negotiations with William Randolph Hearst to merge Hearst's Cosmopolitan Productions (with its star Marion Davies) under the Paramount banner. If a company made money, Zukor tried to buy it, merge it, or squeeze it out of business. He openly stated one clear-cut aim—to own Holly-wood. His former friend and ally Nicholas Schenck was slowly becoming his rival as the president of Loew's, Para-mount's closest competitor.

Zukor also saw the desertion of Hiram Abrams (a former Paramount president and pal from the Brownie Kennedy adventure), with whom Zukor had a falling out over finances and mergers. Abrams teamed up with Paramount's general manager, Ben Schulberg (who also left Zukor after an argu-ment), and approached D.W. Griffith, Charlie Chaplin, Mary Pickford, and Douglas Fairbanks to form their own company which distributed the stars' films produced by other studios. United Artists was born and further threatened to crack Zukor's fortress. The studio wars were on; the battle was fought with money, fueled by wealthy studios with open checkbooks.

As a means of keeping United Artists in check, and rival producer First National (which had theaters in every major city) away from a monopoly, Zukor wooed financier Otto Kahn with $10 million worth of Famous Players-Lasky stock to back the construction of lavish cinemas in cities where First National had a foothold. The scheme worked and Zukor gave the company a run for its money.

When Keaton returned from the war in 1919, he immedi-ately headed to Hollywood to rejoin Arbuckle, St. John, and the gang. He was besieged with offers from film producers who had been trying to star him in their own comedies for as much as one thousand dollars a week. But he chose to return to Joe Schenck, for whom he felt a fondness and loyalty. "Schenck was the nicest man I ever met," he often told reporters. Keaton made three more two-reelers with Roscoe, then was brought to a conference with Schenck.

Schenck presented Keaton with an offer that floored him —he would head his own production unit and star in his own series, to be released by Metro Pictures. (Loew's was negotiating the deal to buy Metro Pictures and Schenck was a silent partner in the deal.) Schenck would serve as producer and would supervise Keaton if he needed it, which he did not. Keaton agreed to the offer and a short time later Schenck bought the Chaplin lot and renamed it the Keaton Studios. The films initially were produced under the Comique banner, and Arbuckle, Schenck, Anger, and now Keaton divided the stock profits from the films. Buster was then handed the Arbuckle unit and a new contract worth one thousand a week plus 25 percent of the profits. Keaton would continue to make two-reelers. As for Arbuckle, Schenck (and Zukor) had other plans, which centered around a so-called "escape clause" in Roscoe's contract with Schenck.

There is a common misconception that Arbuckle and Schenck had only a verbal agreement on their initial five-year deal together. But a written agreement exists in the Paramount archives. It is unthinkable that a cautious and experienced businessman such as Schenck would not put the terms of his agreement with Arbuckle in writing, especially an agreement that involved stock trades, percentages of net profits, and other incentives. And Roscoe had been in the film business too long not to know that a verbal agreement would lead only to misunderstandings, misinterpretations, and trouble.

Under the terms of the agreement, neither Schenck nor Arbuckle could break the contract without significant penalty or loss of work for the duration of the unworked contract. The catch in the contract provided that Arbuckle's contract could be bought out by another studio if the studio reimbursed Schenck for the cash value of the remainder of the contract. There was also another stipulation that directly involved Adolph Zukor.

With the Arbuckle comedies commanding greater and greater return at the box office, and profits for all those involved soaring, Zukor opted to play out the option in

Arbuckle's deal with Schenck. The option left the door open for renegotiations with Famous Players-Lasky if and when the output by Comique was increased. Zukor knew if two reels brought in hundreds of thousands of dollars as a prelude to Paramount features, Arbuckle featured in star billing would quadruple the studio's profits, bringing in millions in rental fees. He also hoped he could woo Roscoe into features without raising his salary.

He made Arbuckle and Schenck an offer that had never before been presented to any actor, let alone a comedian, in motion pictures. Zukor wanted Arbuckle and Schenck to expand their Comique comedies into features beginning in October 1920, with a guarantee of seven features per year for a total of twenty-two features. The contract would run approximately three years. The Comique company would formally fold as far as screen production credit went, and the features would be produced under the Famous Players-Lasky banner.

In exchange, Schenck would continue to receive his 25 percent share of the net, and Arbuckle would receive 10 percent, plus perks if rentals exceeded an unspecified amount "to be negotiated in good faith."

Zukor was a cold and calculating businessman. He knew that Arbuckle was already netting close to $1 million per year under his current deal with Schenck. He had to entice Arbuckle to take the bait, and find a way to do it without costing the studios a minor fortune in salary.

Zukor knew that Arbuckle would jump at the chance to work in features with the promise of complete artistic control —the same environment in which he had established his Comique company—plus a percentage of the net. It was an offer that would boost Arbuckle's prestige and income well ahead of Charlie Chaplin's. (Chaplin was still doing two-reelers for First National Pictures. He would not step into features until February 1922 with the release of *The Kid.*) But Zukor would not come up significantly from the current $250,000 salary.

Relations between Zukor and Schenck had been severely strained for some time. Zukor lost Keaton to Metro and blamed Schenck for letting him slip away, though Zukor openly admitted he would not meet Schenck's financial demands for the comedian and had made no significant offers for Keaton. Years later, Zukor admitted that losing Keaton was a major error in judgment, and that he had underestimated the comedian's abilities and his potential.

Schenck's brother Nick had once been a close associate of Zukor's when Zukor was building his Paramount empire. But while Zukor was building up his studio, Nick Schenck was strenghtening his position with Marcus Loew, the film exhibitor and theater owner. As Schenck rose to become president of Loew's (which eventually was the holding company for M-G-M, which in turn squeezed Zukor and Paramount out of the top seat in film production), he often clashed with Zukor, who considered him a threat and a traitor to their friendship.

Joe Schenck was one of the most powerful producers in Hollywood and a multimillionaire through his representation of such stars as Arbuckle, Keaton, and the Talmadge sisters. He also played a major role in the formation of United Artists, Paramount's competitor in distribution, a fact that did not sit well with Zukor. Zukor was used to, and insisted on, complete control of his stars and producers. He despised clashes with such a formidable opponent, especially when he knew that Arbuckle could pick up a better deal at any studio the very second word got out that Arbuckle and Schenck were looking around.

Studios and many stars had no scruples about jumping ship and breaking a star's contract with a better offer (or dumping a star regardless of the contract if the films failed to show a good profit). Schenck had received a number of offers from rival studios for Roscoe's services. Pushing the hardest was Loew's (through Nick Schenck), which offered Arbuckle $1.25 million a year in salary plus a percentage of the net. Universal Studios (which was considered the bastion of melodramas with its stars Carmel Myers, Lew Cody, Mae Murray, and the youngest Schenck brother, Earl) had also presented a tidy offer in the hope of boosting its prestige and box-office take with a major name. The offers were widely known in the film industry.

But Zukor was not sitting idle either. He had another fat

comedian under contract, a man named Walter Hiers. Hiers had already appeared in features with Paramount and Goldwyn. It seemed odd that Zukor would have two comedians of similar type under contract unless he was either taking a precaution, had plans for one, or needed leverage to keep one of the stars in line. The last assumption seems the most plausible—that Zukor used Hiers as a threat that Roscoe could easily be replaced if he did not meet the mogul's demands.

Schenck also drove a hard bargin. According to the Paramount files, Zukor sweetened the pot with the offer of Paramount stock in unspecified amounts. But the bickering continued. Zukor made his last move—he offered to buy out the remainder of Arbuckle's contract with Schenck for approximately $750,000 in cash, and to up his cash salary offer to $1 million a year, plus added stock incentives. According to published interviews with Joe Schenck, at the end of those three years Arbuckle's contract would revert back to Schenck, and Zukor would have the right of first refusal before Schenck could bargain with any other studio. (Schenck also insisted that reports of the million-dollar contract were greatly exaggerated, that Arbuckle was actually earning far less.)

Zukor and Schenck shook hands on the deal with the formal contract to be signed after minor points were negotiated by attorneys. Zukor was a businessman who respected the need for getting legal matters hammered out before putting any agreements into action. He added only one stipulation to the final agreement. According to papers uncovered in both the Paramount archives and Schenck collection, Roscoe Arbuckle would not begin receiving his $1 million a year salary until all the points of the contract were agreed upon and the final draft was signed by Arbuckle.

Haggling over those unspecified points took more than six months. The contract was officially signed in January 1921, three months after Arbuckle released his first feature for Famous Players-Lasky! It is not known whether Roscoe's salary was made retroactive to August 1920. In any event, Arbuckle still maintained to the Internal Revenue Service that he earned only $250,000 in 1920. No papers could be found in any files indicating the true amount of money paid to Arbuckle, nor when he had received any pay boost.

According to Joe Rock (who had known Schenck well and Zukor on a limited basis), Zukor was angry at the final deal. "Zukor never spent a dime he didn't have to spend. It's very suspicious that he would have agreed to quadruple Roscoe's salary without being forced. No producer would do that, not even me. It's just not good business to increase a star's salary by that much at one time. In the long run, it could break you because the other stars see what's going on and demand the same deal. I wouldn't be surprised if Zukor never paid a dime on that contract. It also makes sense to me that he would do everything he could to put Roscoe back in his place."

Journalist Adela Rogers St. Johns agreed. "From $250,000 to one million a year? Zukor would do that only to keep the others out of his hair—the other studios. He was very shrewd and calculating. He didn't get to be the biggest and most powerful producer in town by being a nice guy."

The fuse was lit for a major blowup, but Arbuckle did not know it. In fact, he had no inkling of the power struggle that was under way between Joe Schenck and Zukor. He cared little for the wheelings and dealings of the business side of filmmaking. He concentrated on creativity and having fun. The rest, he believed, would take care of itself.

When the Comique troops relocated to Southern California, Schenck encouraged Arbuckle to buy a house instead of renting . . . a big house. He believed property was a solid investment as well as a hedge against the future. Spending no time shopping around, Arbuckle paid $250,000 in cash for Theda Bara's mansion at 649 West Adams, considered at the time "the" place to live if you had money to burn. The house was ornately furnished and Roscoe added hundreds of thousands of dollars in furnishings and knick-knacks to the decor. He had a cellar stacked floor to ceiling with liquor (which became his most valuable asset when Prohibition was enacted on January 16, 1920, making his parties the most popular in town). He bought imported paneling, crystal chandeliers, Oriental rugs, marble counters, gold-leaved bathtubs, rare oil paintings, and antique china and crystal services. He had a butler, a chauffeur, and six cars, including a Rolls-Royce that

Schenck gave him as an incentive to leave Keystone and Sennett.

To be closer to Long Beach (where Arbuckle spent a great deal of time not only shooting but relaxing) he bought a second mansion at 1621 East Ocean Avenue. A tunnel extended from his property through a bluff to the beach below. He kept a silver-trimmed touring car at the beach house for convenience. He rode horses on the beach at night and had boisterous parties with imported liquor, exotic food, and a parade of guests almost every weekend.

When he traveled to promote his new features he ordered a specially built railroad car called "The Elysium." He rationalized this extravagance to a reporter. "You know what would happen to me in an ordinary Pullman berth. If it was an upper, I'd fall right through onto the person below, and if it was a lower, I'd fall onto the tracks."

Roscoe also ordered lavish, custom-built dressing rooms while on location during his productions. "An ordinary dressing room is too small because of my size. When I'm making a movie, the first thing the carpenters have to do is build a house—for me."

Roscoe also formed his own clique—his small circle of friends with whom he partied, pulled pranks, and worked. Members of his group were actresses Viola Dana, Bebe Daniels, and the Talmadge sisters, actors Buster Keaton (now a major star in his own right), Al St. John, Lew Cody, Norman Kerry, Buster Collier, and Lowell Sherman, directors Fred Fischbach and Al Goulding. But the real team was Keaton and Arbuckle.

As Roscoe's popularity and wealth grew, so did the zaniness of his pranks. Most were harmless and left the perpetrators and the victims laughing together. One of his most famous was played on Adolph Zukor and carried out by Keaton, who was living with Arbuckle in his West Adams mansion until Buster bought a home of his own.

Several weeks after the feature deal was closed, Zukor came to Hollywood for a visit. Arbuckle invited the mogul to his West Adams home for dinner. It would be their first face-to-face meeting since the new agreement.

Keaton signed on as "the butler," assuming that in the

dimly lighted room Zukor and his small entourage would not recognize him. To make sure the gag came off without a hitch, Arbuckle invited an impressive guest list to keep the conversation flowing and Zukor distracted from getting a good look at Keaton. All the guests, who included Sid Grauman, Viola Dana, Bebe Daniels, and Alice Lake, were in on the setup. They also had orders not to laugh at Keaton or else cover up their laughter with an offhand remark about a joke they had heard or a funny routine they had seen in the movies.

The plan went into action. Keaton, dressed in a waiter's uniform, served a tray of shrimp cocktails to the men first. (Proper etiquette would have been to serve the ladies first.) Zukor dug in, not noticing the break in decorum. Then Keaton served the women. Arbuckle rose from the table and, acting very embarrassed at his help, corralled Keaton into the kitchen for a loud reprimand. Keaton raced from the kitchen and yanked the shrimp away from the men (some right out of their hand) and switched the shrimp with those the women were eating.

Next, Keaton brought out soup bowls and a ladle, but no soup. When he went back into the kitchen he created a racket and came out dripping wet, as if he had spilled the soup all over himself. (It was actually water.) Keaton said nothing and took the soup bowls again.

Roscoe turned on the anger. He worked himself into a rage that threatened to be so violent that Zukor reached over to Arbuckle and tried to calm him down by telling him he did not want soup anyway.

"I'm sorry, Mr. Zukor. But I think I have an awful problem with my servant."

"We have the same problems back east, too, Roscoe. It's impossible to find intelligent servants."

The next phase was the filling of water glasses. Keaton carefully poured ice water into each glass until he got to Bebe Daniels. He flirted with her while pouring the water, not looking where he was pouring, missing her glass completely and dumping ice water on Roscoe. Roscoe screamed and grabbed his "hired help" by the back of the neck and hauled him into the kitchen for another loud scolding. Zukor again tried to calm Roscoe down without success. Then Grauman chimed in that he believed the butler had a drinking problem, accounting for his unusual behavior. Keaton and Arbuckle could barely contain their laughter behind the kitchen door. Once they straightened up, they put the last phase into action.

Buster carried in a massive turkey, complete with trimmings, on a silver platter. Arbuckle gave an approving nod and ordered Keaton to carve it in the kitchen. As he entered the kitchen, Buster dropped his service towel. While he was bending over to pick it up, one of the guests pushed the door open, hitting Buster on the backside, sending him and the turkey crashing into one mess on the floor. Keaton was covered from head to toe with potatoes, parsley, and gravy.

He slowly picked up the bird, nonchalantly brushed it off, and made as if he was going to serve it to the guests. Arbuckle's "temper" could no longer be contained. "I'll kill you, you dumb bastard! I'll kill you!"

By now Zukor was fit to be tied. He pleaded with Bebe Daniels to control Roscoe before he really did kill "the stupid waiter." Daniels opened the kitchen door to let the guests see the full picture of Roscoe crashing a bottle over the poor servant's head. (The bottle was a prop breakaway bottle filled with tea.) The "stupid waiter" ran out the back door screaming.

Arbuckle announced to the group that his chef had prepared a second turkey, and the rest of the dinner proceeded normally.

Moments later the phone rang. Arbuckle answered it, talked for a few minutes, then announced to the party that Buster Keaton was on his way to join them for dessert.

Zukor's face lit up. "Oh yes, Keaton. A wonderful performer." Grauman added the final touch. "He's an unforgettable type of actor."

When Keaton arrived, Zukor and his associates informed him of "the damnedest waiter you ever saw." One man then pointed out a close resemblance to Buster. Zukor gave Keaton a hard look and caught on to the gag.

Roscoe and Keaton played another elaborate gag on a dressmaker who stockpiled vintage wines, but refused to share his stock when Prohibition came, serving cheaper wine, bootleg liquor, or near beer.

His name was Vic Levy, and he opened his vast wine cellar only for the "socially elite," such as visiting dignitaries or royalty. Arbuckle and Keaton thought him pretentious and knew they had to take him down a notch.

Keaton saw a newspaper article announcing the arrival of the king and queen of Belgium and knew Levy would outdo himself trying to impress the visiting royalty. Levy had done a considerable amount for Belgian causes during World War I and did not think twice when he received a telegram from an emissary announcing the couple would pay a social call at his home. The telegram also mentioned the royal couple's interest in American movies, and suggested that Levy might invite several stars for the occasion. Lew Cody, Hoot Gibson, Norman Kerry, and Tom Mix were mentioned.

The telegram was fake, of course, sent by Arbuckle and Keaton, who then hired two actors who were look-alikes for the Belgian rulers. They rented costumes and the gag was off and running.

Levy was out of his mind with excitement. He released his own cook for the night and hired a chef from the elite Jonathan Club. He hired an orchestra, a maid, a waiter, and a butler. He also hired a chauffeur and a limousine to pick up the "king and queen" at the airport and escort them to his home. Upon hearing that news Keaton added one more touch —he hired extras to pose as police bodyguards for his imposters.

Levy's home was specially decorated for the affair and the dinner was lavish with expensive food. Not only did they force him to shell out quite a bit of money, but Arbuckle and Keaton reached their main objective. Levy uncorked an array of expensive imported and vintage wines for the "monarchs," topping off the evening with one-hundred-year-old Napoloen brandy.

The impostors and guests thanked him for a wonderful evening and left, never letting on to the truth!

The party never stopped for Roscoe, who continually burned the candle at both ends. After work Arbuckle, Keaton, and their friends would head out to beach front cafés, nightclubs, and sporting events. Every weekend was filled with sailing, fishing, or letting loose in Catalina, Tijuana, Lake Arrowhead, or San Francisco.

Keaton and Arbuckle went to San Francisco on many weekends, usually joined by friends for the weekend escapades. When the two got together, it was a certainty that practical jokes would follow, even in a hotel.

Buster's wife, Eleanor, recalled one specific incident in which the boys pulled a joke on a hotel maid. "They usually worked six days a week, so when they got time off they used it . . . They used to go to Frisco several times a year to play. One day in a hotel, Buster took his shoes off and went out and scraped them around on the windowsills to get them dirty. Then he did a hand-in-hand with Roscoe . . . where Buster stood upside down in Roscoe's hands . . . he walked up the wall . . . across the ceiling, and then down the other wall, leaving shoe prints all around the room to look like someone had actually walked the walls. They did it just to drive the help crazy! Just a sudden inspiration they had. Just in fun."

San Francisco became the frequent weekend jaunt for many movie people. It was a sophisticated city with more night life than there was in Los Angeles; there was more to do, more to see, and more trouble to find. It was easier to get good bootleg liquor instead of the bathtub hootch more commonly found in L.A. And the city was far and away prettier and more restful than Hollywood.

But San Francisco was also a city that looked down on its southern counterpart. Many of its residents cast a superior eye toward Los Angeles, and looked upon film stars as "trash." They resented their coming to the city and flaunting their nouveau riche wealth. Many of the stars, including Arbuckle, looked upon the city as one big party town, which rankled many native San Franciscans. In 1921 the *San Francisco Examiner* ran an editorial condemning the "rogues and ruffians from Hollywood . . . who disrupt our peaceful city with their ill-mannered ways . . . they behave like children who had not yet experienced the back hand of a parent . . . they spend money wildly, and expect their conduct to be forgiven with the wave of a dollar bill." There was very vocal ill will between San Francisco and Los Angeles and the northern city made its position known.

Several local women's groups were discussing ways to keep visitors from Hollywood out of the city without destroying the tourist trade. San Francisco had a problem on its hands and was looking for a solution to rid itself of the "movie star vermin." With an eye on the governor's mansion, San Francisco District Attorney Matthew Brady promised the people of San Francisco that he would find that "solution" to the problem.

13

The twenties roared through America like an uncontrollable fire. Speakeasies sprang up in every city and town, plying unsuspecting patrons with rotgut gin, spiked "needle" beer, and grain alcohol hootch. It was the dawn of the gangster, the eve of the Charleston, the rise of the flapper, and the beginning of America's ten-year drunk. Prohibition was a knee-jerk reaction by a chosen few who had decided that America's moral decay was being uncorked by the excess of John Barleycorn and Jack Daniel's. But instead of stemming the flow of debauchery, the law made drinking, partying, and sexual immorality wickedly naughty and temptingly fun.

Nowhere did the twenties roar more loudly than in Hollywood, among the young millionaire movie stars who flaunted their dissolute life-style on the screen, enticing other young people to come out and join in the fun. The movies set the pace for Middle America, as millions of housewives copied the fashions of their idols and workingmen tried to emulate the sexual machismo of such stars as John Gilbert, Douglas Fairbanks, and Rudolph Valentino. Movies played fast and loose with the facts of life, and wide-eyed Americans grew discontent and anxious as they lost the battle to keep pace with the stars.

In addition to alcohol, drugs became a major nightmare in Hollywood. Cocaine was as common as aspirin and major stars blew their fortunes on thousand-dollar-a-week cocaine habits. Studios had their own pushers and films often skirted the fringes of cocaine and alcohol abuse in their plots. The industry that was once looked down upon by legitimate actors was now overrun with stage stars, has-beens, and hopefuls looking to crash in and cash in on fortune and life in the fast lane.

In September 1920, Hollywood was rocked by its first real scandal. Olive Thomas, the girl loved by millions around the world as the essence of innocence and sweetness, was found dead in a Paris hotel. The cause of death—suicide by poisoning. There were rumors that she had given up on life, frustrated over her husband's desperate cocaine addiction. Her husband was Jack Pickford, Mary's younger brother, a rising star at Famous Players-Lasky/Paramount, who died a short time later. His death was alleged to be drug-related.

Los Angeles authorities arrested a man nicknamed "Captain Spaulding" on drug charges. He had been a frequent visitor to the Famous Players-Lasky lot and was notorious—and popular—around Hollywood. The "Captain" vowed to name names if the charges were not dropped. They were dropped after a significant amount of hush money was passed out around town. Many who were around Hollywood in those days believed the money came from Zukor, who wanted to avoid a scandal at his studio. The "Captain" reportedly continued his trade at the studio, working alongside his drug-dealing counterparts who managed similar operations on other studio lots in town.

Rumors erupted that beloved Charlie Chaplin's marriage to his child-bride Mildred Harris was in trouble and divorce was imminent. (Charlie was twenty-nine, Harris sixteen and pregnant when they married in 1918.) A shocked nation blamed the affair on Harris, still believing The Little Tramp could do no wrong.

"America's Sweetheart" Mary Pickford divorced movie star Owen Moore and immediately married Douglas Fairbanks. The divorce and seemingly hasty marriage was international news, and within days movie-fan magazines spread stories that Pickford's Nevada divorce was a fraud and accused the star of bigamy.

Adolph Zukor's Paramount seemed to get the brunt of the bad publicity. The studio's biggest heartthrob, Wallace Reid, sustained severe injuries while on a shoot in the High Sierras in 1919. He pleaded with Zukor to fold production so he could return to Los Angeles to recuperate. Reid's movies had symbolized America's fast-driving, hard-driving youth, and Zukor did not want publicity leaked out that his star could not handle his work. Zukor not only ordered Reid to remain on location and continue working, but sent a studio doctor out there with orders to pump Reid full of morphine to keep him on his feet and the film on schedule.

Within days Reid became a morphine addict. In less than one year, his addiction would be so severe that he looked haggard and emaciated, his actions so erratic that he would be confined to a sanitarium. When word of Reid's drug addiction hit the papers, his films were yanked from many theaters and some exhibitors refused to book any more. Though fans eventually rallied behind Reid when he confessed to his problem, he was, for all intents and purposes, washed up, and Zukor refused to pay off the remainder of his contract. In fact, there are rumors still prevalent in Hollywood that when Zukor realized he could no longer make money off the star, he stopped paying Reid's hospital bills and ordered any treatment abruptly withdrawn. Reid went into several severe bouts of withdrawal and died from the shock to his system. Many still blame Zukor for Reid's death.

The stars were out of control, the films degenerating into decadence, and the tabloids soon filled with juicy exploits of the rich and famous.

Since the first frame had flickered against a bed sheet tacked up in an old barn, the moral and righteous had spoken out against the evils of movies. But by 1921, newspapers often ran lengthy editorials lambasting the lecherous lure of Hollywood. The films, they said, glorified sex, adultery, divorce and drugs. They blamed the industry for leading America's youth astray, dragging the country into the gutter, flaunting wealth granted to only a privileged few, and not using the medium for more "upstanding purposes." Churches and temples echoed those cries and demanded reform. Citizens' groups in major cities undertook letter-writing campaigns to the studio bosses, pleading for a curb on the sex and lewd conduct portrayed in the films. Many threatened mass boycotts of "questionable" pictures; some succeeded in their threats and shut down local theaters until more suitable films were booked.

The studio executives had a mess on their hands. They understood and respected the power of the press and the power of the mass audiences. They knew they had to clean up the problem (or at least make it appear that they were getting the problem under control). They needed someone who would establish a code of conduct for the industry and keep close watch on the moral standards of its output. The man the studios began courting was Will Hays, soon to be known and feared throughout the industry as the "Czar of the Movies" with his organization called the Motion Picture Producers and Distributors of America (MPPDA).

In 1920, Hays was heralded as a member of the so-called "Ohio Gang" that helped elect Warren G. Harding president of the United States. With Hays's help, Harding won with one of the greatest landslide victories up to that point in history. Hays became chairman of the Republican party in 1917 at age thirty-eight and carried tremendous political clout. In fact he had his own aspirations for the presidency, but when he could not garner enough support from his party, he reluctantly backed Harding.

As a reward for helping swing the election, Harding appointed Hays U.S. postmaster general on March 21, 1921. He rolled up his sleeves and rammed through major reforms in the system. He established a merit system for promotion, doing away with political favoritism or nepotism in jobs. He extended the length of civil-service jobs, creating the "job for life" categories that later plagued the system with inefficiencies. He beefed up airmail service and enforced efficiency and technical improvements through a watch dog committee. Hays also went public with appeals for literacy and clarity in addressing envelopes. He believed that if the public could not make the effort to address envelopes clearly and literately, it was not the responsibility of the postal workers to do it for them. Hays created the "dead letter office" as a means of storing illegible or undeliverable mail until it was either returned to the sender or thrown away.

Hays was the darling of the press and politicians who extolled the virtues of the man considered above reproach. In fact, some Indiana newspapers even went so far as to compare their native son with Abraham Lincoln! In interviews he described himself as "100 percent American" with a family tree that dated back to the British and Dutch colonists who settled America in the seventeenth and eighteenth centuries. Because of his ancestry, he pompously called himself a branch of the tree that spawned the America we know today. These stories were in turn carried by newspapers in bigger cities such as Chicago and New York until, for many, Hays became synonymous with honesty and respectability. (In truth, Hays was anything but pristine. There were continual allegations of bribe taking and influence peddling from the beginning of his reign as postmaster general. After condemning the movie stars for what he termed "their quick actions toward divorce," Hays himself became entangled in a sticky divorce in 1925. In 1926 he was accused of taking hefty bribes in the Teapot Dome scandal.)

His public image made him the perfect man to set the tone for America's movies. A contingent led by Adolph Zukor (who was frantically trying to clean up the problems with drugs and scandals in his studio), Darryl Zanuck, Lewis Selznick, and Jesse Lasky appointed attorney Charles Pettijohn to make Hays an offer they hoped he would not refuse. Pettijohn, who had known Hays back in their earlier years in Indiana, presented Hays with an offer of $115,000 a year plus additional incentives such as a prepaid life insurance policy, an unlimited expense account, and a full staff with offices paid for by the studios.

Hays wired the group that he needed time to think over the offer. He also cabled Selznick that he believed, at that time, there was no moral incentive for him to govern the motion-picture industry. He expressed concern at the outrage many citizens' groups felt at what was being depicted on the screen. But he said that "all problems were of such a degree as to warrant no outside interference." He indicated he needed something more serious to bring him to Hollywood.

While the studios were trying to entice Hays to Hollywood, the Los Angeles city council swung into action to block the move. An ordinance already existed in Los Angeles that allowed for censorship of the movies according to the dictates of a council-appointed censorship commission. The ordinance, passed in 1917, had never been enforced but was being revived by public groups. It was heavily opposed by the film industry, which claimed censorship stemming from the council would be politically motivated. It also claimed the ordinance would send the wrong message to the rest of the country—that Los Angeles, the heart of the movie industry, had to hire a censorship commission to regulate its business. It said the commission would cost $200,000 a week to operate, the bulk of that money going for staff salaries.

The council suggested charging producers twenty-five cents per reel of film to offset the cost of the commission. But the studios countered that it would cost them fifty cents per reel in time and manpower to hold special screenings for the commission plus costs to reshoot and re-edit to meet the commission's standards. "No," the producers said, "let us police ourselves. It will be far cheaper in the long run if we hire our own committee."

While Hays was mulling over the studio's offer, Arbuckle was working at a frantic pace. He wrapped up a five-reeler called (ironically) *The Life of the Party* and immediately went into production of another feature called *The Traveling Salesman*. On the heels of those films, he started *Brewster's Millions* in July, and *The Dollar a Year Man* in October, followed by *Gasoline Gus* in January. To satisfy the demands of Zukor and an unquenchable thirst for Roscoe's films by exhibitors, Schenck had plunged him into a deadly pace of three features back to back with scarcely a break between. He pushed Roscoe into production six days a week at the studio and on location. Sunday, Arbuckle's official day off, was spent in story conferences, reworking gags for upcoming scenes.

Whether due to exhaustion or maturity, Roscoe refined his character and slowed down the pacing of his films for the 1921 season. He abandoned his famous gag in which he donned a woman's dress and evolved his screen persona into a more dashing, innocent young man. Each feature proved more popular than its predecessor.

138

In *Gasoline Gus*, Roscoe plays the "village pest" who runs a garage, plays a trombone, and loves the ladies. Lila Lee plays the village sweetheart. The film is set in Texas and the plot centers around a bunco artist who swindles an unsuspecting sucker (Roscoe) into buying barren land. In the end the down-and-out Roscoe becomes the hero and wins the girl when he strikes oil.

In *Leap Year* (which was not released because the scandal broke first) Roscoe is an innocent rich boy who finds himself engaged to a bevy of girls. No matter how hard he tries, he cannot escape the clutches of designing women, losing the girl he really loves—a nurse. He feigns sick in an attempt to get the girls to leave him, but they all converge on his home to help him recover. Roscoe eventually finds husbands for all of his fiancées, and wins back the love of his nurse.

Unfortunately, his frantic nonstop pace did not slow Roscoe down. Instead of resting, he stayed up many nights drinking to unwind or partying with friends. He speeded up his buying frenzy, purchasing diamonds and expensive perfume and gifts for friends, filled his closets with imported suits and shoes he knew he would never wear, stocking two refrigerators with the most expensive food he could find. Much of it spoiled and was thrown away. He also invested heavily in so-called "tax-free securities" which were to quickly backfire and ring up a massive bill with the IRS (in addition to the problems of his reported income.) He was a sucker for any sales pitch and a compulsive spender.

Most of what he bought, he bought on credit. Whether he had not been receiving the million dollars plus salary from Famous Players-Lasky, or was just irresponsible with money, Roscoe ran up hundreds of thousands of dollars' worth of bills. When he was jailed in the Rappé scandal, many merchants who had advanced Roscoe for his purchases called in their loans. Schenck covered the debts for Roscoe, who subsequently reimbursed him when Roscoe got back on his feet.

In September 1921, Roscoe took delivery of a $25,000 custom-built Pierce-Arrow touring car. The car was four times the size of an average car, had a full bar and toilet in the back passenger area, leather seats and solid silver accessories.

Arbuckle told interviewers, "Of course my car's four times the size of anyone else's. I'm four times as big as the average guy!" The car was his pride and joy. Roscoe intended to spend the upcoming Labor Day weekend showing off the car to friends and taking it out for a nice long drive up the coast.

The fourth annual "Paramount Week" was scheduled for the Labor Day weekend. Paramount devised the scheme to exploit its films and its stars, and to illustrate the wholesomeness of the motion-picture industry to a skeptical public. The studio's films were booked into expensive "showplace" theaters across the country and Paramount split the cost of promoting the films fifty-fifty with the exhibitors. Paramount stars were ordered to make special appearances at participating theaters, either to perform or to make a short speech extolling the virtues of Hollywood. Tickets were offered either free or at a discount with the purchase of everything from bread to cold cream. The publicity campaign boosted box office receipts for the movie houses, prestige for the studio, and a positive image for Hollywood.

Gasoline Gus was booked into a Grauman's theater in Hollywood. The feature was hyped with a massive advertising campaign. A newspaper ad extolled the friendship between Sid Grauman and Paramount executives.

"Adolph Zukor, Jesse Lasky, Cecil DeMille: This is Paramount week, an international event made possible by your combined efforts in making only high grade artistic productions. Permit me to congratulate you especially, Mr. Lasky, to whom this great week is dedicated. Signed Sid Grauman."

The ad also gave audiences a preview of the show. "Roscoe (Fatty) Arbuckle in 'Gasoline Gus.' His latest, funniest and wholesomest. Cast includes Lila Lee who appears in person with Lois Wilson Wed., 7:15 and 9:15. Mildred Harris appears in person Thursday, same hours. Grauman's symphony orchestra also appears—Mischa Gutterson, conductor. Henry Murtagh at the Mighty Wurlitzer."

Paramount executives also hoped they could convince their biggest star to participate in the personal-appearance aspect of the week. Two telegrams were sent to Schenck from the front offices, one from Lasky, the other from Zukor. Both demanded that Schenck order Roscoe to appear at Grauman's for the Labor Day showing of *Gasoline Gus*, then at another appearance with Wallace Reid, Conrad Nagel, and Agnes Ayres. Roscoe refused on both occasions. He had other plans. The refusal outraged Zukor who called Roscoe an "uncooperative and ungrateful child." When Zukor pressed Schenck for the reason for Roscoe's refusal to comply with orders, Schenck telegraphed Zukor in New York about a "holiday in San Francisco." Zukor was not a man to forgive and forget, especially when he was shelling out more than $1 million a year.

Lasky tried to calm Zukor down. In his autobiography, *I Blow My Own Horn*, Lasky calls Arbuckle "conscientious, hard-working, intelligent, always agreeable and anxious to please . . . he would invent priceless routines and also had a well-developed directorial sense . . . I don't know of another star who would have submitted to such exorbitant demands [as three features in a row] on his energy. But Fatty Arbuckle wasn't one to grumble. There were no temperamental displays in his repertoire. He went through the triple assignment like a whirling dervish, in his top form. They were the funniest pictures we ever made."

Lasky sent a telegram to Zukor telling him to ease up on Arbuckle, that he deserved his rest and relaxation in San Francisco. Zukor was relentless in his wrath. He was not used to being denied anything from his stars and told Lasky so.

Roscoe was exhausted from his work schedule (and from his extensive social life) and booked advance reservations for three rooms at the St. Francis Hotel in San Francisco. Roscoe had stayed there several times before, and he was quite well known as both a movie star and a guest.

Roscoe spread the word around town that he was throwing a big Labor Day blowout up north. It was open house at the St. Francis. He tried to get a caravan to drive up the coast with him. He asked director Al Goulding, who was busy on a film and could not make it. He asked producer Joe Rock, who was also busy. Actor Lew Cody had other plans but said he would try to get away. Roscoe asked Buster Keaton, who begged off and asked Roscoe to join him and his wife fishing instead. Roscoe wanted nothing to do with a quiet weekend. He wanted to party. Bebe Daniels said she would meet him there later. So did several other friends.

Roscoe's actor friend Lowell Sherman was a definite "yes." He thought the drive up would be great fun. Everything was set when something unusual happened. According to a story Roscoe subsequently told several friends, director Fred Fischbach phoned him Friday night, September 2, shortly before 10:00 P.M. Fischbach (who was a friend of Arbuckle's from their days at Keystone) said he had heard about "the shindig in Frisco" and asked if he could come along. He claimed he needed to head north to scout out some seals for the next picture he was directing.

Minta Durfee, Joe Rock, Lowell Sherman, Alf Goulding, and Adela Rogers St. Johns all said that Roscoe suspected something was wrong, that Fischbach was acting rather strangely on the phone. Unfortunately Roscoe ignored his instincts and packed his bags for what he hoped would be a fun and relaxing weekend. Many people who knew Roscoe believe he was driving straight into a trap.

14

The night before the trip, Arbuckle asked his mechanic to give the Pierce-Arrow a once-over to make sure there would be no mechanical problems along the road. (At that time the road north was a two-lane, winding highway with harrowing curves and many unpaved sections. It was a treacherous drive past San Luis Obispo with no readily accessible towns for miles. Roscoe wanted to be certain his car would make the trip without any trouble.)

While watching his mechanic, Arbuckle accidentally sat down on an acid-soaked rag, which was lying on an old crate. The acid burned through his pants and caused second-degree burns on his leg. He was in a great deal of pain and the thought of sitting on hot leather car seats for eight hours seemed excruciating. Because Fischbach had been so insistent on inviting himself, Roscoe phoned him first to tell him the trip was off because of the accident.

Roscoe told friends that Fischbach was irrational on the phone, screaming and demanding they continue to drive as planned. Arbuckle tried to explain that he could not sit very long because of the burn, but Fischbach argued incessantly, finally backing Roscoe down. Again, Roscoe thought Fischbach's behavior was peculiar, but chose to ignore it.

When the conversation quieted down, Arbuckle mentioned that he would pack the trunk with several cases of liquor from his cellars—bourbon, gin, wine, to enjoy during the party. But Fischbach talked him out of it, claiming that it was unwise to travel with "bootleg booze" in the car. "In case we get stopped," the director said, "we'll be clean. Let me take care of everything when we get to Frisco. I've got connections." Roscoe agreed and packed only a small bag for the weekend jaunt.

With Roscoe driving, he, Lowell Sherman, and Fred Fischbach headed off early Saturday morning. Several hours out of Los Angeles, Roscoe's burned leg started hurting and they stopped to buy a rubber ring for him to sit on. The ring kept his leg raised and made it possible for him to sit, albeit uncomfortably, for the duration of the trip.

Roscoe and his friends rented three adjoining rooms—room 1219 (to be shared by Fischbach and Arbuckle), room 1220 (to be used as the party room), and room 1221 (Lowell Sherman's bedroom). Roscoe phoned ahead and asked the hotel to move the twin bed from room 1220 into room 1219 which already had a double bed. Rooms 1221 and 1219 had separate bathrooms. Room 1220 had usually been used as an adjoining bedroom by the hotel and contained no bathroom of its own.

In a newspaper statement, Arbuckle described what happened next. "We got to San Francisco late Saturday afternoon, and tired with the long drive went straight to the hotel, had an early dinner and went to bed. Sunday we did some sightseeing and called on friends across the Bay."

He left one detail out of his account—a bootlegger who turned up at Arbuckle's twelfth-floor hotel suite shortly after the trio arrived on Saturday. Arbuckle claimed it was Fischbach who phoned the man and ordered several bottles of bourbon and gin. Such dealings with bootleggers were so rampant in the twenties, especially among the rich, that neither Roscoe nor Lowell Sherman gave the matter any consideration. In fact, many bootleggers operated freely in the more expensive hotels with hotel managers looking the other way after a bribe of a bottle or a buck.

While the group was sightseeing, three other people arrived in town and checked into the nearby Palace Hotel—movie-star manager Al Semnacher, a friend of his, and his client.

The friend was Maude Delmont, also known as Bambina Maude Delmont, who carried a string of aliases, including

Montgomery and Rothberg. Delmont had an extensive police record up and down the California coast. By 1921, at least fifty counts had been filed against her on crimes ranging from bigamy to fraud, racketeering to extortion. She was known in Los Angeles and San Francisco as a professional co-respondent: a woman hired to provide compromising pictures to use in divorce cases or for more unscrupulous purposes such as blackmail. She was a smooth talker who showed no compunction against lying when it suited her convenience or wallet.

Professionally, she listed her occupation as a gown model or simply as a model. This matter becomes important later, during Roscoe's Labor Day party to which Delmont and the group would be invited.

Semnacher's client was Virginia Rapp, an actress and model who changed her name to Rappé because, she claimed, it sounded "more elegant." Newspaper accounts of her parentage made her anything from the heir of British royalty to the bastard child of a scrub-woman. The truth most likely lies somewhere in between.

According to an interview given to *The Chicago Examiner* by Virginia's grandmother, Mrs. Caroline Rapp, Virginia Rappé was born out of wedlock after an affair between her mother, Mabel, and an English nobleman who was visiting the Chicago World's Fair in 1894. Mabel had been engaged to the son of a Chicago banker, but broke off the engagement during the affair with the nobleman, who broke his promise to marry her. Ashamed at her plight, Mabel fled to New York where Virginia was born. Mabel died there eleven years later. Caroline Rapp sent for her granddaughter and raised her in Chicago. Caroline said that Virginia developed into a strikingly beautiful girl and, in her teens, was flooded with modeling offers. An acting career naturally followed and Virginia moved to Hollywood.

Several significant elements were left out of Grandmother's story. Virginia was fast and free with the men, and had undergone at least five abortions by the time she was sixteen. At age seventeen she was engaged to a forty-year-old sculptor named John Sample, became pregnant, and gave birth to a baby girl. Sample reportedly jilted Virginia and the baby was put in a foster home. Then, under the guise of studying art, she moved to San Francisco, worked as a model of questionable talent (reportedly posing nude for sculptors, which was quite scandalous in the early part of the century), and became engaged to a wealthy dress designer named Robert Moscovitz, who died in a trolley-car accident.

Destitute after the accident, Virginia moved to Los Angeles and rented an apartment at 504 North Wilton Place with her aunt Leora Deltag. In 1917, Rappé met director Henry "Pathé" Lehrman at a war-bond rally. Legend has it that Lehrman was so entranced that he proposed marriage on their first date. He put her in two pictures he was directing, and helped her pick up work at several local studios, including Keystone, where she met Roscoe Arbuckle and Minta Durfee.

There was always a very strong suspicion (many claim it was more than a suspicion) that Rappé was actually a prostitute, hooked into some sort of "white slavery" racket that several studios, including Keystone, had been involved in. Those involved in the racket enticed girls to Hollywood with promises of anything from movie jobs to money to marriage, then whored them out for profit.

"I couldn't stand that girl," Minta remembered. "She was sweet enough, naïve. But had no morals whatsoever. She'd sleep with any man who asked her. In fact Mack Sennett had to shut the studio down twice because of her . . . because she was spreading lice and some sort of venereal disease. She was a sad case."

In 1918, through Lehrman's pull, Rappé was named "Best Dressed Girl in Pictures." Her photo was used on the cover of several sheet-music scores including "Let Me Call You Sweetheart." Interviews with Virginia appeared in movie magazines such as *The Motion Picture News* and in local newspapers.

In one newspaper interview she told how much she disliked Roscoe Arbuckle, calling him "disgusting and crude . . . vulgar and disrespectful of women." She said he approached her on the Keystone lot and made improper advances. The story was fabricated and most likely trumped up under pressure from Lehrman, who despised Roscoe. Virginia later admitted that she ran into Roscoe after the interview and he showed no ill will. In fact he ordered the band to play "Let Me Call You Sweetheart" and was very charming. Virginia said she changed her mind about him after that evening, much to Lehrman's dismay.

A later newspaper account, written by Roscoe's friend Adela Rogers St. Johns, takes the story of Rappé's encounter with Arbuckle one step further, shedding additional light on the actress's dubious character.

St. Johns wrote, "At that time Miss Rappé had been living only a few blocks from me in Hollywood. The day after Fatty had been indicted . . . the man who did my cleaning came to me and told me: 'I did Virginia Rappé's cleaning. I see where one side says she was a sweet young girl and Mr Arbuckle dragged her into the bedroom [of the St. Francis Hotel]. Well, once I went in her house to hang up some cleaning and the first thing I knew she's torn off her dress and was running outdoors yelling, 'Save me, a man attacked me.' There I was standing in the kitchen with my hands still full of hangers with her clothes on them and she was running out hollering I'd tried to attack her. The neighbors told me whenever she got a few drinks she did that. I hated to lose a good customer, but I thought it was too dangerous so I never went back.' "

Rappé had also become friends with another director on the Keystone lot, Fred Fischbach. Fischbach was also born in New York and had little schooling, working at odd jobs from newsboy to a bootblack, boxer to stunt man, before becoming a property man at Sennett's studio. He was assigned as an assistant to Arbuckle, who taught him the fundamentals of directing.

Eventually Sennett gave Fischbach his own comedy unit to direct. Fischbach was considered a capable director who relied on camera tricks as his trademark. In addition to his work with Arbuckle, he later worked with Lloyd Hamilton, Louise Fazenda, and Baby Peggy.

In late 1919, Fischbach and Arbuckle had a falling-out. The circumstances are not clear, but the two remained casual acquaintances at best. Fischbach was also a friend and co-worker of Lehrman's and had known Virginia Rappé quite well from their work at Sennett and, more recently, at the Sunshine Company.

Rappé starred in a film called *A Twilight Baby*, produced by Lehrman and directed by Jack White in 1920. Shortly after the film's release, the couple broke up (as they had done continually since their first meeting). Newspaper reporters said it was Lehrman who kept breaking off the romance. He finally moved to New York, leaving Virginia alone and pregnant once again with a child she did not want.

Newspaper accounts in 1921 claim Rappé had been "prominently associated with successful motion picture comedies in Los Angeles for the past two years. She was at one time a chorus girl in New York musical comedies and was brought to California two years ago by Henry Lehrman.

"Her first picture was made at Fox Studios, but later when Mr. Lehrman erected his own studio at Culver City, she was featured by him in comedies.

"Recently, it is said, Miss Rappé has been featured in comedies made at the Century Film Corporation studios at Hollywood, recently working in a comedy with Lloyd "Ham" Hamilton, which has just been completed and is soon to be released . . . the comedy directed by Fred Fischbach."

Previously published accounts of the Arbuckle story never explained exactly what Rappé, Delmont, and Semnacher were doing in San Francisco. But according to personal interviews with several people who knew Rappé, Semnacher, and Arbuckle, the actress was headed to San Francisco to have an abortion. Semnacher also had business pending in that city.

Shortly before Labor Day Rappé told her manager, Al Semnacher, of her plans for the abortion. Semnacher reportedly advised her to go up north, out of town, to avoid publicity. Virginia was not one to keep a secret and blabbed her business all over Hollywood and by Labor Day everyone in town knew Rappé was on her way north. Everyone in town also knew her penchant for drinking and lewd, alcohol-induced behavior.

It has always been incorrectly assumed that Semnacher headed north simply to accompany Rappé. But newspaper accounts and San Francisco court documents shed some interesting light and also explain Maude Delmont's presence in the scenario. Semnacher had been trying to obtain a divorce from his wife, Lillian, for several months. She refused to grant the divorce and Semnacher had no grounds. The papers were filed in San Francisco on Tuesday, August 2, the case to be heard by a Judge Summerfield, pending the obtaining of proper grounds.

Records show the grounds were subsequently added by Semnacher as adultery and a court date was set for Friday, September 9. Semnacher later stated that he hired Delmont to obtain evidence of his wife's adultery (described in the court documents as "undue attention to Mrs. Semnacher by another man"). He listed Delmont as a witness to Mrs. Semnacher's dalliances. Delmont apparently was going to appear in court for Semnacher after several days' holiday in San Francisco. (The divorce proceeding was stricken from the court calendar on September 9, when the scandal broke).

On Saturday, September 3, Maude Delmont met Al Semnacher at his Hollywood area home. There she was introduced to Rappé and the three drove north to San Francisco.

A number of guests ventured in and out of the Arbuckle suites during Saturday and Sunday, but overall, the weekend proved uneventful for all concerned until Monday morning, September 5, 1921.

A friend of Fischbach's, a clothing and nightgown salesman named Ira Fortlois, was also in San Francisco, staying at the Palace Hotel. According to police reports, Fortlois contacted Fischbach and arranged a luncheon appointment at the St. Francis Hotel. Arriving on time, Fortlois rang Fischbach from the front desk and was invited up to the rooms. (The fact that Fischbach invited a nightgown salesman to the party seems rather odd in itself, but plays an important part in the complete picture.)

According to all accounts Lowell Sherman and Roscoe were still in their pajamas when Fischbach invited Fortlois into the suites. Sherman, Fischbach, and Arbuckle had been up late with several friends the previous night, but Fischbach was the only one up and dressed by noon.

Most of the people involved in the fateful party basically agreed as to the next series of events. A number of people, estimated at anywhere between fifteen and twenty, had dropped by at various times throughout the day, among them Maude Delmont, Virginia Rappé, and Al Semnacher, and two actresses named Zey Prevon and Alice Blake.

Roscoe intially offered one version of how Delmont, Rappé and Semnacher were invited to the party, then later told friends another story. But both versions maintain the trio was invited by Fred Fischbach—against Roscoe's pleas to keep the group away. Roscoe had been well aware of Delmont's reputation as a troublemaker and Rappé's as a prostitute. In fact, he told Fischbach on several occasions that the women meant nothing but trouble, and he was concerned that he would be asked to leave the hotel when word of Delmont and Rappé's visit reached the hotel manager.

By the time they arrived, the party was in full swing with bootleg booze, catered food and snacks, men and women dancing, and a stream of guests filtering in and out of the rooms. There were allegations of drug use on the part of the guests, but the matter was dropped in court in favor of an investigation into the source of the bootleg liquor.

Lowell Sherman eventually got dressed, but Roscoe only threw a bathrobe over his pajamas. Fred Fischbach took off in Roscoe's car, claiming he thought it would be a good time to check out seals along the coast. Another guest, Mae Taub, told Fischbach she needed a ride into town. Roscoe asked Fischbach either not to leave or to return quickly because he too needed the car. Fischbach reportedly nodded and left in an apparent hurry.

The main players were now in place: a nightgown salesman with samples, a model who was also a professional co-respondent, a known prostitute, bootleg liquor, and (allegedly) drugs . . . all ordered to the room by Fred Fischbach who took off leaving Roscoe and Lowell Sherman with a time bomb on their hands.

In the most basic of scenarios, this is what happened next. The rooms being hot and stuffy, Maude Delmont put on a pair of Lowell Sherman's pajamas and continued to down somewhere between fifteen and twenty scotches. She eventually disappeared with Sherman into his suite for a long period of time. Virginia chugged several orange blossoms (gin and orange juice) until she was extremely drunk. Once drunk, she erupted into convulsions and hysterics, and ran through the suites ripping off her clothes.

Delmont had now moved to the bathroom of room 1221 with Lowell Sherman when Virginia suddenly started pounding on the door, screaming for them to let her in. The door was locked, and after a while, Virginia ran out and into Roscoe's bathroom in 1219. Delmont and Sherman reportedly went into Sherman's suite alone.

Unaware that Virginia was in the bathroom, Roscoe casually entered his adjacent bedroom to dress. When he tried to enter the bathroom to wash up, he could not get in. Something was holding the door shut. He pushed several times and finally opened it far enough to allow sufficient room to squeeze through the opening. He saw Rappé kneeling before the toilet, vomiting. She was screaming in pain, so Roscoe helped her up and sat her down on top of the seat. After she calmed down, he helped her to his bed to stretch out—alone—hoping to calm her down. He then got dressed.

When he finished dressing, Roscoe crossed through the bedroom once again and saw Virginia lying on the floor next to the bed moaning. She had apparently rolled off onto the floor. He put her back in the bed, where she vomited on herself and the bedspread and continued writhing in pain. Roscoe left her for only a moment to get a bucket of ice. At least ten minutes had elapsed from the time Roscoe initially helped Virginia from the bathroom to the bedroom to the time he left to get ice.

Sherman and Delmont had now emerged from his room to join the rest of the party. Disgusted at Virginia's hysterics, and Sherman's obvious dalliance with Delmont, Roscoe took his anger out on Fortlois, who was drunk and was using the party to drum up sales. He asked Sherman to order Fortlois to leave, inasmuch as Fischbach was gone and Fortlois had no other friends there. Several minutes later, Fischbach returned from his "scouting" adventure to find the suites in turmoil and the guests in a drunken panic.

Roscoe returned to the bedroom with the bucket of ice which he thought would serve two purposes—one to calm Rappé down and the other to determine whether or not she was faking her hysterics. (Buster Keaton had once told Roscoe that you could always tell whether or not a woman was faking a fainting spell or hysterics by placing an ice cube against her thigh.) He placed several pieces of ice on her stomach, believing it would cool her fever down, and held one against her thigh.

Delmont staggered in to find Rappé in disarray and Roscoe leaning over the girl, holding ice against her thigh. The ice that Roscoe had placed on Virginia's stomach melted slightly and slid down onto her pelvis. He told Delmont about Virginia's illness, and they agreed she was drunk and not in any real pain or danger.

Suddenly, Virginia started ripping off her clothes and screaming that she was hurt and dying. Upon hearing the screams, Zey Prevon and Alice Blake rushed in.

Roscoe, still assuming Rappé was drunk and faking, told Prevon, "Shut her up! Get her out of here. She makes too much noise." Fischbach entered the room and allegedly teased Roscoe that in spite of his sore leg, he was still able to "have fun" with Virginia. Roscoe did not find the joke funny and told Fischbach so in no uncertain terms. Virginia lapsed into semiconsciousness.

Maude Delmont ordered someone to fill the bathrub with cold water to cool Rappé's fever. While the water was running, Virginia snapped back into consciousness and once again started screaming. She looked at Roscoe and made a series of rambling accusations that, at the time, meant nothing to most people at the party but later proved devastating to Arbuckle's defense.

"Stay away from me! I don't want you near me!" she kept screaming toward Roscoe. Then, turning to Delmont, she shouted, "What did he do to me, Maudie? Roscoe did this to me."

They were the two sentences with which the prosecution nailed down its case and the newspapers (and the American public) tried and convicted Roscoe Arbuckle. Up until now those two sentences have been interpreted either as rambling and incoherent accusations, or as statements trumped up by lying witnesses. But as the facts later unfold, those two statements have a very solid significance in the story of what actually happened at the party to set off Rappé's illness.

The cold tub apparently calmed Virginia down, and Roscoe and Fischbach took her into another room down the hall, room 1227. Maude Delmont followed Virginia into the room "to keep an eye on her" and subsequently passed out in the next bed. Sensing that he needed help, Roscoe phoned for the hotel manager and hotel physician. Assistant Manager Harry J. Boyle answered the call but the hotel's physician, Dr. Arthur Beardslee, was unavailable and a message requesting him was left at the front desk. Eventually another doctor was found, Dr. Olav Kaarboe (who was believed to be Mae Taub's doctor), who examined Virginia and determined that she had simply had too much to drink.

A short time later the hotel detective, a Mr. Glennon, turned up at the party in response to a call from Boyle. He looked in on Rappé, and was convinced that nothing was seriously wrong, and left.

With Rappé out of the way, the party continued with guests becoming increasingly wild and intoxicated. There were stories that Sherman, in a drunken state, tried to wrestle two of the female party guests into his bed, and was summarily reprimanded by Arbuckle who wanted no bootleg-induced orgies. Roscoe checked on Virginia one more time. The party continued without much interruption.

Contrary to previously published reports, Roscoe did leave the party. Late that afternoon, he went for a drive with Mae Taub, who had been waiting for Fischbach to return with the car. Roscoe dropped Taub off and drove down to one of the piers to make arrangements to have his car shipped back to Los Angeles on board the *Harvard*, which served as a commuter boat between San Francisco and L.A. Because of Roscoe's leg, which was still quite sore, he knew he would not be able to drive back to Los Angeles.

Roscoe returned just moments before the hotel physician, Dr. Beardslee, arrived in room 1227. It was just after seven o'clock. Virginia suddenly started screaming again and Beardslee injected her with morphine to ease the pain and quiet her down. Maude Delmont was awakened by Virginia's screams and got out of bed to see what was going on. Dr. Beardslee turned to Delmont and asked her what had happened to Virginia. When Maude Delmont responded, she spun a treacherous tale.

15

Early the following morning, Virginia woke again, screaming in pain. Delmont quickly summoned Dr. Beardslee,
who returned and gave Rappé another morphine injection.
Four hours later, Delmont again called Beardslee because of
Virginia's screaming. When he returned, Delmont informed
him that Virginia had not urinated since the vomiting began
more than fifteen hours earlier, and that might be the cause
of her stomach pain.

The doctor catheterized the girl, which, he later testified,
produced a small amount of urine, about five ounces, and the
urine was tinged with blood. He said the blood was dark,
brownish-black, indicating that whatever had triggered the
injury had happened hours before. The blood was apparently
old and partially clotted. If the injury had been fresh, the
blood would have been bright red.

Beardslee also said there were indications of bladder
trouble—an issue the prosecution would incorrectly use to
indicate Roscoe had jumped upon the girl.

In all, Beardslee checked on Virginia four times during the
day, and contradicted Doctor Kaarboe's findings that the
actress was merely drunk. Beardslee said there were strong
indications of problems with Rappé but gave no orders to
move her to a hospital. He believed that catheterizing her,
releasing the urine and blood from her bladder was enough,
and with rest she would recover. Instead, Rappé's condition
continued to deteriorate.

Delmont phoned another doctor, Melville Rumwell, who

was quite prominent in San Francisco and also associated with a local sanitarium/medical center called Wakefield. Wakefield specialized in maternity and postnatal care. Delmont apparently knew Dr. Rumwell quite well because during the course of his treatment of Virginia, Delmont called him by several "pet" names, including "Rummy" and by his first name. Dr. Rumwell agreed to take over the case after Beardslee was formally relieved by Delmont, who had now placed herself in charge.

Rumwell examined Virginia and found nothing unusual. Virginia was conscious but sore, and said she had no recollection of the specifics surrounding her illness. She vaguely remembered Roscoe carrying her into the bedroom, but she could remember nothing else. Rumwell found no signs of violence, no signs of "attempted rape," no unusual marks or bruises, and agreed with Dr. Beardslee's conclusions. Rappé drifted back to sleep and Delmont repeated the tale she had privately told Dr. Beardslee. Like Beardslee, Rumwell ignored Delmont's ramblings.

Several nurses were called in by Dr. Rumwell to assist with Virginia's examination. The first was Jean Jameson, who was ordered to remain at Virginia's side in case her condition took a turn for the worse. Jameson later admitted in court she saw no sign of any physical violence against Rappé and believed the actress was another victim of bootleg alcohol. But during her stay, Delmont once again expounded her version of what had happened at the party. Jameson took a note, but paid little attention because Delmont's story was inconsistent with the physical evidence (or lack of physical evidence in this case).

When Jameson examined Virginia she noted an amount of dried blood and a vaginal discharge. Rappé claimed she was sore from "excessive intercourse with [Lehrman]" and that she had had the problem for at least six weeks. Jameson believed the girl was suffering from some sort of venereal disease such as gonorrhea, which is highly contagious and, at that time, not readily treatable.

Jameson took herself off the case on Tuesday afternoon, believing her services were no longer needed.

Tuesday afternoon, Arbuckle, Fischbach, and Sherman

checked out of the St. Francis. Arbuckle picked up the tab for the entire weekend, including the bill for room 1227 and meals to that room (Delmont and Rappé's room). Under assurances from Drs. Beardslee and Rumwell that everything was in proper order and there was no cause for concern, the trio drove Roscoe's Pierce-Arrow to the pier, loaded the car, and boarded the *Harvard* for Los Angeles. They did not personally check in on Virginia nor confront Delmont again. At this point Roscoe had no inkling that Delmont was quietly spinning her web of lies to anyone within earshot.

Roscoe later said that Fred Fischbach was very edgy and irritable on the ferry ride home. He brought up Rappé's illness several times; each time Roscoe shrugged it off, believing the girl was merely ill from too much liquor. Finally Roscoe pointedly asked Fischbach why he was so concerned about the girl (whom Roscoe referred to in this conversation as a prostitute), asking if he had "something going" with Rappé. Fischbach shut up and remained silent the remainder of the journey.

During the trip home, Roscoe met Doris Deane, the woman who would become his second wife. Deane was a friend of a man named Irvin Weinberg, who was an acquaintance of Roscoe's. She was traveling to Los Angeles with her mother, and Weinberg thought it would be an ideal time for an introduction.

In a newspaper interview given twelve years after the San Francisco indicent (and several days after Roscoe's death in 1933), Deane recalled Roscoe as being very calm and very gentlemanly on board the boat. He chatted freely with her about a number of subjects. The two seemed to hit it off immediately and were quite taken with one another. She believed that if anything "below board" had happened between Roscoe and Virginia at the St. Francis Hotel, it did not show in Roscoe's face nor in his actions. Roscoe, she felt, was too honest and open to be able to hide anything that well.

The following day, Wednesday, September 7, Roscoe returned to wrap up final editing on a feature called *Freight Prepaid*. He was also sketching out story ideas for a forthcoming feature titled *The Melancholy Spirit*. The story line of that movie is odd in light of the drinking incident at the St.

Francis Hotel. It revolves around a feisty, drunken spirit named Ek which does not have a body and comes down to earth "through" a professor of a spiritualistic society. When it takes over the professor's body, it gets drunk and takes on several scheming politicians. Roscoe reportedly mentioned Doris Deane to director James Cruze as a possible player in the feature, which was later assigned to Will Rogers after the San Francisco "scandal" hit the newspapers.

During a Thursday afternoon meeting with Joe Schenck, Roscoe talked about the weekend in San Francisco and how Fischbach invited Rappé, Delmont, and Semnacher up to the party. In a later interview, Schenck related details of that conversation.

"When Roscoe told me that Rappé and Delmont were at the party I laughed. I remember telling him, 'I'm surprised anyone stayed with those two there.' Having Virginia Rappé at a party was a sure ticket to a quick wrap-up. She was well known everywhere, and her reputation was bad, to say the least. When Roscoe told me Freddy Fischbach was the one who invited them up, I thought to myself, 'That's odd.' I thought Freddy would have known better. I asked Freddy about it a while later and he refused to say anything about it. There was something very strange about the whole affair. I had a feeling something was wrong with the guest list at the party."

Roscoe was very casual about the party and he certainly would have been uneasy talking about Rappé if he had had anything to hide. But he was free and open to friends, who later related details in newspaper interviews or personal accounts of Roscoe. He even menioned the bootleg liquor, but told only close friends that it was Fischbach who ordered it into the room. When he mentioned Fischbach's involvement it was not with the intention of "tattling" on the director, but simply relating the story to those close enough to know that bootleggers were part of daily life among the wealthy movie crowd.

Back in San Francisco, Virginia's condition took a turn for the worse. She broke out in cold and hot sweats and once again started rambling about the party. This time another nurse, Victoria Cumberland, heard Virginia's ramblings and suspected something was seriously wrong. It may have been from overhearing Delmont's lurid stories or her own fever-induced imagination, but once again Rappé mentioned Roscoe bringing her into the bedroom. She also reportedly asked if the nurse knew of a good abortionist in San Francisco. The actress started hemorrhaging once again and Nurse Cumberland restarted the catheterizations and compresses on Virginia's stomach.

According to *The Day the Laughter Stopped*, Delmont allegedly sent two highly suspect telegrams hinting at possible collusion or conspiracy to set Arbuckle up for a trumped-up case of rape. One was supposedly sent to a San Diego area attorney, the other to an attorney in Los Angeles. Author David Yallop claims the telegrams stated that "we" have Roscoe Arbuckle in a hole and there was a chance to make some money. Who the "we" was in the telegrams was never specified.

That evening, Nurse Cumberland took herself off the case after Maude Delmont refused repeated requests to call Dr. Rumwell back in to check on Virginia's deteriorating condition. Cumberland later testified that she felt Rappé's treatment was handled in a sloppy fashion because the proper medical procedures had not been taken (such as cultures to determine what disease, if any, Rappé carried, and X Rays and tests to see if her bladder had ruptured as some suspected).

Dr. Rumwell returned to check on Virginia the next day and noted he suspected Rappé had indeed contracted a case of gonorrhea, which needed immediate treatment. He also said he suspected some sort of kidney problem and that she had a severe infection. Rappé was taken to Wakefield Sanitarium on Thursday afternoon.

Later that night, Rumwell returned to Wakefield to find Virginia in dire straits. She was shaking from a fever, her abdomen was noticeably distended, her heart rate was rapid and irregular, and her blood pressure had dropped to dangerously low levels. Two other doctors were called in to assist in the diagnosis, which Dr. Rumwell now listed as peritonitis—acute infection caused by a rupture of the bladder. He surmised that the infection from the rupture had spread throughout Virginia's body. Drs. Read and Rixford agreed with Dr. Rumwell's conclusion.

They also agreed that Virginia's condition was too delicate at this time for any surgery, that because of the infection she probably would not survive any operation on the bladder. Dr. Rumwell ordered significant doses of opium to relieve the pain and to allow Rappé to rest quietly. He believed, at this time, rest was the most helpful course of action. He also prescribed various doses of general antibiotics (sulfur among them) and hoped the drugs would help fight the infection.

Dr. Rumwell returned to the sanitarium just before midnight Thursday to have one last look at the actress before he retired for the night. Rappé had lapsed into a coma, her skin was a grayish-yellow, and her eyes were dark and sunken. She was drenched in sweat and nearly dehydrated. Her lips were cracked and parched. The doctor realized the drugs had been administered too late to do any good. Rappé was also too far gone for surgery. Dr. Read was called in for a second opinion and, after a brief consultation, backed Dr. Rumwell's assertions. The end was invevitable and only a matter of a very short time.

Virginia Rappé died on Friday, September 9, at 1:30 in the afternoon. The initial cause of her death was listed as "rupture of the bladder." Dr. Rumwell then called in Dr. William Ophuls, a Stanford University professor of pathology, to assist in a postmortem examination. There are uncomfirmed reports that Rumwell ordered that portmortem an hour and a half before Virginia died. He also ordered the operation to be performed without the consent of the San Francisco County coroner's office, which was illegal.

At two thirty, Drs. Ophuls and Rumwell conducted their autopsy of Virginia Rappé and concurred in the conclusion that she had died of acute peritonitis from rupture of the bladder. Dr. Ophuls signed the death certificate, and the bladder, uterus, sections of the rectum, ovaries, and Fallopian tubes were removed and placed in specimen jars (which were later secretly destroyed). The body was driven to Halsted's Mortuary on Sutter Street for embalming.

In addition to the illegal and suspect postmortem, the death certificate was filled out and signed by Dr. Ophuls, not by Dr. Rumwell who was considered the physician of record for the case. Dr. Ophuls gave no specific details about Rappé's background other than that she was a motion-picture actress, white, single, and female, "about 25" years old. There was no record of her father, mother, birthplace, nor when he last saw the deceased alive (he had never seen her alive). He listed Rappé's residence as Los Angeles, with no other information. Her stay in San Francisco was given as four days. He stated there was no operation before her death. He confirmed there was indeed an autopsy performed, but drew a line through the area that asks what tests confirmed the diagnosis (of peritonitis and rupture of the bladder.) He signed the certificate on September 10, and gave his address as that of the Wakefield Sanitarium at 114 Walnut Street. The informant, the one who gives information on the deceased and "claims" the body, was given as the Halsted Company. Where was Maude Delmont?

Late that afternoon, about the time Drs. Ophuls and Rumwell were about to begin their examination of Virginia Rappé's body, a woman, believed to be a secretary from the Wakefield Sanitarium, phoned the coroner's office inquiring about the autopsy. Deputy Coroner Michael Brown of the San Francisco Homicide Department received the call and asked what the woman was talking about. Before she could explain, a second woman from the sanitarium apparently covered the phone, there was an exchange of muffled whispers, then the line went dead.

Deputy Coroner Brown phoned the sanitarium to try to find out exactly which autopsy the woman had referred to in her mysterious call. The same woman answered and sounded very alarmed. She denied calling the coroner's office and claimed she knew nothing of an autopsy. Brown paid a personal call to Wakefield.

During the subsequent coroner's inquest, Brown said he was blocked by the staff in his quest for information on an alleged autopsy. He was finally told to speak with Dr. Rumwell. After more than two hours' wait Brown spotted Drs. Rumwell and Ophuls walking through the halls carrying glass specimen jars. It was apparent to him that an autopsy of some sort had been performed and that the coroner's office had not been contacted in regard to the operation.

"What you have done is an illegal autopsy and you have exceeded your place within the confines of the law. You are required by law to contact the coroner's office before such an operation is to take place. As the physician of record I am holding you personally responsible."

Dr. Rumwell remained unusually casual in his response to Brown. "I did not attend the woman, but was only called in for the autopsy. If there is any problem with the autopsy you will have to take the matter up with the attending physician." He brushed past Brown without further comment.

Brown insisted on inspecting the organs and the body. Dr. Rumwell obliged and Brown arrived at the same conclusion as the other physicians—Virginia Rappé's bladder had been ruptured by a blow or fall, and she died of subsequent complications from the rupture, specifically peritonitis.

But Brown still suspected something was amiss at the sanitarium, especially in light of the unusual call and denial by the secretary and the quirky behavior of Rumwell. He phoned his office to request an investigation.

At this point, the organs of Virginia Rappé were summarily destroyed by Rumwell, and along with them, all evidence that could have cleared Roscoe Arbuckle of any wrongdoing and implicated at least one doctor in Virginia Rappé's death. That doctor was Melville Rumwell.

San Francisco Department of Health files trace a very intriguing path back to Dr. Rumwell. They show he had not only been "associated" with the Wakefield Sanitarium, but had been listed as a staff physician there as well. The sanitarium had been known in certain circles as an illegal abortion clinic, and had reportedly been involved in hundreds of illegal abortions for the wealthy or the prominent by 1921. Dr. Rumwell had also garnered a reputation in the Hollywood community as an abortionist. It is alleged that he routinely performed abortions for one thousand dollars and up, depending upon the finances of the client and her medical condition. When Virginia Rappé attended Roscoe's party, she claimed she needed money for an abortion, and it was commonly assumed that she needed money "to get" the abortion. Gossip in the Hollywood community suggested that

162

she had already had the abortion, that Maude Delmont had fronted the money, and that now Rappé needed to reimburse Delmont for the operation.

Exactly how Maude Delmont knew Dr. Rumwell is a matter of conjecture. Several people who knew Roscoe, Rappé or Delmont, or knew of the Wakefield Sanitarium, all arrived at the same conclusion—independent of one another. That conclusion was that Maude Delmont had accompanied Rappé to the sanitarium for the illegal operation, which was performed by Rumwell. The doctor must have noticed that Rappé was scarred from previous abortions and certainly had to see the lesions and infection from the gonorrhea. Yet, by all medical accounts, he had taken no precautions nor prescribed any further treatment for Rappé.

If this story is true, that Delmont went with Rappé to the sanitarium, and that Rumwell performed the operation, then the events after Delmont fired Dr. Beardslee would all add up. This explains why Delmont phoned Dr. Rumwell and made no further attempt to see Virginia after she was taken back to Wakefield. It also explains Rumwell's hurried post-mortem examination and his insistence that he was not the attending physician on Rappé, that he was called in after she died. It also explains why he was so careful to destroy the organs, which would have certainly showed evidence of a recent abortion.

County medical reports also indicate that there was an investigation into Dr. Rumwell's record and allegations that he was an abortionist. Whether the investigation turned up any evidence against the doctor was not indicated, and the final records on the outcome of Dr. Rumwell's career have apparently been lost.

While Dr. Rumwell tried to spirit away his involvement in the Rappé case, Maude Delmont was seeking audiences with the local press. She contacted the San Francisco Police Department and swore out a complaint against Roscoe Arbuckle. The stories she had quietly told to the succession of doctors and nurses in the hotel were finally made public. Virginia Rappé died because Roscoe "Fatty" Arbuckle dragged her into his bedroom, against her will, and tried to rape her!

16

ACTRESS DIES MYSTERIOUSLY, ROSCOE ARBUCKLE SOUGHT IN HOTEL ORGY DEATH, PLAN TO SEND ARBUCKLE TO DEATH ON GALLOWS, COMEDIAN LINKED TO BOOTLEG BOOZE—ACTRESS' DEATH, RAPER DANCES WHILE VICTIM DIES.

The newspapers quickly jumped on the story, the first article appearing on Saturday morning, September 10, the day Rappé's death certificate was signed. The newspapers had already printed statements from Maude Delmont, who wasted no time getting her story out to millions of eager readers. Though it changed with each telling, this is the basic story she initially told the press:

"Mr. Arbuckle entertained a number of men in his rooms and there was much drinking and many women guests. He had made a number of advances toward sweet Virginia who rebuffed him each time.

"Finally, when he succeeded in getting Virginia drunk, he leered at her and said, 'I've waited five years and now I've got you.' He then dragged the poor girl into his bedroom and locked the door. I could hear Virginia kicking and screaming violently and I had to kick and batter the door before Mr. Arbuckle would let me in. I looked at the bed. There was Virginia, helpless and ravished.

"When Virginia kept screaming in agony at what Mr. Arbuckle had done, he turned to me and said, 'Shut her up or I'll throw her out a window.' He then went back to his drunken party and danced while poor Virginia lay dying."

Delmont took other incidents out of context and twisted facts about the party. She never mentioned that she had left the party for a while with Lowell Sherman, implying that she had witnessed the entire sequence of events from Roscoe's alleged rape to Virginia's death. She told the press that Virginia had pointed to Roscoe, accusing him of raping her. (Rappé's statement of "he did this to me" or "What did he do to me?" was true but was not an accusation as Delmont made it out to be.)

Of course, not one word of her story was true. It was fabrication at best, vindictive hatred at worst. Roscoe Arbuckle did not even know Virginia had died until two men from the San Francisco sheriff's office turned up at his West Adams home.

"You are hereby summoned to return immediately to San Francisco for questioning . . . you are charged with murder in the first degree."

Roscoe still was not quite certain the men were not hired as part of a practical joke. "And who do you suppose I killed?"

"Virginia Rappé."

Roscoe spoke with Joe Schenck, who advised him to retain legal counsel. Outwardly, Roscoe did not let on that he considered the situation at all serious. In fact he joked about the murder charge to several friends. But Roscoe was never one to openly display any sort of negative emotion such as worry, fear, or anger. He put up a great front.

When he finally read the account in the newspaper, Roscoe told friends that Delmont was "simply sore at me . . . After Miss Rappé became ill and threw a fit after a couple of drinks, Mrs. Delmont came back into the rooms and became so objectionable that I ordered her out . . . She talks about the party being the roughest she ever saw. She was the only one who was pulling rough stuff. She got into a pair of men's pajamas and acted so rough I ordered her out."

When confronted by newspaper reporters, he calmly related his account of the party. "We ate and had a few drinks. After Miss Rappé had a few drinks she became hysterical, and I called the hotel physician and the hotel manager. By the time they arrived some other girls who were there had taken off her clothes and put her into a bath of cold water. Then we carried her to another room and put her to bed. The doctor and I thought it was nothing more serious than a case of indigestion, and he said a little bicarbonate of soda would probably straighten her out.

"To show how serious we thought it was, I and the other men of the party danced that night. Tuesday we left, according to our previous plans, and came back by boat."

Early Saturday morning, Roscoe left for San Francisco. With him for the return trip to San Francisco were his chauffeur, his attorney, Frank Dominguez, and Al Semnacher, who agreed to act as a witness on Roscoe's behalf. Dominguez advised Roscoe to remain silent from this point forward and let the police play out their hand.

Upon their arrival, they checked into the Olympic Athletic Club on the outskirts of downtown San Francisco. Word of the alleged rape had already spread through the town, especially among the hotels; several had already refused Roscoe's attempts to book advance reservations. The Olympic was the only place that would agree to put the men up on the proviso that they keep their stay quiet.

The group then drove to the Hall of Justice, where Roscoe was summoned for questioning. He still assumed it would be a matter of routine questions and he would be exonerated of any wrongdoing. He was concerned, though, that reports of bootleg booze at the party had already surfaced in the newspapers, partly through his own admission and Maude Delmont's stories. Dominguez told Roscoe to admit only to having the liquor in small quantities at the party and to refrain from offering any further details about who ordered it and the amount in the room.

When he entered room 17 of the Hall of Justice Saturday evening, he was greeted by several police homicide detectives and two assistant district attorneys, Isador Golden and Milton U'Ren. They promptly informed Roscoe of the murder charge and that they had sworn affidavits from three witnesses, Maude Delmont, Zey Prevon, and Alice Blake—all claiming that Arbuckle had forced Virginia into his bedroom and attempted to rape her. Once again Dominguez advised his client to remain silent, both frustrating and angering the interrogation team.

After nearly three hours of intense grilling, sharp accusations, and twisting of facts to "catch" Roscoe in a trap, the men asked Arbuckle to step into the corridor so they could conduct a private conference. Roscoe waited silently with Dominguez. Now the casual air that Roscoe once possessed had disintegrated. He was sullen and nervous. He now recognized the peril he might actually face and he realized that the detectives were dead serious in their allegations of murder. Dominguez tried to assure Roscoe that the matter would be quickly cleared up and he would be released within minutes.

"How can they know I'm innocent when I could not tell them my story? The only version they have is what Maude Delmont told them and she told them a pack of lies. How can they release me if they don't know the truth?"

"Roscoe," Dominguez patronizingly explained, "they'll know you didn't have anything to do with any murder."

"How can they know that when you wouldn't let me talk?"

Dominguez had no reply. Roscoe sat somberly on the bench and stared at the marble floor. The reporters were kept at bay, closeted in another room until the detectives were ready to make their move.

Moments later the door opened and Milton U'Ren walked out toward the two men.

"Roscoe Arbuckle, you are under arrest. The count is murder in the first degree. You are hereby ordered into custody in the State of California, County of San Francisco, City of San Francisco."

As Roscoe was taken up the stairs for processing, word of the arrest blazed through newspapers and radios in "Extras" and "Special News Bulletins" across the country. Millions of movie fans and murder buffs snapped up every newspaper they could find and ate up every lurid detail about the party and the arrest of "The World's Richest Comedian." Many believed Roscoe, "the party boy," had finally gotten his comeuppance, regardless of his guilt or innocence. Others felt he was being railroaded because of his stature and wealth. In either event, the arrest of Roscoe Arbuckle meant the sins of the entire movie industry were to be aired in public like dirty laundry. The movie fans would be judge and jury on the future of Arbuckle and the movies themselves.

Studios panicked that the arrest would mean a massive boycott of all films. They were terrified of a possible witch hunt, that the overly eager righteous would uncover the rampant drug abuse among the stars and blatant sexual degeneracy in the films. Leading the pack were Adolph Zukor and Jesse Lasky who huddled together in an eleventh-hour meeting, determined to give Will Hays enough incentive to bring him out of Hollywood to put a bandage on the now-gaping wound.

The swiftest knee-jerk reaction to Roscoe's arrest came from his longtime friend Sid Grauman. While Roscoe was being fingerprinted, photographed, and treated as a desperate criminal in San Francisco, Grauman was severing their relationship in Los Angeles. When word of Roscoe's arrest hit the papers, Grauman abruptly withdrew *Gasoline Gus* from his Hollywood theater, called "The Million Dollar Theatre," where it had only one more day to run. It was withdrawn without a formal statement or any announcement in the newspapers. Grauman told reporters only that he had "no comment." Another Paramount feature, *The Great Impersonation* (a spy movie starring James Kirkwood,) was put on for an eight-day run instead of the usual seven-day run to account for the one-day loss of the Arbuckle film. There reportedly were no complaints from patrons about the switch.

Grauman then phoned Jesse Lasky and Adolph Zukor advising them that he was canceling all outstanding contracts on Arbuckle features. Following Grauman's lead, another theater also backed out of its commitment for the Arbuckles. Word of that action would soon spark a chain reaction.

The early editions of the Sunday newspapers carried a formal statement from Captain of Detectives Duncan Matheson, who pulled no punches in his press briefing.

"Arbuckle was charged with Section 189 of the city penal code providing that a life taken in rape or attempted rape is considered murder. Neither I nor Mr. U'Ren nor the Chief of Police O'Brien, feel that any man, whether he be Fatty Arbuckle or anyone else, can come into this city and commit that kind of an offense. The evidence showed there was an attack made on the girl.

"On Monday, a formal complaint will be filed against Arbuckle."

The temporary complaint was filed by the detectives from the interrogation—Harry McGrath, Thomas Regan, John Dolan, and Griffith Kennedy—after Arbuckle refused to answer any questions or offer any information about the incidents at the St. Francis Hotel . . . All attempts to obtain statements from him were fruitless.

"Witnesses whom we have examined today have given us information, that in my mind, leaves no doubt as to his direct responsibility for Miss Rappé's death . . . The evidence disclosed beyond question that [Rappé's death] was caused by Arbuckle. We know from the evidence that Arbuckle seized Miss Rappé and dragged her into his bedroom . . . and raped her. We don't feel that a man like Fatty Arbuckle can pull stuff like that in San Francisco and get away with it.

"District Attorney Matthew Brady has stated that he would spare no effort in his prosecution of this case, and said he expects to oppose the cleverest lawyers and the greatest influence which money and fame can purchase.

"Bail has been denied for Roscoe Arbuckle."

Roscoe was booked, searched, and locked up in cell 12 of the city jail, in an area called "Felony Row," a section used exclusively for men involved in serious crimes such as murder and armed robbery. The walls were solid steel, which was corroded and moldy; the ceilings were lined with bars and blanketed with dust and filth. The mattress was thin and worn and had the stench of stale sweat and urine.

When he entered the cell, the first thing the meticulously clean Roscoe asked for were toilet articles. During a line-up with eighty other felons, Roscoe asked the guard if he had any soap, a towel and a comb. He said his cell had no essentials. He even turned his uniform pockets inside out as a demonstration but the guard only laughed.

The prisoners were tough, hardened criminals with no sense of humor and little respect for one another. Most said they did not even know who Arbuckle was because the prison did not show films and most of them had been confined for years. Roscoe turned to one man in line to protest his innocence. The inmate sneered at Arbuckle mockingly, telling him that they were all inoocent. Roscoe knew he would be in for a long and difficult period.

Two separate investigations into the alleged murder were launched simultaneously, one by the San Francisco County Grand jury, the other an inquest by the San Francisco County Coroner.

One of the key pieces of evidence, Virginia Rappé's torn clothes, was missing and unaccounted for by all the witnesses. (Maude Delmont and Al Semnacher later admitted they took the garments and destroyed them without thinking.) SFPD Detectives Vail and Parson traveled to Semnacher's home on Pinehurst Road in Hollywood, hoping to recover the garments. Only a small piece of Rappé's shirtwaist was found.

By Sunday afternoon the police department had been deep into its interrogation of the witnesses at the party and had already noticed that many of the statements carried major discrepancies, such as Arbuckle's exact whereabouts when Virginia started screaming, Rappé's words and alleged accusations against Arbuckle, and whether Roscoe dragged the actress into the bedroom or if he followed her in. The biggest discrepancies were between the testimony of the men and the women.

Three women, Delmont, Alice Blake, and Zey Prevon, all offered similar stories that Arbuckle and Rappé were together in the bedroom half an hour before Virginia started screaming for help. They claimed that Lowell Sherman told them that Virginia and Roscoe were in the bedroom together, and when Maude Delmont tried to enter the room the door was locked. "About a half hour later," they said, "Arbuckle came out and sat down with us and said, 'Go get her dressed and out of here. Take her back to the Palace [Hotel]. She makes too much noise.' Miss Rappé was lying on the bed screaming that she was dying."

Nurse Jameson also told police that Virginia gave her two versions of what happened—one that Roscoe attacked her, another that she did not know what had happened. Jameson also added one of the most damaging

statements yet—that Rappé told her if she got well she would
drop the matter, but if she had to go to the hospital she would
make Roscoe Arbuckle pay for her expenses because he was
responsible for her injuries! She also allegedly told Jameson
that she wanted Arbuckle punished.

Three men at the party (Semnacher, Fischbach, and Fortlois) all denied the women's claims. They said Miss Rappé
had only two drinks or so and became ill and medical assistance was summoned. They also said there were no locked
doors in the suites and there was nothing unusual except for a
significant amount of alcohol. They all stated they remained
at the party during the crucial time in which Rappé became
ill. They all said Arbuckle tried only to attend to the girl.
(Fischbach never told authorities that he left the party.)

On Monday morning, September 12, as the coroner's
office announced it would begin a formal inquest into the
allegations, Virginia Rappé's "fiancé" stepped before the
press in New York. Though Virginia's death had been
published in the newspapers for three days, Henry Lehrman
remained on the East Coast with no attempt to head west.
Nevertheless, he vowed to send Roscoe Arbuckle to the
gallows.

During the interview he showed reporters a pair of cuff
buttons with the inscription: "To Henry, my first and sacred
love, Virginia." The stage was set.

> I would not wish to go to the coast now because I
> would not [go] with safety for Arbuckle. I would
> kill him.
>
> Mrs. Sidi Spreckles, former wife of John D.
> Spreckles, Jr., told me in a conversation over the
> long-distance telephone that when Virginia did not
> think she was going to die she kept repeating,
> "Don't tell Henry." To me this message meant that
> she had done her best to defeat the attempt made by
> Arbuckle and failed. She did not want me to know,
> because she knew what I would do.
>
> For a year and a half I was Arbuckle's director.
> He is merely a beast. He made a boast to me that he
> had torn the clothing from a girl who sought to

repulse his attentions. That is what results from making idols and millionaires out of people that you take from the gutter. Arbuckle was a spittoon cleaner in a barroom when he came into the movies nine years ago. He was a bar boy—not a bartender —cleaning glasses and spittoons . . . I would kill him if I had the chance.

While this was running in the press, a second attorney, Milton M. Cohen, arrived in San Francisco to assist Frank Dominguez. Described in the newspapers as the attorney for both Roscoe Arbuckle and the estate of Virginia Rappé, he said he was making arrangements to have Virginia's body shipped back to Los Angeles. His second action was to work with Dominguez to try to get Roscoe released on bail, which they initially failed to do.

It seemed anyone who had ever heard of Roscoe Arbuckle was calling the New York, Los Angeles, and San Francisco newspapers and offering their personal accounts of "the monster" Arbuckle. Most had never met him.

Kevin Kingsley, the director of publicity for the Keith vaudeville circuit, claimed he knew Virginia Rappé well, and that she frequently told him that her life would come to a violent end.

A chambermaid at the St. Francis claimed she heard Virginia Rappé through the door of the suites screaming, "Oh, God! No! Please don't," at Arbuckle.

But once again, Maude Delmont stole the show. Now she claimed she was being harassed and bribed to remain silent.

While the grand jury debated the charge against Arbuckle, civic groups and women's groups were forming and demanding his lynching. If not physically, certainly professionally, Roscoe Arbuckle was a dead man.

17

"We, with complete knowledge of all the facts, know that Arbuckle is innocent. The patrons of the silent drama, having the knowledge of the smile of the famous Fatty Arbuckle, will not believe that he is guilty of the charges made against him until proven in a court of justice.

The Christian sentiment of this God-fearing nation will not adjudge any person guilty of an alleged crime until the same has been proven in the spirit of our Master, who said, 'Judge not lest ye be judged.'

The whirlpool and typhoon of the unjust criticism is now on. Truth will dispel the clouds of falsehood, and will sustain the basic principle of the Anglo-Saxon ideal that the presumption of innocence prevails until the same has been proved beyond a reasonable doubt.

Comedy and tragedy came into the lives of fortunates and unfortunates. In God's plan the two are essential. With the abiding confidence that the Christian charity of the civilized world be manifest in this case, we appeal to conscience and hearts of the American people to hold in abeyance any judgement until the court has determined the guilt or innocence of our client.

To our countryman and his admirers we positively

declare that the charges made against him are false and the same will be established in due time in the courts of Justice in California. Bias and prejudice cannot prevail.

Signed: Frank Dominguez, Charles H.
Brennan, Milton Cohen."

Roscoe had not eaten since his arrest on Saturday. On Monday morning he ate a light breakfast of ham, eggs, and toast and was then escorted to the prison barbershop for his first shave in two days.

John Gallagher (described as a tonsorial expert who ran the haircut and shave concession in the prison) and Harry Heid (who was a free-lance barber who had many of the city officials as customers) actually came to blows over the privilege of shaving him. Arbuckle was waiting his turn and Gallagher was shaving a prisoner when Heid entered the "shop" with a straight razor and cup of lather. The two barbers started arguing, then started swinging at one another. Heid ordered a prisoner to call Chief O'Brien in to resolve the fight, which cooled tempers slightly. When asked to choose between the two, Arbuckle replied that it didn't matter to him, as long as he got a shave. Heid stormed off, insulted.

"Well, I'm not crazy to shave Arbuckle. All those muggs look the same to me when they need a shave."

Arbuckle was called to appear twice before the coroner's inquest on Monday, September 12. Each time he related only the abbreviated story of the sequence of events at the party, and remained silent (on the advice of Dominguez) when asked to elaborate. Once, Roscoe tried to speak in his own defense but Dominguez put his finger against his lips signaling his client to remain silent. This angered his interrogators, who interpreted his refusal to answer as an attempt to cover up the facts. Detective Matheson made a point of this in the newspapers.

Sensing the public ground swell against Roscoe because of his silence, Dominguez briefly explained his strategy—he would reserve his "evidence" during the proceedings before the grand jury and coroner, using it if and when the case headed to Superior Court. He believed that if he held back, the witnesses could not further fabricate stories and refute Arbuckle's statements with lies.

Roscoe entered a formal plea of "not guilty" to the charge of first-degree murder, and sat somberly in the courtroom listening to testimony.

Dominguez had another ploy. The prosecution tried to delay the start of the coroner's inquest until Thursday, September 22, on the grounds that it needed more time to properly present its evidence. Dominguez argued that the delay was detrimental to both the health of his client and the right to a speedy trial. Dominguez won that round.

But he lost a major battle when he tried to force Bambina Maude Delmont to the stand as the first witness. Dominguez claimed that her testimony had been the most damaging, and in fact the prosecution's most crucial evidence in the case. Dealing with this at the beginning of the inquest, Dominguez argued, would bring the case to a rapid conclusion.

The point touched off a heated argument between Assistant District Attorney Milton U'Ren and Dominguez. Dominguez accused U'Ren of suppressing evidence and playing games with Arbuckle's life. U'Ren fired back that it was inadvisable to put Delmont on the stand until the district attorney had had more time to review Delmont's testimony. The argument became so hostile that U'Ren had to be restrained. He accused Dominguez of manipulating and forcing issues prematurely to block justice. Dominguez maintained the only way the truth could be revealed was by bringing the accusers face to face with the accused.

Coroner Leland stepped in to defuse the situation. He gave the prosecution one day to present Maude Delmont in court to be cross-examined by the defense. He said he believed there was "no harm" in putting the witness on the stand to bring her testimony out in court. U'Ren was angered by the order but reluctantly agreed to comply.

The first witnesses called were Dr. Olaf Kaarboe and Dr. Rumwell. Kaarboe offered little evidence for either side, simply stating that he saw the suite occupied by Arbuckle and his friends when he was called in on the case. He claimed Rappé refused to answer questions and was in a stupor, and that he attributed her condition to an excess of alcohol. He said he left without prescribing anything for the girl and asked those at the party to notify him if the girl's condition became worse. Kaarboe said he never returned to the suites.

Rumwell cautiously left out major facts in his testimony, and the prosecution helped guide him through potential land mines. Unfortunately the defense was not yet privy to the outlandish lies and statements made by the key witnesses, and therefore left serious allegations unchallenged.

Dr. Rumwell claimed he attended Rappé for two days in the hotel, then insisted she be taken to a hospital. He claimed his examinations did not lead him to believe that there was anything unusual in the case, but he finally determined she was suffering from peritonitis; that the case did not yield to treatment as it should have, and he was not at all satisfied that he had made the proper diagnosis.

Dominguez dropped the bomb about the illegal post-mortem, believing that if Rumwell was forced to admit to criminal acts, his testimony would also be suspect. But Rumwell remained calm as he continued to speak.

He said he called the coroner's office and learned that Dr. Leland was out of town and therefore unable to sanction an autopsy. He said he then phoned Dr. Ophuls, who assisted in the "unofficial" postmortem. It was during this unofficial examination that the men found a puncture in the woman's bladder. Rumwell stated he believed it was then a matter for official investigation and phoned Deputy Coroner Brown to come into the case.

Again, Dominguez had not been apprised of all the facts and did not challenge Rumwell's statements that he magnanimously "called" Dr. Brown in on the case.

During the course of the day, the reasons for the prosecution's refusal to put its star witness on the stand to open the proceeding were evident. While U'Ren was battling with Dominguez in court, he was buying time for Maude Delmont and the district attorney's team of investigators. Delmont was in Police Chief O'Brien's office, swearing out the formal complaint against Arbuckle, at the exact moment Dominguez was insisting she be brought into court for examination. U'Ren could not produce Delmont until the complaint and formal statements were completed. Also, each time Delmont repeated her story of the "rape" of Virginia Rappé, the facts varied dramatically—from the length of time Roscoe was in with Virginia to Virginia's rambling statements to Delmont's whereabouts and participation in the scenario. Even at this very early stage in the case, the investigators were suspicious of Maude's testimony, but were backed into a corner and had to play out their hand. The last thing they wanted to do was put Delmont on the stand. They knew her testimony would not stand up under scrutiny.

The D.A. also had another problem—Zey Prevon, who had earlier backed Delmont's basic story, now refused to sign her statement, claiming it was untrue.

During a recess in the proceedings, Roscoe was taken from the courtroom to Chief O'Brien's chambers. Pushing past a crush of reporters, Roscoe and his attorneys refused to answer questions. He made only one remark in answer to a reporter's request for him to "smile." "No, boys. Not in a situation like this."

The worst was yet to come. Movie theaters across the country started canceling Roscoe's films in droves. *Gasoline Gus* was yanked from theaters from coast to coast and in Canada. His next feature, *Crazy to Marry*, was canceled in advance of its release in many areas, including Chicago, where the film was pulled citywide. In addition to Chicago, among the cities pulling the films were Butte, Montana; Fresno, California; Memphis, Tennessee; Toledo, Ohio; Detroit, Michigan; Oklahoma City, Oklahoma; Medford, Massachusetts; Sacramento, California; Vancouver, British Columbia, and of course, San Francisco. The Motion Picture Theater Owners of Southern California placed a so-called "absolute ban" on all Arbuckle pictures for their region, leveling the most severe blow yet. The group held jurisdiction over 98 percent of the theaters in the area.

It seemed that even those who did not hate Roscoe found ways to use the scandal to their advantage. Initial reports claimed a band of 150 armed cowboys shot up the movie screen, and seized and burned an Arbuckle film that was being shown in a Thermopolis, Wyoming, theater. The manager said that earlier in the day members of the Purity League had asked him not to run the film. The gang burst in after the theater refused to withdraw it. But it later came out that the shooting was a hoax, dreamed up by the manager as a publicity stunt. The locals had considered taking action against the manager. Nevertheless, the "prank" gained national attention and the feeling against Roscoe was snowballing and picking up speed.

The press apparently went out of its way to make him out to be a coldhearted monster. A small article with a big headline, published on September 13, claimed that Arbuckle had neglected his mother's grave, that the grave in Santa Ana was marked only by a wooden slab with the name all but obliterated by the sun. A local contractor stated that six years ago he offered to put in a cement headstone if Roscoe would pay the cost of materials, but, he said, Roscoe refused. He did stipulate, though, that the offer was made to Arbuckle's sister Maggie and not directly to Roscoe, and he was not positive that the offer ever reached him.

There were also rumors that Minta Durfee had sent a telegram to Arbuckle saying she would take the first train back to Los Angeles from New York if it would help. Though Minta flatly denied it, word of such an offer sparked an idea in Joe Schenck that would come into play in the near future. During the subsequent trials, he asked Minta to come down to Los Angeles to help give the impression that Roscoe was a "family man." Schenck believed pictures of Roscoe with his wife would help dispel stories of his being a party boy and a seducer of innocent women. (Though Minta insisted she paid her own way, papers found in Joe Schenck's files show that he paid her five thousand dollars "to cover travelling expenses." Minta moved into Roscoe's house.)

Roscoe's friends converged at his West Adams home in a show of support (some were turned away from the jail, and many could not break away from their own shooting schedules to travel to San Francisco). When some of Roscoe's closest friends—Buster Keaton, Viola Dana, Lew Cody, and Bebe Daniels—tried to speak to the press about Arbuckle's gentle nature and innocence, they were ordered by studio heads and producers (including Adolph Zukor and Joe Schenck) to remain silent and stay out of trouble. There was a great fear that any association with Arbuckle would result in a backlash against his friends. Some still spoke out against studio orders. Zukor suspended Arbuckle's salary until the matter could be cleared up, and went on record as having no further obligations to the comedian.

But some film industry leaders did speak out about the case. Irving Thalberg (who was general manager of the Universal City Studios) said, "If Roscoe Arbuckle isn't guilty, he has been badly treated. But it is unfortunate that isolated cases of misbehavior and crime cast as black a shadow on the business that thousands of quiet, law-abiding people who form the rank and file of the profession should have to share in the disgrace of one or two."

Tom Mix: "I keenly resent the published statement of San Francisco officials [who say] that the influence and money of the Los Angeles picture colony will be behind the accused in this case. I want to say that there are in this city a great number of honest home-loving picture players, and happily they represent more than 90 percent or more of the screen actors who do not countenance this sort of thing, nor would they uphold a man charged with such a violation of the law just because he is a picture player. We don't want such men among us."

Viola Dana: "He was like a big brother to us all. I don't believe he is guilty."

Alice Lake: "All I can say is that when I was struggling along to make a name for myself and was playing in Roscoe Arbuckle's comedies, he was wonderfully kind and helpful. I can never say anything of him that is not good. He was always doing kind things. Remember his work in the Liberty Bond sales [in 1918]? I wish that not be forgotten."

Joe Schenck spoke out on behalf of Comique: "Fatty Arbuckle is a great, big, loveable, good-natured sort of chap and I think he is not guilty of the charges that certain California public officials seeking notoriety are trying to hang on him. When the truth comes out it will be an entirely different story. I know no finer man than Roscoe Arbuckle, whom I call my friend."

With Roscoe in jail, theaters banning his films, and his income suspended, Roscoe's debtors closed in. When Arbuckle bought his West Adams home, he bought many of the furnishings on credit. Retailers used the purchases to boost their own sales and prestige among the wealthy and were falling all over themselves to offer credit in exchange for the use of his name in advertising. Now that name carried dark overtones and the creditors wanted to cut their association short.

Deputies from the Los Angeles Sheriff's Department served papers attaching twenty-five pieces of furniture on behalf of the California Furniture Company for an unpaid bill of more than $6,500. Then, attachments were also served on two pieces of real estate owned by Arbuckle as "investment" property. Within one day, additional papers were served attaching his cars and other items within his home.

Much of Roscoe's money was tied up in investments; the rest he had spent wildly, assuming he would be set for life with his million-dollar-a-year contract. He was now broke and on the verge of bankruptcy. If he liquidated all his assets, he could scrape together slightly less than $200,000, still quite substantial in 1921 but not enough to cover the impending legal costs if the case headed to trial. It would be worse if the trial dragged on for any length.

To get some quick cash together, Roscoe sold his shares of Comique, which was still producing the Buster Keaton shorts for Metro. He also sold his share of the Vernon Ball Club and other properties and stocks in which he had invested with Lou Anger. The money was immediately confiscated by the authorities to pay off the outstanding debts on his West Adams furniture. He was financially back to square one.

On top of that, the Los Angeles Athletic Club summarily dropped Roscoe from its membership list. The vote was unanimous. In a brief statement, club president William Garland said, "We do not want that kind of man in the club for we do not care to associate with that class. The events as far as they have gone, show that Mr. Arbuckle is not a proper person to be a member of the club, therefore he ceases to be a member."

Then, another bomb was dropped. Federal authorities were called in to investigate the bootleg liquor at the party— a fact to which everyone, including Arbuckle, admitted. The flagrant violation of the Volstead Act was a federal offense and authorities said it appeared likely charges would be filed against Arbuckle and others involved in the party.

In the separate federal investigation, St. Francis Hotel manager Thomas Coleman and assistant manager Harry Boyle were the first called to testify. Both, of course, testified they knew nothing of any illegal liquor in the hotel.

But the main witness was Fred Fischbach, who, Sherman and Fortlois claimed in sworn statements, had ordered the liquor. Fischbach denied any knowledge of the source of the liquor and statements made by Delmont that there was liquor in Arbuckle's car during the drive north.

"I am not a drinking man. I never took a dozen drinks of whiskey or gin in my life [as Delmont claimed]."

Investigators then searched Arbuckle's home and found a stash of liquor and no record of permission to stock it, as was required by Prohibition law. Arbuckle claimed the liquor was left by the former owner and because he did not buy it, he required no permit. But investigators disagreed and maintained they had enough evidence to nail Arbuckle with many counts of violation of the Volstead Act.

While the coroner's jury wrapped up its probe, the grand jury also concluded its hearings into the alleged murder. Reviewing evidence given at the inquest and statements made by witnesses under oath in its own court, the jury prepared to adjourn to deliberate.

Roscoe had been returned to his cell and Dominguez and his partners remained within earshot expecting the jury to return with its decision on the murder charge sometime during the evening. The prosecution also hoped for a quick decision, but it looked for an indictment on a unanimous vote. There arose a major snag that presented a serious problem for both sides.

After they had deliberated for more than three hours, there were rumors the group was undecided and that it would be dismissed until the following Monday. When the men of the jury started leaving their room, District Attorney Matthew Brady protested and demanded the group remain until a decision was reached. Dominguez saw the recess as a hopeful sign that the jury was undecided and would ultimately move for acquittal.

But the men returned and within half an hour handed up a indictment. Both sides were called in and Arbuckle was rousted from his cell. The court waited until he dressed and was shaved.

The charge: one count of manslaughter, on a twelve to two vote, reduced from the charge of murder. Brady was furious and Dominguez remained silent. Roscoe turned red in the face and lowered his head, trying to hold back the tears. He had hoped for dismissal, though had no real reason to expect it due to his silence throughout the proceeding. He was informed that the manslaughter charge carried a maximum prison sentence of ten years.

As Roscoe was ushered out of the courtroom, Frank Dominguez huddled with his colleagues to arrange bail, which was allowed under a manslaughter charge.

When questioned, the jury claimed it believed that Rappé had sustained injuries inflicted by Arbuckle, but the evidence showed lack of premeditation or death due to criminal assault. They all agreed the injuries were not deliberate, therefore not indicative of murder.

The jury also had one more problem with the evidence— the testimony of Zey Prevon, which had been a sore point with the prosecution. Earlier she had refused to sign her statement to the police; now she changed her testimony in court, denying that Virginia Rappé had said, "I am dying. I am dying. He hurt me. Arbuckle hurt me." She had also given several names including Sadie Reiss and Zey Prevost, adding to the jury's confusion. But it cited the abrupt switch in her testimony as the primary reason for the delay in its verdict.

After Prevon recanted her testimony on the stand, she was immediately escorted off by D.A. Brady's men. Newspaper accounts say she was in the group "for hours" and it was taken for granted that she would return to her original story. There were confirmed stories that she (and Alice Blake) were browbeaten by the district attorney's office and intimidated into lying on the stand. Records indicate Brady threatened to charge them with perjury if they recanted their initial testimony and told the truth (that Virginia did not name Arbuckle as her assailant) and vowed to lock them in jail.

This terror tactic was enough to frighten the girls into going along with Brady.

Upon word of the grand jury's indictment, Joe Schenck telephoned Minta in New York and asked her to take the first train back to Los Angeles.

"Roscoe needs you now, Minta."

Minta, who had moved into her sister's apartment on West Ninety-seventh Street, packed her bags immediately.

"I'm going to him because I think it is my duty to be near him—I want to help him in every way I can." She claimed she had not read the newspapers and did not know Roscoe was in trouble until she received a telegram from Mrs. McLean (who had loaned them the railroad car for their earlier cross-country tour). She said Mabel Normand had expressed her concern and assured her that "everything will come out all right."

She said there were no hard feelings between her and Roscoe, that they had agreed to remain friends and due to his generosity she had not had to work for five years. She claimed he had presented her with an expensive automobile several months prior to the San Francisco party. She even mentioned a possible reconciliation if Roscoe was acquitted.

Word of the indictment triggered another wave of creditors grabbing at Roscoe's property. The second attachment was filed by an interior decorator named Raymond Gould, who claimed Arbuckle owed him $11,400 for decorating the West Adams home. Because other attachments were already in force, Gould filed liens against the home and two other properties that Roscoe had purchased in Culver City. The properties were empty lots situated (oddly enough) next door to the Pathé Lehrman Studios. The lien also named Lou Anger as trustee of Arbuckle's estate, the first time the extent of Anger's hold on Roscoe had become public.

Several days later two more attachments were leveled against Roscoe's property—one filed by a tailor demanding $60 and another by a tire maker who stated the comedian owed him $296 for the tires he supplied for Roscoe's infamous $25,000 Pierce-Arrow. The court placed an attachment on the Pierce-Arrow in lieu of payment of the outstanding bill.

The world continued to crash down around Roscoe. He knew he was being railroaded but felt helpless to stop it. His mail had not been forwarded to him in jail. Frank Dominguez offered him little news of the outside world and no messages from friends or co-workers. Dominguez later said he believed such news would only further distress Roscoe. Not knowing that most of Hollywood had supported him, Roscoe believed his friends had deserted him and that he was all alone.

As Roscoe waited the verdict from the coroner's inquest, a small item ran in the *Los Angeles Times.*

> Fatty Arbuckle has one sincere mourner whose love and faith no reports can shake. That mourner is Luke, Fatty's old bulldog. Luke usually goes with Fatty on his long trips, but the comedian didn't take him to San Francisco with him.
>
> This is the longest time that the comedian and Luke have been separated. And out at Fatty's house, Luke sits, disconsolate, at the door, waiting for the familiar step and his well-known voice. He doesn't eat. He waits.
>
> Whatever befalls Fatty, Luke will not forget.

18

"We, the Coroner's jury, find that the said Virginia Rappé, age 25, single, resident Los Angeles, came to her death on September 9, at the Wakefield Sanatorium [sic] from a ruptured bladder, contributing cause peritonitis.

"And we further find that said Virginia Rappé came to her death from peritonitis caused by a rupture of the urinary bladder, caused by the application of some force which, from evidence submitted, was applied by one Roscoe Arbuckle.

"We, the undersigned jurors, therefore charge the said Roscoe Arbuckle with the crime of manslaughter.

"We, the undersigned jurors, recommend that the District Attorney, Chief of Police, Grand Jury and Prohibition officers take steps to prevent a further occurrence of affairs such as the one which caused this young woman's death, so that San Francisco will not be made the rendezvous of the debauchee and the gangster."

With the coroner's jury backing the grand jury, Dominguez and his partners realized that chances were slim that bail would be granted. They had believed the coroner's jury would rule in their favor because it based its finding solely on the medical evidence, which, they claimed, clearly showed no violence had been involved in Rappé's death.

Dominguez assured Arbuckle that the coroner's jury's finding was not as important as the grand jury's finding, and that the jury had been divided in its decision. Roscoe said that did little to comfort him and, for the first time, expressed actual fear that he would serve jail time for a crime he did not commit.

Before the coroner's jury announced its findings, it, too, had a spat with D.A. Brady over the testimony of Zey Prevon and Alice Blake. Coroner Leland had requested that the women offer their testimony firsthand to his jury. Brady argued that the two had already told everything they knew to the grand jury and that they were now confused by the barrage of questions, that their testimony was not only tainted but could be detrimental to the prosecution. After deliberating with the jury for nearly twenty minutes, Leland agreed with Brady and kept the women off the stand.

The decision sparked an outburst and a very terse verbal battle between Dominguez and Brady, with Dominguez accusing Brady of suppressing testimony and even going so far as to tamper with the witnesses. Though he was correct, Dominguez had nothing more than a suspicion and a knowledge of Brady's background and motives.

Brady was a native San Franciscan, a fact he used freely, calling himself the city's "native son" when running for office or drumming up support for causes. In 1899 he graduated from Hastings College of Law and set up a reasonably successful private practice. In less than ten years he worked his way through the legal system and city politics, garnering an appointment on the Civil Service Commission until he replaced that with an appointment to the Police Court bench. The appointment earned him the title of "judge," a title he continued to use for purposes of status after he left the position. In 1919, Brady defeated the incumbent district attorney, Charles Fickert, and openly voiced plans for bigger and better things—the governorship of California.

Those who knew Brady described him as self-serving and arrogant, a ruthless man with blind ambition and a quick temper. Many believed that when Maude Delmont entered his office he saw a chance to seize the governor's mansion with the conviction of the country's most popular comedian for the city's most heinous crime. The case would bring him national notoriety, citywide adoration, and respect from his peers. He pinned his future on destroying Roscoe Arbuckle.

When he realized that something was seriously wrong with Maude Delmont's story, that she could not keep her story straight and casually added and deleted major details, he knew he had to act fast. He instructed his men to keep Maude Delmont off the stand at all costs in future proceedings.

When he checked into Delmont's background, he found a string of convictions for charges from fraud to racketeering. But the ace he would soon use to "protect" Delmont from the defense was the fact that she had an outstanding conviction for bigamy. He waited until the time was right to show his hand.

He was also afraid that Alice Blake and Zey Prevon would break under cross-examination by the defense. He demanded the two girls be drilled and grilled by the D.A.'s office until they were too frightened not to comply. If it ever became public that he had based his case on lies and unreliable witnesses, he knew he would be ruined. Matthew Brady neded to win this case—at all costs.

Upon receiving the findings from the coroner's jury, a jubilant Brady stepped before the newspaper and radio reporters.

"I am very pleased at the decisions made by both the grand jury and the coroner's jury. I believe these good men had a difficult task before them and they voted according to the evidence presented to them by this office. I believe the findings of these juries will stand during trial and Mr. Arbuckle will be found guilty beyond a shadow of a doubt. His conviction will also serve as an example to everyone that the fair city of San Francisco will not tolerate such behavior.

"We think we have sufficient evidence to convict Arbuckle of murder, but of course that is up to the committing magistrate.

"In the event we decide on the murder charge and he is given a preliminary hearing, it will mean that we will have to disclose all of our testimony to the defense and we have no desire to do that. If we go ahead with the manslaughter charge we do not have to have the preliminary hearing.

"I am going to push the prosecution of this case as speedily as possible. I expect to be ready to go to trial within three weeks and I believe the defense will also be prepared."

Brady was relentless in keeping the word "murder" connected to the Arbuckle case, though two juries had already reduced the charge. He had gone out on a limb and could not back down without giving the impression that he believed Roscoe was guilty of something less than murder.

While Roscoe prepared to return to court (for the plea on the manslaughter charge), his attorneys finally agreed to give him the week's worth of newspapers which detailed the events up until the present. Arbuckle sat quietly and glanced through each edition, then finally looked up at Frank Dominguez.

"I guess this looks like I did it, huh?"

They also allowed a visitor to the cell—Lou Anger, who chatted privately with the comedian for about fifteen minutes. He then prepared to go back into court.

The arraignment was scheduled for Friday, September 16, in San Francisco Superior Court. It was well attended by women who claimed they were from various vigilante groups (many unnamed), there to make sure justice was carried out. One of the women, the president of a club called Papyrus, Mrs. Edward Place, met in conference with D.A. Brady to offer their support and to seek his approval for a plan to fill the court with members.

'It is our plan," she said, "to watch this overwhelming indecency [so] that nothing can thwart our high standards for truth in this proceeding. We do not want to wait until Arbuckle is out on bail and then try to remedy the matter. The presence of women at the trial will guarantee to the woman witnesses that representative members of their sex will stand by them, regardless of the revelations they may have to make in the interest of justice."

When Judge Shortall called the court to order, more than 150 women and 100 men packed the 200 seats and the aisles, waiting for Roscoe to enter. The women became raucous at times and started a near riot when the judge tried to remove them from the court. Instead of evicting them forcibly, he sent word to "keep Arbuckle safe in jail, do not let him attend the proceeding for his own protection." His attorneys agreed Roscoe was better kept in his cell.

When the charge of manslaughter was read, Brady insisted he was holding to the murder charge and had no intention of trying Arbuckle on the lesser charge.

Shortall assigned the bail hearing to Superior Court Judge Harold Louderback, who agreed to grant Roscoe's release on $10,000 bond of $5,000 cash. But there was a major road-block—Roscoe could not be freed until Brady backed down. According to state law at that time, the murder charge super-seded the grand jury's manslaughter indictment.

The moment the bail amount was set, Attorney Milton Cohen left the courtroom and withdrew $5,000 in a cashier's check from the Bank of Italy, now the Bank of America. The money was from a Famous Players-Lasky/Paramount "slush fund" made available to preapproved individuals in case of an emergency. (Fragmented records of the "slush fund" were turned up about ten years ago in the Paramount archives.) When Cohen returned with the cash, it was deposited with the court clerk.

Judge Louderback then handed the case over to Police Judge Sylvain Lazarus, who specialized in court cases invol-ving women. The decision on the bail matter was postponed to give Judge Lazarus time to review the case.

News of Roscoe's possible release sparked another round of slander from Henry Lehrman, who was putting on a big display for the newspapers, making arrangements to have Virginia's body shipped back to Los Angeles. He ordered a lavish flower arrangement to drape Rappé's casket: one thou-sand pink lilies with the message TO MY BRAVE SWEETHEART, LOVE HENRY emblazoned in gold letters. The flowers cost upward of seven hundred dollars, and Lehrman refused to pay the bill. He was sued by the florist.

While funeral arrangements were being made, Lehrman also sent this illiterate and incoherent letter to the San Francisco and Los Angeles newspapers.

> I am related to this girl that he is no doubt respon-sible for the death of, and if Mr. Arbuckle success-fully cheats the law and justice with his money and able attorneys I say here and now he will not succeed.
>
> I will say here and now he can not cheat me. I will shoot him down if it were the last act of my life.
>
> I will wait a time with patience for justice and if it

can not be weighed out justly then Mr. Arbuckle
will answer to me.

My only hope and prayer is that the law shall find
its course.

With me it is affection and such act as this is what
my answer will be—an eye for an eye, a tooth for a
tooth.

I have determined he shall answer for it—no
pleasure to travel the rocky road blight, there seize
this defenseless girl in the valley of the shadows.

While this letter was published, Lehrman was traveling
with his new girlfriend, a model named Jocelyn Leigh, on
whom he spent a small fortune, showering her with gifts of
fur coats and expensive jewelry. Lehrman married her on
April 17, 1922, in Santa Ana, shortly after his "dearest love"
Rappé's funeral.

The fact that Arbuckle was returned to jail spared him
from an odd and macabre coincidence. If he had been freed
that night, he would have taken the only train back to Los
Angeles, the very same train that was transporting Virginia
Rappé's body.

Lerhman asked Maude Delmont to supervise the funeral
arrangements (he was too busy in New York with his girlfriend to take the time to travel west). He sent a telegram to
the undertaker asking him to "whisper in her [Rappé's] ear
that her Henry still loves her. She will hear."

A wake was held at the Strother and Dayton Funeral Home
on Hollywood Boulevard. The coffin and room were jammed
with flowers from women's groups, movie fans, "friends,"
strangers who bought into the pack of lies perpetuated by
Brady and his team. Virginia was laid out in a white dress
with delicate pink roses in her hands. A rosary was also
draped across the casket, giving an impression of her
character that was at odds with the true one.

The service was set to begin at 10:30 A.M. on Sunday,
September 18. By ten o'clock the sidewalks surrounding the
mortuary were jammed with more than three thousand
visitors and sightseers who stood in line to get a look at poor
Virginia. A count showed there were twice as many women as

men, and most of the women brought their children to show them, many told reporters, "the evils of Hollywood."

By the time of her burial, theaters were clamoring for Virginia Rappé movies. She had minor roles in five films, and any theater showing one of them had standing room only for the shows. For the first time Virginia Rappé was big box office, although the backlash of moral outrage became so strong that First National eventually canceled all bookings of the actress's films.

Though Frank Dominguez and the studio heads asked Roscoe's movie-star friends to steer clear of the jailhouse, Arbuckle's two brothers, Arthur and Alfred, paid a surprise visit. It was the first time they had seen their brother in years.

The three sat on a narrow bench outside the cell and talked for several hours. Roscoe told them he passed his time by reading the newspapers and still felt confident that the matter would soon be cleared up and he would be freed. He also told his brothers that he was sleeping well (which was an obvious lie evidenced by the dark circles under his eyes, his pale color, and the drawn, tired look on his face). Other prisoners said that Roscoe smiled occasionally, which was the first time they had seen the comedian smile since his initial imprisonment. Little else of the conversation was revealed.

Minta Durfee had now arrived in San Francisco and went straight to meet attorney Milton Cohen, who arranged for a private office. There, Cohen told her that he had been unable to get a hotel room for Minta and her mother, Flora Adkins Durfee, who traveled with her daughter. Minta then realized the seriousness of the situation and the outpouring of hate for her estranged husband. They were checked into the Olympic Athletic Club for the night.

The following day after a light breakfast, Cohen escorted the two women to the city jail to meet Roscoe. Minta said he was sitting on a couch, looking very drawn.

"Roscoe, I have only one question to ask you. Please don't get angry but I must know. Were you in any way responsible for Virginia Rappé's death?"

Roscoe looked up at the wife and said solemnly, "Minty, I swear to God I never touched that girl like they say I did."

Minta and her mother posed for photographers (per

191

Schenck and Dominguez's request to keep up the appearance of Roscoe being a family man), then left. Minta stayed by Roscoe's side, in court, during the preliminary hearing, then returned to Los Angeles and moved into the West Adams home until she was needed again in San Francisco.

As Roscoe awaited word on his possible release, federal agents were rounding up his friends to grill them about the bootleg liquor. Lowell Sherman and Fred Fischbach were recalled for questioning; each offered a different account of how the liquor got to the suite. Sherman said he saw all the liquor but thought "it was impolite as a guest to question where it came from, that he left the room for a short time and when he returned "the party was in full swing and the booze was flowing."

When the federal agents questioned Roscoe, he refused to divulge how the liquor made its way into the party. He said the liquor was brought up while the party was already going, that there were so many people in and out of the rooms that anyone could have brought it in. In short, he refused to blow the whistle on Fred Fischbach, though Fischbach and Sherman laid the blame for the bootleg booze right at Roscoe's door.

When the jury indictments were returned, D.A. Brady and his team kicked into high gear in their push to pin the murder charge on Arbuckle. Brady believed that even if the murder charge would not stand up in court, he would be prepared to put Roscoe behind bars for the maximum sentence of ten years for manslaughter when the case went to trial. He recalled the major witnesses (Delmont, Prevon, Blake, and Rumwell) and issued summons for others involved in the party (Fishchbach, Fortlois, Semnacher, Mae Taub, and Lowell Sherman).

Taub and Sherman could not be located and the office enlisted the help of Los Angeles authorities to bring the two back to San Francisco for questioning. Taub was quickly found and brought in without any problem. But Sherman was missing. Brady issued a fugitive warrant and contacted federal authorities.

There were reports that Sherman was in hiding in Hollywood, in San Diego, in New York, in just about every major city in America. After a week's search he was finally located in Chicago, staying with relatives. He said he did not know he was being sought for questioning and was on his way to New York to speak with some unnamed producers about an upcoming project.

When cornered by the authorities, Sherman issued a statement detailing his participation at the party that coincided with his earlier accounts, once again leaving out his involvement with Maude Delmont. He again stated that Arbuckle had nothing to do with Virginia Rappé's death.

The statement was sent in the form of a telegram to Matthew Brady, and a formal deposition was taken by the district attorney's office in Chicago. He thought nothing more of the affair and continued to New York.

Upon his arrival, he received an abrupt telegram from what the newspapers described as "a major studio," stating that his contract had been canceled. The name was not specified in the report, but it is assumed the studio was Mack Sennett's. Sherman had just completed work in Mabel Normand's feature *Molly O'*, which was wrapping up production when the scandal hit. It was copyrighted October 24, and premiered in November. (Sherman later found work with Goldwyn and made three or four films per year, usually playing the unlucky lover or heavy, and worked briefly as a director.)

Federal authorities, in their quest to trace the source of the bootleg booze, placed Sherman under surveillance. A similar order was also issued for Fred Fischbach, Al Semnacher, and Ira Fortlois. Mae Taub, Maude Delmont, Alice Blake, Zey Prevon (listed as Prevost), St. Francis bellboy John Pickette, maid Josephine Kessler, and guest Joyce Clark were also asked for information but never formally subpoenaed by the authorities.

The federal agents eventually claimed that they were able to trace the connection to "several prominent Beverly Hills and Hollywood men" but never offered names. They also said the "bootleg connection" ran from Mexico, up the California coast, and through the rest of the country (similar to the drug connection of today).

While the federal authorities questioned their witnesses,

Matthew Brady launched another investigation into charges of witnesses tampering and bribery. He claimed an unidentified woman overheard one witness say, "There is money in this case and I'm going to get some of it."

Delmont claimed she had been approached by "two men" who tried to pay for her silence. There was no proof of this and, as usual, Delmont changed the story with each telling. Brady also said that several other "lesser" witnesses were approached by "one or two men offering sums of money." He was apparently stacking the deck against the defense because the only people Brady found who had allegedly been approached were witnesses for the prosecution.

The preliminary hearing on the manslaughter/murder charge was scheduled for Thursday, and once again the court was packed. Everyone had assumed the hearing would focus only on the charge against Arbuckle and would wrap up within a day or so. But that charge wound up taking a temporary backseat to another leveled by Frank Dominguez against Al Semnacher, then a counterattack fired back by Semnacher. Semnacher was considered a troublesome witness by both sides because he had problems remembering exactly what had happened at the party. He, like so many other witnesses, repeatedly changed his testimony.

In court Dominguez stated he had evidence that Semnacher had tried to extort money from Arbuckle to offer supporting testimony. Dominguez filed the charge with Brady and asked the matter be brought before the grand jury. When Judge Lazarus called a temporary recess, Semnacher told a gathering of newspaper and radio reporters that he was immediately wiring his attorneys in Los Angeles to file defamation of character charges against Dominguez.

Dominguez then took down another witness, Maude Delmont. He claimed Delmont and Semnacher had deliberately taken Virginia Rappé's torn clothes to use as blackmail against Arbuckle. He also said he had proof of collusion between the two in more "intimate" matters. Brady had no choice but to pursue the matter in court, which was considered the first victory for the defense.

"If I can show, and believe I can, that Semnacher, in his conversations with Mrs. Delmont and someone else, plotted and conspired with the idea of blackmailing Arbuckle through Miss Rappé's torn clothes, then it is my duty to do so," said Dominguez. "If I can show the existence of intimate relations between Semnacher and Mrs. Delmont, it is my duty to show it, and I intend to do so."

When court was reconvened, Brady went back on his promise and blocked all attempts to put Maude Delmont on the stand. Semnacher was called instead. Dominguez led the questioning.

"When you were registered at the Palace Hotel [with Delmont and Rappé], you occupied one room, the ladies the next one to it?"

"Yes."

"There was a door between the rooms?"

"Yes."

"Could that door be opened?"

"Yes."

"You opened it, didn't you?"

"No."

"You say you were Miss Rappé's manager?"

"I have been misquoted."

"You knew her about five weeks?"

"About five years."

"But you knew her well only about five weeks?"

"About six weeks."

"You didn't attempt to place her in any pictures?"

"Yes, one."

"You knew Mrs. Delmont?"

"Yes. I met her three times in four years."

"The last time was in Los Angeles?"

"Yes, on August 30, on a Tuesday."

"And she agreed to go to Selma, California, with you?"

"Yes."

"You introduced Miss Rappé to Mrs. Delmont."

"The other way around."

"Don't you know the door between your room at the Palace and the ladies' room was unlocked day and night?"

"It could have been."

"Did you visit the ladies' room at the Palace?"

"Yes, when I went to take them breakfast."

"When you took those torn garments into room 1227, where Miss Rappé lay suffering, and Mrs. Delmont watching her, did you have a conversation as to these clothes?"

"No, sir."

"Now, Mr. Semnacher, I want you to follow me closely."

Assistant District Attorney Isador Golden chimed in, "But not too closely."

For the first time Roscoe smiled, laughed, and stamped his feet at the remark. Attorney Milton Cohen placed a glass of water on the table for Dominguez. Roscoe jokingly reached over and gulped some down before the attorney got to it.

Dominguez zeroed in on remarks attributed to Roscoe that Semnacher first told authorities he heard, then denied, then restated. Dominguez claimed Semnacher made the last switch after he failed to extort money from Arbuckle.

"Mr. Semnacher, did you ever state that you saw Roscoe Arbuckle forcibly applying ice to Miss Rappé's genital area?"

"I believe so. Yes."

"And did you not later deny that statement?"

"I might have. I do not recall."

"And now you state you did indeed see the act committed?"

"Yes."

"Are you aware that there is no medical evidence to back your claim?"

"I saw ice there."

"But you did not see Mr. Arbuckle put it there."

"No, probably not."

With Semnacher's testimony broken, Dominguez went back to the blackmailing charge.

"Did you have any conversations with Mrs. Delmont regarding Miss Rappé's torn clothes?"

"I do not recall."

"Did you knowingly remove the clothes from the hotel suite?"

"Yes."

"For what purpose."

"I do not recall."

"You remove women's clothes and do not know why?"

Roscoe smiled once more as Semnacher twisted on the stand.

"Let me ask you this, Mr. Semnacher. What did you intend to do with Miss Rappé's clothes once you brought them back to your home in Hollywood."

"I don't recall."

"Did you approach my client or anyone associated with my client regarding these clothes?"

"I do not recall."

Though neither side was able to prove attempted bribery by Semnacher or Delmont, the defense believed it had cracked Semnacher's testimony far enough to hang a cloud of suspicion over him for the remainder of the case. Semnacher eventually dropped his defamation of character suit against Dominguez.

The preliminary hearing then veered back on track, and the witnesses were once again called to the stand. The examination and cross-examination dragged on for more than a week while Roscoe Arbuckle remained a prisoner. Each witness, from the four doctors involved in the examination and post-mortem to the hotel chambermaids to the men and women at the party, repeated the testimony they had given to the grand jury, the coroner's jury, and the police.

This time around, Alice Blake and Zey Prevon repeated their well-rehearsed testimony without any problem. But Brady was still terrified to put Maude Delmont under oath. By keeping her off the stand, he could continue his charade as a solid prosecutor with an ironclad case.

Finally, on September 28, Judge Lazarus announced his decision. "I have overruled a defense motion to dismiss this case on lack of evidence. There is enough evidence here—I may say barely enough—to justify my holding the defendant without further facts and circumstances which would more strongly establish the fact that Roscoe Arbuckle is guilty of the crime of murder.

"This is an important case. We are not trying Roscoe Arbuckle alone. We are not trying the screen celebrity who has given joy and pleasure to all the world.

"Actually, in a large sense, we are trying ourselves. We are trying present day morals, our present day social conditions, our present day looseness of thought and lack of social balance.

"Roscoe Arbuckle will be held over to the Superior Court on a charge of manslaughter. He has already posted the required bail and is free to return home to Los Angeles."

Apparently the convoluted stories of the witnesses had a positive effect on Judge Lazarus. They also seemed to sway the audience back in Roscoe's favor. When the decision was read, the court, which was packed with women, erupted into loud applause and cheers. They stampeded toward Roscoe to shake his hands and congratulate him on the victory.

Reporters ran to nearby telephones to phone in the news. Roscoe unconsciously rolled a brown-paper cigarette while his hands shook uncontrollably. He embraced Minta and shook hands with his attorneys, then, for the first time, broke into uncontrollable tears. The weeks of stress, the hatred he sensed, the shock of the ordeal was finally releasing itself. Though he was far from being a free man, he sensed the tide was finally turning in his favor.

Brady and his team were obviously angered by the decision. He angrily accused the judge of giving Arbuckle special consideration because of his celebrity status, and claimed the judge was swayed by Arbuckle's reputation as a screen comic. He claimed the murder charge would have been upheld if anyone else had been caught in such a violent act as the one Arbuckle (allegedly) committed against Virginia Rappé.

"Judge Lazarus openly stated that more evidence should be required in this case than any other case for the reason that the defendant was an important celebrity."

Brady agreed to try Arbuckle on the coroner's indictment, which would bring the case to the so-called police court of Judge Lazarus. He put aside the grand jury indictment, which would have landed the case back in Louderback's court. Brady met reporters in the hall outside the courtroom.

"You say that Roscoe Arbuckle cannot be considered a dangerous criminal because of the circumstances surrounding the death of Virginia Rappé.

"I say, are we ever safe when a murderer walks the streets? A murder is a murder, my friends. And I believe Arbuckle is guilty of murder. No, he should not be free, but he is today because of one man's decision. I vow that when this case goes to trial I will prosecute Mr. Arbuckle as if the charge were murder. And I promise he will serve the full sentence punishable by law until he has paid for his crime . . . no matter what I have to do."

One *Los Angeles Times* reporter offered his opinion of Roscoe Arbuckle upon hearing Brady refer to the comedian as a "has-been with no future in films."

"In this he is correct. Fatty Arbuckle, the comedian, exists no more. He is no longer the backstop for custard pies. He is Mr. Roscoe Arbuckle, the most serious visaged personality existent. His conduct and appearance . . . made Hamlet and Macbeth and Jean Valjean look like circus clowns."

19

Outside the courtroom, Roscoe was mobbed by hordes of women with hatpins, women who shouted at him, calling him a monster, a beast, a pervert, women who spat on him. Some brought their children and pointed in hate. Men glared, only a very few shouted good wishes. They all apparently believed Matthew Brady's slander.

That night, Arbuckle arrived in Los Angeles, setting foot in the city for the first time in three weeks. The *San Francisco Examiner* claimed he was stoned and angry women spat on him at the Union Station train terminal. In truth, he was met by a mixed crowd. There were numerous well-wishers and fans who had turned out in force to show their support, to touch him and present him with flowers and cards. There was another group that pelted him with eggs and shouted obscenities. Roscoe later said he was amazed at the reception. He had convinced himself that the exhibition outside the San Francisco courtroom was to be expected and indicative of the public's feelings toward him. He was at least heartened that some people believed he was innocent.

Throughout the night, scores of friends turned out at the West Adams home to show their support. The first to arrive was Buster Keaton, followed by Al St. John, Lew Cody, Bebe Daniels, Viola Dana, and at least forty others who arrived in everything from expensive limousines to taxis. They tried to make the best of the occasion, but as Buster Keaton said, "What could you say to the poor bastard?

After all he'd been through. A funeral would have been more cheerful. Half of us whispered and tiptoed around afraid to say the wrong thing, the rest laughed too loud pretending they were having a good time."

There was no liquor served, just light snacks and soft drinks. "I learned my lesson—no more drinking from now on," Roscoe told the group. It was a disaster as parties go, but if nothing else, it was a clear demonstration that Hollywood had not abandoned Roscoe Arbuckle. The last guest left at 4:00 A.M.

The following morning, he greeted reporters who converged on his mansion. An affable Arbuckle told how the prison cot was too small and the previous night was the first decent night's sleep he'd had in nineteen days. He joked and smiled but refused to answer any questions about the party or about the proceedings, only to say he still believed he would be proven innocent of any wrongdoing.

Meanwhile the ground swell against Arbuckle's films continued. In addition to scores of theaters across the country banning the films, a Los Angeles area coalition of women's groups voted to protest the showing of any Arbuckle films in the city. They told their women to storm any theater showing his films and shout "Remember the Arbuckle Horror" as their battle cry, driving out customers until the films were pulled.

While Arbuckle tried to shake off the stress of the last month's ordeal, Lou Anger was called out to New York on urgent business. An emergency meeting had been ordered by Adolph Zukor, Jesse Lasky, and Joe Schenck to decide the future of Roscoe Arbuckle. With both the grand jury and coroner's jury indictments pending against him, and theaters across America refusing to show his films, the studio knew it could no longer carry him as a million-dollar-a-year star. Famous Players-Lasky had three Arbuckle features in the can and no place to show them. Paramount stock had plummeted since word of the scandal first broke. A massive amount of money was at stake, millions had already been lost. Something had to be done. The studio needed a way out without appearing that it, too, had prejudged the comedian.

The following day, Roscoe received a tersely worded telegram stating that he was in breach of contract for failure to appear for the shooting of the upcoming feature, *The Melancholy Spirit*. He was also suspended until he was cleared of all wrongdoing. The telegram was signed by Adolph Zukor. Rumors of the severance spread quickly, and the New York offices of Famous Players-Lasky/Paramount denied the story, claiming it was taking no stand until the outcome of the criminal trial. This was an outright lie—the studio did take a stand even though it denied the telegram. Paramount led the drive to enact a so-called "morals clause" in stars' contracts—giving the studios a loophole to release a player if he or she violated what the studios considered the proper code of conduct. Every other studio followed Paramount in adding the stipulation to its contracts. Roscoe Arbuckle was the first victim.

The group took up other business—Roscoe's legal defense. Roscoe told Anger that Frank Dominguez had refused to let him speak in his own defense, despite pleas to do so. Both Anger and Arbuckle agreed that if he had been allowed to tell his version of the story, the case probably would have been dismissed. They believed Frank Dominguez had fumbled the ball, and by doing so triggered the backlash of hatred and the boycott of Roscoe's comedies. They agreed he had to go before the case went to trial.

Anger related the conversation to the group. Earlier, through Joe Schenck's insistence, Paramount had given Dominguez carte blanche to spend as much money as necessary to secure an acquittal. Now Schenck insisted (on behalf of Roscoe and Anger) that Dominguez be dismissed from the case.

Zukor was angered by the entire situation. He had little regard for Roscoe; to him he was just another contract player who was overpaid and rebellious. Zukor told Schenck that, in a way, Roscoe had got what he deserved for disobeying a company order.

"If Arbuckle had stayed in Los Angeles as I requested him to do, and if he had appeared [on stage for Paramount Week] as he was told, he never would have gotten into this mess."

Schenck disagreed and convinced Zukor that the prudent course of action was not to throw Arbuckle to the wolves but to salvage what they could of the case and the comedian's reputation by hiring a better lawyer who could secure an acquittal.

Finding that attorney was not easy. When the charges were first filed against Roscoe, Schenck had actively sought the best lawyers in town but hit a series of roadblocks.

The first considered was Clarence Darrow, but he was unable to take on the case because of his own legal problems. Darrow had been charged with two counts of jury tampering. For one he obtained the legal services of Earl Rogers (who was considered the best criminal laywer in the country), who won an acquittal. But Darrow defended himself on the second count, which ended in a hung jury. To avoid a retrial, he agreed to stay out of California courtrooms.

Schenck then went after Rogers and drafted a check for $50,000 as a retainer. Rogers was in frail health and begged off the case on doctor's orders. His daughter, Adela Rogers St. Johns, said her father sensed that Roscoe was in for a very rough ride, and he had told Schenck so.

"Arbuckle's weight will damn him. He is charged with an attack on a girl, which resulted in her death. He will no longer be the jolly, good-natured fat man that everybody loved. He will become a monster. If he were an ordinary man, his own spotless reputation, his clean pictures would save him. They'll never convict him, but this will ruin him and maybe motion pictures for some time."

Rogers's prediction was on target. Schenck's third choice was Frank Dominguez who had a good reputation as a criminal attorney in Los Angeles. He was also hefty, and Schenck believed that the presence of another fat man near Arbuckle would offset his weight, making him appear less threatening and gain a psychological advantage. Now, the hunt was on again.

Zukor, Schenck, and Lasky agreed the best choice now was Gavin McNab, who was well known in the motion-picture industry and in San Francisco, his hometown. McNab had stepped in to iron out problems with Mary Pickford's divorce from Owen Moore when charges of collusion hit the papers. (Pickford was seen with Douglas Fairbanks, her former husband, shortly after the divorce decree and Moore's attorneys claimed the two had conspired to get their client out of the way.)

McNab was also well respected in San Francisco politics and had tremendous influence in City Hall. Schenck believed a jury of San Francisco residents would be more open and less resentful to "one of their own," playing down the Los Angeles-San Francisco rivalry. Schenck, Zukor, and Lasky agreed that if anyone could free Roscoe, it would be McNab.

Papers in Schenck's files show that McNab was paid $50,000 to handle the case, more than double his usual fee because of the notoriety and possible consequences of being associated with such a volatile situation.

Roscoe later said that according to Schenck, Zukor initially refused to put up studio money to pay the legal fees. But after Schenck explained the financial loss to the studio in completed and unreleased features alone if Roscoe was convicted, picking up the tab was by far the wiser action. Zukor wrote the fees off by recording them in Paramount's book as Roscoe's salary, which provided a better tax deduction than listing it as legal expenses. (This also gave the appearance that Roscoe was still on the payroll and not fired.)

Though Zukor had written off the fees, and recorded them as salary payments to Roscoe, he later insisted Arbuckle repay the fees to Paramount. Zukor claimed it was only a "loan" and the studio had disassociated itself from the star. Schenck told Roscoe that if those films had not been in the can, Zukor would have let him swing in the breeze. A group of Roscoe's friends got together and took up a collection to help offset the tab, quickly raising close to $45,000.

Attorney Milton Cohen, McNab, Dominguez, Schenck, and Anger held a late-night conference in Roscoe's home to make the transition smooth and to avoid giving the impression Dominguez was either being forced out or quitting because of the apparent hopelessness of the case.

On October 5, Dominguez officially withdrew.

My Dear Roscoe:
It is with profound regret that I am compelled to advise you that, because of my business affairs in Los Angeles, I am obliged to withdraw from the

defense of your case. As I indicated to you at the conference held in your home the other day, it will be impossible for me to spend the necessary time in San Francisco for a proper defense of your matter.

In withdrawing from this case, I am pleased through sheer admiration of your conduct, to say that it has been a great pleasure for me to have met you and that you have a heart of pure gold.

I know you are innocent of the charges made against you, and that a jury of your peers in the court of justice of San Francisco will acquit you. The good people of that wonderful city will see justice is done. I am convinced from my knowledge of you, and the evidence in that case, that a great triumph awaits you. The people of San Francisco will give you justice and fair play.

God is just, and justice will be yours. Then you will be restored to the hearts of the people of our country, to whom you have given unbounded pleasure and joy.

I am proud to be your friend, and whenever I can be of service I am yours to command.

Your sincere friend, Frank Dominguez.

There was also pressure placed on Attorney Charles Brennan (who was a native San Franciscan) to resign, but after consideration, the executives believed it was best to keep him rather than risk dismissing an attorney from San Francisco. Two more attorneys were added, Joseph McInerney and Nat Schmulowitz, giving Roscoe a team of five competent and well-respected attorneys. Matthew Brady called them Roscoe's "million-dollar defense team" both as a joke on their stature and reflecting the amount he believed it cost to retain the group. (The actual cost was about one quarter of that amount, which was still sizable.) They were ready to fight for Roscoe.

As the defense shuffled its players, the San Francisco Coroner's Office swore out an official complaint against Dr. Rumwell on November 1, charging him with performing an illegal autopsy. The offense was considered a misdemeanor under a city ordinance. Dr. Rumwell paid a five-hundred-dollar fine and the issue of the autopsy was dropped. But the action did spark a quiet investigation into the doctor's background and allegations that he had been performing illegal abortions at Wakefield. The outcome was never made public.

McNab's first action as Arbuckle's attorney was to order a complete probe into Virginia Rappé's background. Charles Brennan pulled strings in Chicago and found several witnesses who said they would testify that Rappé had been in bad health for years and had undergone several abortions. Dr. Maurice Rosenberg (no relation to Maude Delmont who used Rosenberg as an alias) said the girl had been treated for chronic cystitis, a complaint that could have caused the infection and inflammation that started her problems at the party. Mrs. Joseph Roth, who ran a home for unwed pregnant girls and mothers, said Rappé was there for treatment for venereal disease five or six times between the ages of fourteen and sixteen.

Upon hearing the news, Brady sent one of his men, Assistant District Attorney Alden Ames, to Chicago to "talk to" the witnesses. Upon his return he assured Brady that he had nothing to worry about, and that he had uncovered enough evidence against the witnesses to assure their cooperation.

Then another bomb exploded. Federal agents said they had enough evidence against Roscoe to convict him for violation of the Volstead Act. They filed charges on October 7. Roscoe headed north with McNab and Cohen and posted five hundred dollars bail. Authorities would notify him when a hearing date was set. (The case was ultimately dropped.)

On the return trip, McNab told Roscoe that the charge could not have come at a worse time. Not only was the comedian now considered by many to be a rapist and murderer, but a bootlegger as well.

As both sides readied to present their cases in court, Brady had a scare. He had placed Zey Prevon and Alice Blake "in protective custody" for several days, again making sure their testimony would hold up under cross-examination. They were finally released and placed under "protective surveillance" to prevent the defense from tampering with them. But

Alice Blake slipped away, right under the nose of Brady's men.

She turned up at a friend's home in Alameda County, saying she was frightened about the "ordeal." She never specified what that meant and Brady made sure reporters were left with the impression that she was receiving pressure from the defense. Brady placed her under subpoena to "make sure she is available to us any time we need her." Blake was ordered to appear in court November 15.

On Monday, November 14, an odd set of occurrences happened involving Joe Schenck, Adolph Zukor, and the Bank of Italy. They are apparently connected in some fashion, but exactly how is a matter of speculation.

That morning, it was announced that Joe Schenck had accepted an advisory position with the Bank of Italy, which was headquartered in San Francisco with offices in Los Angeles. The bank also catered to the movie industry, which helped establish it as a financial leader. Schenck's duties included working as a liaison between the studios and the bank and developing the best systems to help studios get the necessary financing for their films, answering directly to Motley Flint, a bank executive.

In connection with the position, Schenck and his wife, Norma Talmadge, moved to Los Angeles, arriving on Monday and setting up temporary quarters in the Ambassador Hotel. Schenck said the move west had a dual purpose —besides his work with the Bank of Italy, he believed it was better to base his residence nearer the studios and his stars.

Also on Monday, November 14, Adolph Zukor sent a ten-thousand-dollar check to San Francisco District Attorney Matthew Brady; the check was a Bank of Italy draft note, signed by Zukor and co-signed by someone named Woods.

The "Woods" is most likely Frank E. Woods, Paramount's chief supervising director. Woods had worked under Jesse Lasky just prior to signing with Zukor. Among the productions under his control were the Arbuckle features. If this "Woods" is indeed Frank E. Woods, it is also likely that the checks were "laundered" through production. It was common among the larger studios to use the production budget to absorb costs of nonproduction and questionable items such as cars, furs, lavish dinners, and in this case, bribes.

It is interesting that the draft was made from the Bank of Italy, which was a San Francisco-based bank, because Zukor was still in New York. It would have made more sense for Jesse Lasky, who was in Los Angeles at that time, to sign the check. Was Zukor trying to bury the funds and hide the check from Lasky? Or did Zukor sign the check at the demand of Joe Schenck? Was Schenck somehow implicated in a bribe scheme? Did Frank Woods know the checks were being illegally laundered through his department?

Was it a bribe to quash the case, or keep certain witnesses off the stand? Was it a payoff to stop Brady from digging too deeply into certain aspects of the San Francisco party? It seems unlikely that Zukor would be willing to shell out ten thousand dollars to help Roscoe when he had done nothing to help him prior to this. He blamed Roscoe for the Brownie Kennedy party that Roscoe did not attend, he signed another hefty comedian as leverage against Arbuckle, he openly expressed hostility for Roscoe, and he agreed to front the legal fees only upon insistence from Joe Schenck and a promise that Arbuckle would pay back the money.

It seems more likely that, as in the Brownie Kennedy affair, Zukor was paying out money to cover himself; for what purpose may never be known. But the tie-in with the Bank of Italy and Schenck's sudden affiliation with the bank cannot be overlooked.

The date of the check is also important for another reason —it was the day that jury selection began for the first manslaughter trial of Roscoe Arbuckle.

20

"We're ready to shoot." With those four words, Roscoe Arbuckle and his defense team, led by Gavin McNab, announced that the manslaughter trial was ready to get under way.

A list of 207 potential jurors had been drawn, and McNab hoped the bulk of the jury would be made up by those who had served on two previous Superior Court panels. Brady expressed indifference to the jury, claiming any panel would rule in his favor. But once the questioning began, they both changed their attitude.

The first jurors were interviewed on Monday, November 14, at 10:00 A.M. Presiding was Superior Court Judge Harold Louderback.

The district attorney said he would reject any prospective jurors who said they were movie fans or that they had read the newspapers (which, except for the Hearst papers, had leaned in favor of Arbuckle's acquittal). Brady also made one more stipulation—he would turn down anyone with "political aspirations who chooses to run for office during a Democratic Administration."

The defense said it would reject any woman associated with a women's club or organization, or anyone who had heard that the Volstead Act had been violated during the St. Francis party.

The ground rules were laid.

No sooner had the questioning gotten under way than a vicious battle erupted between Brady and McNab, with Brady

209

screaming, pounding his fists, throwing papers, and threatening to resign from the case unless McNab changed his line of questioning. At the center of the controversy: allegations that Brady had forced witnesses into signing statements under the threat of imprisonment. The witnesses in question were Alice Blake and Zey Prevon.

McNab questioned the first potential juror, John C. Medley.

"Would you take into consideration as evidence in the case the fact that witnesses for the prosecution had been threatened with imprisonment in the county jail if they refused to make certain affidavits?"

U'Ren jumped out of his chair shouting, joining Brady who was pounding the desk.

"That statement is untrue and a vile lie aimed at influencing prospective jurors against the prosecution. If you believe such slander will win your case you are sadly mistaken, Mr. McNab. We will reject every juror on those grounds if necessary."

"Mr. U'Ren, I will bring seven witnesses into this court to prove that this is more than an allegation, this is a charge. You have tampered with, threatened, and intimidated witnesses into lying. You know this is true and I know this is true. By the time this trial is done, the world will know this is true as God is my witness."

"This is a lie!" Brady was red in the face as he spoke. He leaped to his feet and waved a clenched fist at McNab. "If you can prove it I will resign from this case!"

McNab dropped his line of questioning. He had made his point. Mr. Medley was passed for cause.

The next prospective juror called was a woman. Again, McNab led the questioning.

"Are you a member of, or do you have any affiliation with, any women's mob?"

"Objection! You cannot call women's groups mobs."

"Then I'll call them vigilance committees."

"Objection. We have no such vigilance groups here in San Francisco."

"How about vigilante, then?"

When McNab asked the juror if she knew of any such

women's groups in San Francisco, Brady screamed that it was not the women of the city who were on trial, but Arbuckle. The argument grew so hostile and unruly that Judge Louderback stepped in with a severe reprimand for both men.

During the battle, Roscoe sat quietly behind his attorneys. Next to him were Minta and her mother, and his brother Alfred.

McNab returned to his original questioning when the next juror August Fritze, a broker, stepped into the box.

"Would you consider all the testimony of witnesses, even if those witnesses had altered or completely changed their testimony several times?"

Again, Brady pounded the desk.

"It is prejudicial for counsel to take an isolated portion of the testimony and hammer and hammer and hammer at it!"

Mr. Fritze was accepted.

Wholesale grocer Fred Jordan (who was a personal friend of U'Ren's) was on next. McNab focused on Rappé's health and spoke in a flippant tone.

"Would you consider previous testimony of bladder trouble a reflection on an unfortunate girl's morals?"

"When Mr. McNab puts in that evidence, he is to introduce it with intent to attack the morals of the girl. His proposal is to tie up the jurors as to the effect such evidence will have on his or her mind. A juror at this time cannot tell what effect certain statements will have on his mind later," U'Ren protested.

McNab listened, then ignored U'Ren.

"If it is shown by scientific testimony that the unfortunate girl had a diseased bladder from an immoral life—would that prejudice you?"

Again Judge Louderback intervened. "Gentlemen, are we arguing the case or drawing a jury here?"

The haggling went on for five days. Forty-three people were called; finally both sides agreed on seven men and five women. One of the women was Helen Hubbard, the wife of a prominent San Francisco attorney. She admitted she was a movie fan but vowed that would not influence her decision. She was to become a key player in the outcome of the trial.

Though a panel was selected, the fighting and the accusations against the defense and prosecution were just getting started. Matthew Brady put Prevon and Blake in "protective custody" once again until the trial started to prevent the defense from getting at them. Brady accused the defense of spiriting away several witnesses on John and Jane Doe warrants for the same reason.

Then he pulled off the ultimate coup. Brady learned that the defense had centered its case around breaking Maude Delmont. The charges were based on her claims, and by now both sides had no doubt that she was a liar and a woman of questionable repute. McNab knew if he could put her on the stand, not only would the prosecution's case be shot down, but quite possibly Brady's reputation would be severely damaged (if not destroyed) as well. He would be laughed out of town for pinning a case on the accusations of such a woman. Brady made sure Delmont's testimony would stand. He locked her in jail on bigamy charges and refused to release her to testify. Defense requests to release her to testify were turned down by the court. Brady won another, decisive victory.

Brady called his first witness: Grace Halston, a Wakefield Sanatorium nurse. She emphatically stated that Virginia's body was riddled with bruises, that she found numerous organ ruptures, and that both had most likely been caused by force—from a man. Newspaper reporters in the courtroom claim that Halston continually glared at Arbuckle and demonstrated obvious hatred for the man by her looks, actions, and tone of voice. She also seemed extremely nervous, bit her lip, and repeatedly looked at Brady before answering delicate questions. It seemed obvious to even the most casual observer that something was amiss with this witness's testimony. McNab also sensed the irregularities and closed in during his cross-examination.

"Miss Halston. You claim you saw several organ ruptures and lesions on the bladder during your examination. I would like to know what qualified you to examine the body because you are neither a physician nor a graduate nurse."

"Yes, this is true."

"I demand her testimony be stricken from the record."

The request was denied by Judge Louderback.

Through the precise wording of questions, McNab ascertained that the ruptured bladder and lesions could have been caused by cancer, thereby refuting brute force as the only possible explanation for the condition of the bladder. He also showed that the alleged bruises Halston identified were most likely caused by jewelry that Virginia wore. The defense won a major point and opened the door to alternative causes for Virginia's injuries other than rape or attempted rape by Arbuckle.

Dr. Arthur Beardslee was the next witness to testify about Virginia's injuries, which, he observed, seemed inflicted by an outside force. He said he tried several times to get the "history" of Virginia Rappé from Maude Delmont, who proved uncooperative.

McNab hoped to shoot down claims that Rappé had accused Roscoe of raping her.

"Did Mrs. Delmont or Miss Rappé intimate to you that Mr. Arbuckle was responsible for her condition?"

The prosecution team of Brady, U'Ren, and Leo Friedman objected in one loud voice. Another verbal battle between the sides erupted. Calling McNab's questions "poison," U'Ren begged the court's indulgence to temporarily dismiss the jury until the dispute was settled, further infuriating McNab, whose voice cracked under the strain of anger.

Nat Schmulowitz shouted at U'Ren to sit down, that the defense had the floor. U'Ren grudgingly obliged after receiving a nod from Brady. Judge Louderback ordered Schmulowitz to return to his seat. The cross-examining continued.

"Doctor, did you ask Miss Rappé if Mr. Arbuckle had anything to do with her injuries?"

"No."

"Did you ask her if Mr. Arbuckle had assaulted her?"

"I did not."

"Did you ask Mrs. Delmont if anybody had assaulted Miss Rappé?"

Brady objected and the objection stood.

"Did Mrs. Delmont tell you anybody had injured the girl?"

213

"Objection!"

Once again, Brady's objection held.

Dr. Beardslee finally offered a glimmer of light to the case, but by doing so opened another can of worms.

"It was evident that I was dealing with an operative case. I saw no evidence of intoxication. If there had been any evidence [of intoxication] it was overshadowed by the girl's extreme pain."

"Then, Dr. Beardslee, let me ask you this. If you saw evidence that Miss Rappé would benefit from surgery, why was no surgery ordered at that time?"

"I have no answer for that."

As he returned to his seat, McNab dismissed the witness with an "aside" that was fiercely objected to by the prosecution.

"You have no answer. I wonder if Miss Rappé might be alive today if you had."

On Monday, November 21, the trial was ripped wide open by a bombshell dropped by a model named Betty Campbell. Campbell was called to testify as a guest at the fatal party. She claimed she arrived one hour after the alleged "rape" incident and found Roscoe, Lowell Sherman, Fred Fischbach, Al Semnacher, and Zey Prevon (called Zeh Prevost during the course of the trial) relaxing together in one of the suites. Brady tried to use this in an attempt to show Arbuckle had neither remorse nor concern for the condition of Virginia Rappé.

But while answering questions from McNab, Campbell claimed that Arbuckle showed no signs of intoxication, that his steps were even while they danced together, and he appeared casual in his manner. It seemed unlikely to her that this could be the conduct of someone who had just violated a woman.

Then McNab and Campbell changed course and weaved their way through the testimony that turned the tide in Arbuckle's favor. Campbell claimed the San Francisco district attorney had threatened her with prison if she refused to testify against Arbuckle! McNab shouted over Brady's objections as Brady claimed that this had not been brought up in direct questioning, and was therefore inadmissible as evidence. McNab said he had evidence to back his claim and to establish grounds for the questions. He presented affidavits by Campbell, Blake, and Prevon—all backing claims of Brady's intimidation tactics.

"Zeh Prevost is being held right now by the district attorney's office. She has been held there for more than two months and subjected to repeated interrogation and intimidation by the district attorney to sign false statements against Roscoe Arbuckle. Here is her sworn statement and a statement by Alice Blake."

Exactly how McNab wangled a statement from Zey Prevon is a mystery (or his claim could have been a bluff) because she had been spirited away by Brady for nearly two months. But records show McNab obtained his statement from Alice Blake sometime between her escape from Brady's custody and her subsequent "recapture" in Alameda County—the only time she slipped through Brady's fingers. Blake was released shortly after her rearrest and put in her mother's custody. But Zey Prevon was still being held.

She was then called to the stand to testify about the allegations. Prevon testified that she had been held captive, against her will, by an employee of the D.A. and had been repeatedly interrogated by Brady and his staff in Brady's chambers. Prevon claimed Brady kept insisting she sign the statement that Virginia Rappé said "he had killed me," when she had already told the grand jury that she was mistaken when she first made the statement, and that the statement was not true.

As shock waves rippled through the court, Judge Louderback ordered Prevon immediately released from custody. Without missing a beat, McNab subpoenaed her as a witness for the defense. But first, she had to face questions from the prosecution. Leo Friedman handled this series of questions.

Prevon told the story that the newspapers had already printed in great detail—the party, the list of guests, the eating, drinking and dancing, Virginia going into the bathroom in room 1219: Arbuckle's suite.

"Mr. Arbuckle followed her and closed the door."

She said that half an hour later, Maude Delmont kicked at the door [of the suite] several times.

" 'Open the door,' Mrs. Delmont called. 'I want to speak to Virginia.' "

"Objection! Hearsay testimony."

The defense was overruled.

"Who opened the door?" Friedman asked Zey Prevon.

"Mr. Arbuckle."

"What was he doing?"

"He was fumbling with his robe."

"Did Mr. Arbuckle say anything after opening the door?"

"He said nothing."

"Did you observe his face?"

"It was red."

Gavin McNab objected that Friedman was leading the witness. Overruled.

Prevon went on to say that she and Delmont entered room 1219, where Virginia was already lying on a bed. She claimed Arbuckle entered later without his bathrobe and his back was wet.

"Miss Rappé was lying on the bed. Her hair was down and she was fully dressed, moaning and moving around."

"Did she say anything at this time?"

"Yes. She said, 'I'm dying. I'm going to die.' Then she began tearing at her waist . . . Mr. Arbuckle entered the room, grabbed at Virginia's waist, and laughing, began fooling with her. Miss Blake came in and we undressed Virginia. Mrs. Delmont and I removed all her clothing."

"After the bath did she say anything?"

"Yes. She said, 'He hurt me.' "

At this the defense was pleased. Prevon did not say "Arbuckle hurt me" as Brady had tried to force her to say. Her statement was later to show that the "he" in question was Fred Fischbach! Fischbach was the one who placed Virginia in the bathtub. Virginia's screams and apparent accusations were now linked to that incident, not anything Roscoe had tried to do.

"Did the defendant say anything?"

"Yes. He said, 'Aw, shut her up. I'll throw her out the window if she don't stop yelling.' "

Roscoe leaned forward to one of his attorneys, Brennan,

and asked him to object to that statement. Brennan whispered back and no objection was raised.

Prevon related the story of how Roscoe placed ice on Virginia to "get her to come to." Recess was called.

Alice Blake was then called to the stand. She reiterated much of Zey Prevon's testimony, again refusing to name Roscoe as the man Virginia indicated as the one who "hurt her." She was also visibly frightened when the prosecution questioned her and obviously relieved when McNab stepped in.

McNab asked for the initial statement she made to the police shortly after the party—the statement made before Brady locked her away and worked on her. Friedman said the prosecution no longer had that statement but would gladly supply—for the record—the statement made later by Blake.

"Your Honor. I ask for a fish and the prosecution offers me a serpent."

With both women on record as having been threatened and intimidated by Brady, and both refusing to name Arbuckle as the man singled out by Rappé, the D.A.'s case was crumbling. If Brady could not prove Arbuckle actually attacked Virginia at the party, then he had to show Arbuckle had plotted to "have his way" with Virginia for several years.

Jesse Norgard, a former security guard at Henry Lehrman's Culver City studio, was sworn in as the next witness for the prosecution. The defense team voiced strenuous objections at his being called as a witness, claiming any testimony from Norgard was irrelevant because he was not involved in the party. Brady's men insisted that he was there to testify about Arbuckle's prior knowledge of Rappé and prior intent. Roscoe asked McNab to allow the testimony because he believed it would provide nothing harmful.

Norgard said he met Arbuckle in August of 1919, when the comedian tried to get onto the lot. He said Arbuckle first used the excuse that he had forgotten his hat and wanted to retrieve it. Then, he testified, Arbuckle asked for the key to Rappé's dressing room. Norgard refused to surrender it, and Roscoe supposedly insisted he only wanted to play a joke on Rappé.

"Did he offer you anything for that key?" U'Ren asked.

"Yes. He showed me a big roll of money and said he would trade it for the key."

"How much was in the roll?"

"I could only see two twenties and one ten."

"Were there any other bills?"

"Yes, there were other bills."

"What did you say to that proposition that he submitted to you?"

"I said, 'No, sir,' and walked out."

Roscoe found the line of questioning funny and burst out laughing in court. He was ordered by the judge to remain silent. He quickly discovered the story was no laughing matter when the evening papers reported that he had offered a guard fifty dollars to sneak into Virginia Rappé's dressing room. A slight twisting of facts with major ramifications. Several newspapers printed Roscoe as a crazed man with a long-burning lust for Virginia Rappé.

Prosecution witness Josephine Keza, a hotel chambermaid, told stories of hearing a woman scream, of seeing Lowell Sherman wandering through the suites with a woman dressed only in her underclothes, of seeing Roscoe with Virginia (she did not recall whether or not they were kissing), of seeing bootleg booze, dancing, and a phonograph playing jazz music. She painted a lurid tale of a drunken orgy. The defense hoped to tear her testimony apart but managed only to puncture a few holes.

Dr. Edward Heinrich was called next and identified himself as a criminologist and fingerprint expert. He testified he sealed Roscoe's suite (1219) at the St. Francis (on Matthew Brady's orders) eleven days after the party took place. On October 7, he removed the bedroom doors and shipped them to his laboratory for examination. There, he claimed, he found partial fingerprints of Miss Rappé on the inside of the door, and Arbuckle's prints were superimposed over them. He said this seemed to be an indication that Miss Rappé had been struggling to open the door and that Roscoe had pushed them back closed.

Gavin McNab challenged Heinrich as an expert witness by showing he had never testified on such cases before in the state of California. He hoped to disqualify his testimony by introducing his own witness, Ignatius McCarthy, who was a former federal investigator. McCarthy said he could prove the fingerprints on the door were faked, and strongly implied that the culprit was Matthew Brady. Brady and U'Ren objected in turn to McCarthy's testimony and asked that he be disqualified and McNab's objection to Heinrich overruled. Judge Louderback agreed and let Heinrich's testimony stand.

Then McNab tried to call his own fingerprint expert to refute Heinrich's testimony, but he failed to qualify and the court refused to allow his statements.

In a last attempt, the defense called a hotel maid who said she had gone over the door with a feather duster several times after the suite had been vacated and long before it was ordered sealed by the D.A.

"I will accept the statements made by Dr. Heinrich on this basis . . . that the fingerprints be put upon a door, that a chambermaid take a rough cloth and rub them every day for eleven days. Then, whatever remains can be entered into evidence."

The courtroom went up for grabs between uncontrollable laughter from the audience and angry objections by the prosecution. McNab scored another round.

On Tuesday, November 22, the defense presented its opening arguments. McNab's speech brought down the ire of the prosecution team, especially Assistant District Attorney Friedman, when McNab pointed out that it was the duty of the State to prove its case beyond a reasonable doubt, and in that, " . . . the State has miserably failed to perform." Friedman admonished the defense counsel and ordered him to cut short the accusations and declare what the defense intended to prove.

"We intend to show you by the best evidence that it is possible to produce, the words of the dead girl at or about the time of the sad events, exonerating the defendant."

The defense called in its own medical experts who backed early claims that Virginia's bladder could have ruptured through disease and not necessarily through force. It obtained surprisingly solid testimony from Dr. Rumwell, who swore the actress had gonorrhea and was definitely not a

219

virgin. Though Friedman and U'Ren angrily objected to all so-called aspersions on Rappé's character, the testimony stayed. It was the first time the defense had won a point on establishing the true character of Virginia Rappé. Until this time she had been painted by the prosecution as an innocent young victim. Rumwell also stated that Rappé never indicated she blamed Roscoe Arbuckle for her injuries.

Another medical witness, Irene Morgan, testified she had treated Virginia as both a nurse and a masseuse at Henry Lehrman's home in Hollywood (where Virginia had stayed on occasion). Morgan said she had been told that the actress had suffered from severe abdominal cramps and had several catheterizations performed because she had trouble urinating. U'Ren's objection on the grounds of hearsay was sustained. Morgan then claimed Rappé would tear off her clothes and run through the streets naked after a few drinks. The second objection from U'Ren was overruled.

Morgan proved the most damaging witness to the prosecution so far. She also came dangerously close to becoming a macabre sidebar to the story. Two days before she was to testify, she was found lying on the bedroom floor of her hotel. She had been poisoned. She also claimed she had been threatened by an anonymous phone caller who said he would kidnap or kill her if she testified. The allegations were never proved. Brady poked fun at Morgan in the newspapers, calling her the "lithping nurth who worked ath a mathooth."

The prosecution still had to do something to swing the mood back in its favor. A defense witness, Mrs. Minnie Neighbors, was the wife of a former Los Angeles policeman and had lived near Lehrman's home. She made the same claim as Morgan—that she had seen Rappé rip off her clothes while drunk.

Brady proved she lied on the stand and also filed felony perjury charges against another defense witness, Harry Baker, who claimed to be a former lover of Rappé's. Baker said he, too, had seen Virginia clutch her stomach and run naked through the streets. Brady found a woman who refuted Baker's testimony, saying she knew Virginia during the time Baker claimed he dated her, and Virginia was definitely not seeing anyone named Harry Baker.

Baker changed his tune when perjury charges were filed. Brady dropped the charges against Baker and obtained a warrant for Mrs. Neighbor's arrest. She was released on two thousand dollars bond and pleaded "not guilty." Brady finally dropped the charges when the trial ended in a hung jury . . . on the proviso she would not testify again.

Then Fred Fischbach took the stand. He admitted he invited Virginia to the party. He admitted he heard Virginia "moaning or screaming" when he returned and "dunked her in a cold bath to quiet her down." But he said he knew nothing of the events that triggered Virginia's hysterics because he was "gone for a few hours in the automobile . . . out of the room." At Roscoe's insistence, McNab steered clear of asking Fischbach about the bootleg booze, Maude Delmont's purpose at the party, the ordering of the phonograph, and why he took off so quickly when all the key elements were in place.

"I'm on trial here, not Freddy."

Roscoe later told friends that he knew the truth would never come out in court—why Fischbach insisted on bringing the people, the bootleg booze, and the phonograph to the party, and why he made a hasty exit. He also said he was afraid of finding out that his suspicions about Fischbach were correct.

The court was adjourned for Thanksgiving. Roscoe and Minta spent the holiday with his brother A.C. Arbuckle and sister-in-law and mother-in-law. Roscoe cooked the turkey and Minta helped prepare the trimmings. Reporter Otis Wiles described the meal.

> It was a turkey he had prepared himself, a big bird, juicy and browned and tender as a lullaby—a turkey grabbed in its flapper stage and stuffed with oysters and sage and other nice things.
>
> Fatty ate it in the midst of his family . . . He didn't have to go out in the chill rain to have a Thanksgiving to give thanks for. And he could sit in a big easy chair and digest his dinner in peace and smoke brown paper cigarettes and crack jokes and listen to the records on the phonograph.

Fatty tried the turkey and found it innocent.

The jury that is trying Fatty also tried a turkey today, but refused to render a verdict.

The jury . . . went out in the rain and the chill to a restaurant. The turkey was brought to them on plates.

Then through the chill and rain again, back to the hotel, and so to bed to be refreshed for the trial tomorrow.

On Monday, November 28, nearly eleven weeks after the fatal party, Roscoe Arbuckle was the last witness called—finally taking the stand in his own defense for the very first time.

21

As Roscoe entered the court he was flanked by reporters and well-wishers anxious to get a quote or look at the star. The defense apparently had done a terrific public-relations job and turned much of the sympathy back toward Roscoe. The vigilante groups were still represented, but they were now less hostile and far less vocal. This was the day both sides had been waiting for.

"Hey, Roscoe? How does she look now?"

"Well, I'm not losing any weight. There's nothing for me to worry about. I see they're betting ten to six for my acquittal. Maybe I should get in on that action?"

Arbuckle rolled a brown-paper cigarette as he pushed past the crowd.

Before the proceedings got under way, Brady was called to the bench to answer charges leveled by Bailiff Harry McGovern, that he had placed certain members of the jury under detective surveillance, and that four detectives were ordered to follow the jury, eat lunch and dinner with the members, and talk about the case in "loud tones" and speak against Arbuckle. McGovern also claimed that two detectives were seen talking with the one male alternate juror, Stephen Hopkins, patting him on the back, asking about his health and calling him "Whiskers." Brady, of course, denied the charges and the matter was discussed privately in Judge Louderback's chambers. There was no further record of the outcome of the charges.

Roscoe was sworn in and remained unusually calm, almost

relieved at finally getting the chance to speak. His story was well rehearsed. After hours of planning and practicing answers to possible questions that could be asked of him by Brady's men, he appeared ready to clear his name. He was on the stand for four hours and fifteen minutes.

"Mr. Arbuckle, where were you on September 5, 1921?"

"At the St. Francis Hotel occupying rooms 1219, 1220, and 1221."

"Did you see Miss Virginia Rappé on that day?"

"Yes, sir."

"At what time and where did you see her?"

"She came into room 1220 at about twelve o'clock noon."

"Who was there at that time?"

"Mr. Fortlois, Mr. Fishbach, and myself. Mrs. Delmont came a few minutes later but I did not invite her."

"Who else was there?"

"Miss Blake."

"Did you invite her?"

"No."

"Who else?"

"Miss Prevon came later."

"Did you invite her?"

"No."

"Who else?"

"Mr. Semnacher."

"Was he invited by you?"

"Absolutely not."

"Did anyone come to your room at your invitation?"

"Yes. Miss Taub and another lady."

Roscoe then related how he agreed to take Mae Taub into town and needed to get dressed in the bathroom where he found Virginia Rappé.

"When I walked into 1219 I closed and locked the door, and I went straight to the bathroom and found Miss Rappé on the floor in front of the toilet. She'd been vomiting."

"What did you do?'

"When I opened the door, the door struck her, and I had to slide in this way to get in, to get by her and get hold of her. Then I closed the door and picked her up. When I picked her up . . . she vomited again. I held her under the waist . . . and

PLACE OF DEATH 3801

California State Board of Health
BUREAU OF VITAL STATISTICS

City and County of SAN FRANCISCO

NON-RES STANDARD CERTIFICATE OF DEATH

State Index No. _____

Local Registered No. _____ 5182

(No. _Wakefield Hospital_ and)

[If death occurred in a hospital or institution, give its NAME instead of street and number and fill out Nos. 11a and 11b.]

FULL NAME _Virginia Rappe_

PERSONAL AND STATISTICAL PARTICULARS

COLOR OR RACE _White_   SINGLE, MARRIED, WIDOWED, OR DIVORCED (Write the word) _Single_

married, widowed, or divorced
HUSBAND of
(or) WIFE OF

DATE OF BIRTH _____ 18__ (Day) (Year)

AGE _Abt 25_ years _____ months _____ days   If LESS then 1 day ____ hrs. ____ min

OCCUPATION
(a) Trade, profession, or particular kind of work _Motion Picture Actress_
(b) General nature of industry, business, or establishment in which employed (or employer)

(c) Name of employer

BIRTHPLACE _No Record_
(state or country)

NAME OF FATHER _No Record_

BIRTHPLACE OF FATHER (city or town) _No Record_
(state or country)

MAIDEN NAME OF MOTHER _No Record_

BIRTHPLACE OF MOTHER (city or town) _No Record_
(state or country)

LENGTH OF RESIDENCE
At Place of Death _____ years _____ months _4_ days
If nonresident, give city or town and state) _Los Angeles Calif_
in California ? years _____ months _____ days
How long in U.S., if of foreign birth? _____ years _____ months _____ days

THE ABOVE IS TRUE TO THE BEST OF MY KNOWLEDGE
(Informant) _Halsey Co_
(Address) _1122 Sutter St_

HOME ADDRESS Los Angeles, Calif.

Filed SEP 15 1921   WILLIAM C. HASSLER
Registrar or Deputy

MEDICAL CERTIFICATE OF DEATH

DATE OF DEATH _September 9th_ 19_21_
(Month) (Day) (Year)

I HEREBY CERTIFY, That I attended deceased from _____ 19__, to _____ 19__

that I last saw h___ alive on _____ 19__

and that death occurred on the date stated above at _1.30_ p.m.

The CAUSE OF DEATH* was as follows: _Rupture of the Bladder_

Inquested by Coroner—Sept. 12, 13, 14, 1921. Peritonitis following rupture.

Urinary Bladder due to external force

Manslaughter (Duration) _____ years _____ months _____ days

Contributory _Acute peritonitis_

(Duration) _____ years _____ months

Where was disease contracted
If not at place of death?

Did an operation precede death? _No_   Date of _____

Was there an autopsy? _yes_

What test confirmed diagnosis? _N. Ophüls_

(Signed) _Sept 10_ 19_21_ (Address) _114 Walnut St_

*State the DISEASE CAUSING DEATH, or, in deaths from VIOLENT CAUSES, state (1) MEANS OF INJURY; and (2) whether (probably) ACCIDENTAL, SUICIDAL, or HOMICIDAL. (See reverse side for additional space.)

PLACE OF BURIAL OR REMOVAL _Los Angeles Calif_   DATE OF BURIAL _Sept 16_ 19_21_

UNDERTAKER _Halsey & Co_   EMBALMER'S LICENSE No _1316_

ADDRESS _1122 Sutter St_

Virginia Rappé's death certificate . . . quickly filled out. Note manslaughter remains listed as the cause of death.

Maude Delmont, aka Montgomery, aka Rosenberg. A bigamist and professional co-respondent with a long police record and a nefarious reputation. AP/Wide World Photo

The first jury missed settin[g]
Roscoe free by one vote.
The woman who held out [was]
Helen Hubbard, second
from right in top row. Was
she pressured by Brady?

After being ordered to
remain silent during the
preliminary hearing,
Roscoe finally takes the
stand in his own defence.
Nov. 28, 1922.

Will H. Hays and Adolph Zukor at the 1926 opening of the New York Paramount Theatre. Were they secret allies five years earlier? Author's Collection

The telegram written by Hays in Zukor's office. 45 words that smashed Arbuckle's career and destroyed his life. Author's Collection

Roscoe returns to San Francisco with his $25,000 Pierce-Arrow touring car. He expected a quick dismissal of the charges.
Author's Collectio

Minta Durfee, Roscoe and Flora Adkins Durfee (Minta's mother). They stayed by Roscoe's side through the ordeal.
AP/World Wide Pho

The Schencks work a deal in which all benefit at no risk to the studio and no apparent profit to the I.R.S. The mystery name at the end was Will Hays.
Author's Collection

WESTERN UNION TELEGRAM

NEWCOMB CARLTON, PRESIDENT   GEORGE W. E. ATKINS, FIRST VICE-PRESIDENT

RECEIVED AT

D154N XSJ 131 BLUE

HD LOSANGELES CALIF 1240P JAN 22 1923

NICHOLAS M SCHENCK   0974

1540 BROADWAY NEWYORK NY

R CAN NOT ACCEPT A FLAT SALARY HE OWES TOO MUCH MONEY TO GOVERNMENT FOR BACK INCOME TAX AND OTHER PEOPLE WE HAVE EXCELLENT COMEDIAN HERE POODLES HANNEFORD WHOM R COULD DIRECT IN TWO REELERS THAT WOULD NOT COST OVER TWENTY THOUSAND INCLUDING RS SALARY WHICH WOULD BE ONE THOUSAND PER WEEK ARRANGE WITH A DISTRIBUTING COMPANY THROUGH ASSOCIATIC IF NECESSARY TO DISTRIBUTE AND FINANCE COMEDIES ON A THIRTY SEVENTY BASIS UNTIL THEY RECOUPED COST OF COMEDIES AND PRINTS AND THEN FIFTY FOR R AND FIFTY FOR DISTRIBUTING COMPANY IN THIS WAY NO ONE WILL LOSE ANY MONEY I AM QUITE SURE AND R WILL HAVE A CHANGE TO GET ON HIS FEET PLEASE GET QUICK ACTION ON THIS PROPOSITION ALSO WIRE ME RESULT OF CONFERENCE WITH

JOE SCHENCK

No longer a pariah . . . at Norma Talmadge's Santa Monica home – May 1926.
TOP ROW – Roscoe Arbuckle, Mae Murray, Ward Crane, Virginia Vallee, Ronald Coleman, Bessie Love, Jack Pickford, Rudolph Valentino, Pola Negri.
2ND ROW – Raymond Griffith, Chris Goulding, Louella Parsons, Lila Lee, Carmel Myers, Allan Forrest, Bert Lytell, Claire Windsor, Richard Barthlemess, Constance Talmadge, Beatrice Lillie, Al Hall, Mrs. Jack Mulhall, Mrs. John Robertson, Julianne Johnson, Agnes Ayers, John Robertson, Mrs. Talmadge, Henri the Marquis de Falais, Micky Neilan, Howard Hughes.
BOTTOM – Tony Moreno, Prince David Mdivani, Charles Lang, Edmund Goulding, Marcel Desano, Manuel D'Arce, Harry D'Arost, Doris Deane Arbuckle, Mrs. Antonio Moreno, Eddie Lane, Natalie Talmadge, Mrs. Ed Sedwick, Christine Francis, Allie MacIntosh, Kitty Scola, Blanche Sweet.

The Plantation Club. A money-maker until a Pub Nuisance Ordinance and the Stock Market crash shut it down.
Author's Collection

Roscoe, Bill Heyes and A
Goulding in a production shot from "HEY POP".
Author's Collection from Bill Heyes

Bill Heyes and Roscoe in a rare still – a deleted scene from "HEY POP". The film was Arbuckle's much heralded return to the screen in 1932. *Author's Collection from Bill Heyes*

Shortly before his death, Roscoe attends a movie premiere with friend Lew Cody. Is the woman on Roscoe's right remembering the tragedy that dethroned Hollywood's biggest star? *Author's Collection*

Roscoe Arbuckle. Always a gentleman. His friends never called him Fatty.

the forehead, to keep her hair back off her face so she could vomit. When she finished, I put the seat down, then I sat her down on it."

"Can I do anything for you?" I asked her. She said she wanted to lie down. I carried her into 1219 and put her on the bed. I lifted her feet off the floor. I went to the bathroom again and came back in two or three minutes. I found her rolling on the floor between two beds holding her stomach. I tried to pick her up but I couldn't. I immediately went out of 1219 and 1220 and asked Mrs. Delmont and Miss Prevon to come in. I told them Miss Rappé was sick."

He told of how Virginia sat on the bed tearing off her clothes. His description of the actress painted a picture of a mad dog foaming at the mouth, which brought out a strong objection from Friedman.

"She had a black lace garter and she tore the lace off the garter. Mr. Fischbach came in about that time and asked [her] to stop tearing her clothes . . . she was tearing off her dress and she had just one sleeve hanging by a few threads. I said, 'All right, if you want that off, I'll take it off for you.' And I pulled it off for her and went out of the room."

Roscoe related how Fischbach hauled Virginia off into the bathroom and put her in a tub of cold water to calm her down. He avoided any further details that could have been interpreted as hearsay or as unrelated testimony about Fischbach that might have sparked another objection from Friedman.

He testified that it was Maude Delmont who put the ice on Virginia, that she had already been rubbing the girl down with ice by the time he returned to the bedroom. Roscoe claimed he picked a piece of ice off Virginia's body and asked Delmont what it was for, to which Delmont replied, "Leave it here. I know how to take care of Virginia." Arbuckle claimed Delmont told him to leave the room when he tried to cover Rappé with the bedspread, and that Delmont became quite hostile.

"I told Mrs. Delmont to shut up or I would throw her out of the window, and I went out of the room. Mrs. Taub came in and telephoned for the hotel manager. I told Mrs. Delmont that the manager was coming up . . . Mrs. Delmont put a bathrobe on Miss Rappé. We then took her to room 1227."

McNab gave Roscoe the chance to refute Brady's charges.

"While in 1219 with Miss Rappé did you ever at any time place your hand over Miss Rappé's on the bedroom door?"

"No, sir."

"At any time on that day did your hand come in contact with her hand on the door?"

"No."

"Have you ever had a conversation with Jesse Norgard at a Culver City studio regarding the key to Miss Rappé's dressing room at the studio?"

"Never had such a conversation."

"Are there any other circumstances that occurred in 1219 that you have not told this jury?"

"No, sir."

"Cross-examine the witness."

Roscoe fared quite well under the skilful guidance of his attorney Gavin McNab. From this account, Roscoe was an innocent man who was only trying to help a sick girl. But this account was carefully edited. There was no mention that he pressed ice to Virginia's thigh to see if she had been faking hysteria, as Roscoe had already admitted to friends and his first attorney. There was no mention of excessive drinking nor of anything but casual dancing by only a few guests. From this version, the get-together was more of a formal, sedate gathering then the three-day free-for-all painted by the prosecution.

When Assistant D.A. Leo Friedman began his cross-examination it was gloves off. He pounced on Roscoe with everything he had, twisting facts, hammering away at seeming insignificant details to frustrate and anger the witness, and repeating the same questions over and over again. The grilling was frequently interrupted by objections from the defense. It was the most vicious court battle since the trial began. The prosecution was out for Roscoe's blood and had no alternative but to destroy him on the stand.

The first questions centered on the allegations by Norgard.

"You state you had never seen Mr. Norgard of Culver City?"

226

"I stated I had no conversation with him."

"Where were you employed in August of 1919?"

"I was not employed. I had my own company. I rented a studio."

"Mr. Lehrman's studio?"

"Yes. It was the only way I could get back money he owed me."

"Do you recall having seen Miss Rappé there?"

"Oh, yes."

Then Friedman abruptly shifted his line of questioning.

"What time did you say Miss Rappé entered your rooms?"

"Around twelve o'clock."

"You had known her before?"

"Uh-huh. About five or six years."

"Nobody told you she was coming to your rooms?"

"No, sir."

"Didn't you know how Mrs. Delmont happened to come up there?"

"No. They all kept stringing in. I didn't know who they were then. I didn't invite them."

Roscoe testified he did not know any of the uninvited guests. He also said it was Virginia Rappé who requested the Victrola be brought into the room. He admitted to drinking "a few" highballs and dancing, and said he did not pay much attention to Virginia Rappé's actions prior to her getting sick.

Friedman picked at little points in an effort to trip Roscoe —whether or not a clock was working, how many drinks he had, whether or not the windows were open—hundreds of obscure questions. Roscoe answered each one patiently and unshakably.

"What was the first thing you did in room 1219?"

"I closed the door and locked it. I wanted to dress."

At this point, Judge Louderback called a noon recess. Moments after his announcement, Virginia Rappé's bladder was carried into the courtroom and entered as an exhibit. Gavin McNab objected strenuously, calling the display, "disgusting and obscene."

When the session resumed, Friedman picked up where he had left off—why Roscoe entered the bathroom of 1219. He tried to get Roscoe to admit to another reason other than his getting dressed. He hoped to get Arbuckle to admit he knew Virginia Rappé was already in the room.

"There was no other reason?"

"No—no other reason. I went straight to the bathroom and opened the door. The door struck Miss Rappé, as she was lying on the floor. She was holding her stomach and moaning . . . she looked sick, as if she was short of breath."

Brady repeatedly motioned to Friedman and whispered in his ear. Friedman paused after each session, then began again.

"Did you hear anybody kick or knock at the door?"

"No."

"How were you dressed when you came out of 1219?"

"Had my bathrobe on."

Arbuckle repeated his story of Virginia sitting on the bed tearing off her clothes.

"Did you tell the hotel manager what had caused Miss Rappé's sickness?"

"No. How should I know what caused her sickness?"

"You didn't tell anybody you found her in the bathroom?"

"Nobody asked me."

"You didn't tell anyone you found her between the beds?"

"Nobody asked me, I'm telling you."

"You never said anything to anybody except that Miss Rappé was sick?"

"Nope."

"Not even the doctor?"

"Nope."

"After Mrs. Delmont entered the room and you went back to 1219, how did you find Miss Rappé?"

"Nude. Mrs. Delmont had some ice in a towel. There was ice on the bed and a piece of ice on Miss Rappé's body. I picked the ice up from her body. I asked Mrs. Delmont what the big idea was. She told me to put it back, that she knew how to care for Virginia, and ordered me out of the room. I told her to shut up or I would throw her out the window."

"And you never told this story to anyone since that time?"

"Oh, yes. I told it to my attorney, Mr. Dominguez, while I was in jail."

The interrogation went on for another hour and forty-six minutes. Roscoe never broke.

A series of rebuttal witnesses was called, among them Jack White (brother of Three Stooges' producer Jules White), who had directed Virginia in *A Twilight Baby*. They covered well-trodden ground and no startling relevations were uncovered until two witnesses were called to testify about the bladder: Dr. William Ophuls for the prosecution, and Dr. G. Rusk for the defense. Judge Louderback denied Dr. Rusk as a defense witness and appointed Dr. Daniel Ervin in his place. Even with that setback, the defense won the point.

The center of the debate was whether or not Rappé's bladder was diseased or inflamed prior to the party, or if it ruptured from external force. It was the last evidence debated before both sides rested their cases.

The experts agreed on four points: that the bladder was ruptured, that there was evidence of chronic inflammation, that there were signs of acute peritonitis, and that the examination failed to reveal any pathological change in the vicinity of the tear preceding the rupture. In short—the rupture was not caused by external force.

Without a doubt this was the most crucial finding in favor of Roscoe's innocence. There was no longer any doubt that Virginia was in pain and ill before she went to the party and her subsequent death was not directly caused by any outward aggression. The defense team shook hands and Roscoe grinned from ear to ear. They all seemed confident that the ordeal would finally be over after the formality of the closing arguments and the jury's verdict.

Leo Friedman gave the first summation for the State. He recounted the events at the party, then laid into Roscoe's friend Fred Fischbach in an effort to show that Roscoe associated with men of questionable repute.

"Miss Prevon told us he [Roscoe] followed her [Virginia] into room 1219 and closed the door. Yet this man, who makes a living by acting, takes the stand and tells you he didn't see Miss Rappé go into 1219, this man who says he can't remember.

"He didn't dare tell you he followed her into that room immediately.

"What occurred then? Did the door open? No. Eventually the door is opened and Miss Rappé is suffering on the bed, and the defendant announced simply that Miss Rappé is sick.

"Mr. Fischbach, who braces his shoulders and says he is proud to be a guest of the defendant. Mr. Fischbach, this model young man, this paragon of virtue, who never took a drink in his life, this model young husband who walks into a room where a nude, young woman lies writhing in agony and performs such as he has testified to.

"Mr. Fischbach says with his enormous hands he grabbed Miss Rappé, a poor, weak suffering girl. He says he grabbed her by the right arm to place her in the tub and therefore caused the bruises on her arm. But when he attempted to demonstrate his actions he had to admit it was the left arm he grabbed.

"The statements of this big, kindhearted comedian [Roscoe] who has made the whole world laugh; did he say 'Get a doctor for this suffering girl'? No. He said, 'Shut up or I'll throw you out the window.'

"He was not content to stop at throwing her out the window. He attempted to make sport with her by placing ice on her body. This man then and there proved himself guilty of this offense. This act shows you the mental makeup of Roscoe Arbuckle."

Friedman went on to criticize the defense witnesses, questioned why Roscoe had never told anyone his version of the party, accused Roscoe of lying, and challenged the jury to find any reason why Roscoe Arbuckle should be let free. He pounded his fists, he waved his finger at the jury, glared at Roscoe to make crucial points, he shouted and whispered. Friedman had the skills of a modern-day hellfire and brimstone evangelist.

When he finished, after a ten-minute recess the defense was called to speak. Gavin McNab had one half hour to present his summation before the court was adjourned for the day. He spoke calmly and carefully to the jury; he did not wave his arms or use elaborate gestures. He was the antithesis of his opponent.

"May it please the Court and the ladies and gentlemen of

the jury. King David the Psalmist said, 'In my house all men were liars.' Had he listened to Mr. Friedman, he might have said that in anybody else's house, everybody was a liar. But it seems to me needlessly cruel to make the attacks upon the witnesses, especially the attacks that have been made upon the women in this case.

"You have heard throughout this case the name of Bambina Maude Delmont . . . why has not the District Attorney produced this witness, so long associated in gathering evidence? Why has he not placed this witness on the stand so you, the jury, might see and hear her?"

McNab went over the testimony of the witnesses who backed Roscoe's claim that Virginia suddenly became ill and Arbuckle apparently tried to help her. He stressed that it was Virginia who tore at her own clothes and that it was Maude Delmont who ordered Roscoe out of the room. McNab also pointed out that the "throw you out the window" statement was for the sharp-tongued Delmont and not aimed at Virginia.

"Miss Prevon and Miss Blake, prosecution witnesses, were imprisoned and gave up their homes under the coercion of the district attorney. They were put into a private prison. Has he the right to take away the liberty of those two girls that they might swear with him to take away the liberty of an innocent man.

"We sent 2,000,000 men overseas to put an end to that sort of thing forever. Why should we allow it to continue in San Francisco?

"It was a deliberate conspiracy against Arbuckle. It was the shame of San Francisco. Perjured wretches tried, from the stand, to deprive this defendant, this stranger within our gates, of his liberty.

"The prosecution has shown that Miss Rappé was a young and vital woman with tremendous athletic abilities. If this was so, if she was in excellent physical condition as the prosecution has tried so diligently to show, then why didn't this girl scream if she was being attacked? If she was trying to get out of the room as the prosecution claimed by the alleged fingerprints on the door, why didn't anyone hear her cries for help?

"The evidence presented on both sides has proven that Virginia Rappé was not a girl in excellent health, but a sickly, broken down woman as testified to [by the prosecution's] own witnesses. That woman lying there writhing and vomiting would not have excited the passions of the lowest beast that was ever called man.

"You have to take one theory or the other—there isn't any escape from it. If she was in that condition, no man would have touched her. And if she was in the condition of a giantess and an athlete, no man could have touched her without the knowledge of everybody in that part of the building. In the period of ten minutes nothing could have been done.

"We don't ask any special consideration for Arbuckle because he is a great artist. We claim nothing in him superior to any other American. Only consider him as if he had never been heard of. This man who has sweetened the lives of millions of little children comes here with his simple story and submits it into your hands. There was no crime here, and Roscoe Arbuckle has needlessly endured enough suffering for one lifetime."

The prosecution closed with another elaborate speech by U'Ren, who compared the St. Francis party to a Babylonian feast and an orgy. He called Roscoe a modern day Belshazzar and a moral leper. He implied that no woman in America was safe on the streets as long as a man like Roscoe Arbuckle was free. He asked for a guilty vote to ensure the safety of all women, to "let the Arbuckles of the world know that womanhood of America is not their plaything."

With that, Judge Louderback read the jury its instructions. The defense submitted eighty-five instructions; only eighteen were read by the judge, who added nine more of his own. The prosecution submitted only eight, all of which were read to the jury. The judge read for twenty-five minutes before the case was handed to the jury for a verdict. The group left the jury box on Friday, December 2, at ten minutes past four.

It was a long and stressful night for both sides. Roscoe paced in the courtroom and through the halls, rolling cigarettes and biting his lip. He answered reporters' questions with vague answers and stared at the crush of spectators being kept at bay by a crowd of policemen. Minta appeared extremely nervous and anxious and remained silent most of the night. Roscoe's brothers and his sister Nora St. John, also waited silently. Lou Anger sat next to the family.

But the defense attorneys and the district attorney's staff tried to appear confident of victory. The jury called for the bailiff several times during the evening, raising hopes that they had reached a verdict, but the calls were for paper, further instructions, or refreshments. Finally, just after eleven o'clock, the jury retired for the night after two ballots. No verdict was reached.

After forty-one hours, the jury remained hopelessly deadlocked—eleven to one for acquittal. One woman remained firm in her belief that Roscoe was guilty, and she refused to listen to any reasoning or consider any evidence that could prove her wrong. There were rumors of fierce arguments between the woman and the other eleven jurors. She shouted at them, accused them of being bought and paid for by Arbuckle, threatened to claim that she was being coerced into going along with the group, and covered her ears when statements not to her liking were voiced. Her name was Helen Hubbard.

After twenty-two ballots, the jury returned to the courtroom on December 4. The final ballot recorded ten votes for acquittal and two votes against. During the balloting two other jurors wavered and continually switched their votes. Jury Foreman August Fritze made the announcement.

"We have taken many, many ballots and find it a physical and moral impossibility to reach a verdict."

Mrs. Hubbard did not stop at a hung jury. She claimed she was threatened into casting a vote in favor of acquittal. U'Ren and Brady agreed to pursue her claim to the grand jury. She claimed that a police commission associate, Gus Oliva, approached her husband and suggested he use his influence on Mrs. Hubbard to force her to change her vote. She claimed the man phoned her husband the night before the final ballot and asked him to slip his wife a note. Helen Hubbard said that when her husband refused, explaining that it was impossible to reach the jury, the caller threatened both her and her husband with "harm." Mrs. Hubbard boasted that no one could change her mind—that she intended to vote for conviction from the very minute she heard Arbuckle was arrested!

Upon hearing the statement, Gavin McNab said he knew Mrs. Hubbard had a working relationship with the district attorney's office and that, from the start, he saw hostility and prejudice on her face toward every defense witness. He also said he had believed the outcome would be a hung jury of mistrial because of this juror.

There were uncomfirmed suspicions that she had been influenced by the D.A.'s office. There are also serious questions as to why McNab did not boot her off the jury at the beginning of the trial.

As both sides prepared for round two, the studio moguls were preparing to take matters into their own hands. The first trial lasted eleven days and cost only $2,389 in food and hotel bills for the jury. But it was going to cost Hollywood much more.

22

The hung jury devastated Roscoe. He returned to his West Adams home with Minta where he sat for hours in the dark, alone, refusing to speak. He was severely depressed and alternated between crying jags and vacant stares. And he started drinking once again, more heavily than before. Minta described him as "a shellshocked war veteran who had seen too much fall apart around him." The man who appeared so confident of acquittal a few days before now dwelt on the possibility that he would be convicted and sentenced to death.

"Minty. We proved to them all that I had nothing to do with that girl's death. We proved there wasn't even a crime committed. Why do they hate me so? Why do they want me dead?"

Vicious rumors and outright lies had been perpetuated throughout the ordeal, many of the stories instigated by the Hearst newspapers. Two of the most popular are still taken as fact by many people today.

One of the stories is that Roscoe had leered at Virginia at the party and said, "I've waited five years for you, and now I've got you." Or that he shouted at her while chasing her into the bedroom, "I'm coming, Virginia."

The first had been claimed by Maude Delmont in her initial statement to police, but she quickly recanted and the matter was never entered into testimony (partly because Delmont was never called to testify). The other was drummed up by enterprising reporters.

The second lie connected to the Arbuckle case involved an alleged rape with a Coke bottle or champagne bottle. There are two persistent stories, neither of them in any way credible.

To this day many people "remember" Roscoe as "that fat comedian who raped that girl with the bottle." They believe that Roscoe was impotent from too much liquor or the drugs that were rumored to be at the party, and finding himself unable to perform, used a bottle, which ruptured Virginia's bladder and caused the internal injuries. Another account claims that when Maude Delmont broke into the room and saw Virginia lying in bed bleeding, either she or Roscoe grabbed a bottle and jammed it inside the girl to "catch the blood" or stop the bleeding. When the police entered the room, Roscoe reportedly tossed the bottle out the window shouting, "There goes the evidence."

Nowhere in any testimony in the court transcripts, police reports, or personal interviews did this story appear. The only newspapers who carried it to any degree were the Hearst papers. Everyone connected with the case vehemently denied it, yet it is the most popular story, and one of the most ugly lies, still connected with the ordeal. The fabrication haunted Roscoe throughout the remainder of his life.

While Arbuckle was fighting for his life in the courtroom, the Hollywood studio bosses made a major assault on Will Hays. The Los Angeles City Council was still locked in a debate over film censorship. After nearly six months of wavering, the council appeared headed to establish a city-run censorship committee to police the industry. This the moguls did not want. They refused to submit to such outside interference, especially when it smacked of political manipulation. Their only hope was to lure Postmaster General Will Hays to align with the motion-picture industry. After months of negotiations they enticed him with money, power, and the chance to stake out his new position with the Arbuckle controversy.

On December 8, a letter drafted and signed by twelve of the industry's most powerful men was hand delivered to Hays by Lewis Selznick and Charles Pettijohn (who had been in negotiations with Hays for months). After some haggling, Hays finally agreed to accept a salary of $115,000 per year (rumors incorrectly persist to this day that he was paid $150,000), plus a $2 million life-insurance policy and other bonuses including an unlimited expense account. The price tag of the package was divided up among the studios.

In return, Hays was to serve as the head of a censorship board for three years, with renewable options by mutual agreement. He announced his decision to accept the proposal on January 14, 1922, officially taking office on March 14.

His first move as head of the newly formed Motion Picture Producers and Distributors Association (MPPDA) was to open offices on Fifth Avenue in New York. He hired Pettijohn as his chief assistant. Within one week he managed to open a multimillion-dollar line of credit for the association and (by pulling political strings) derailed legislation in Massachusetts that would have severely censored movies in that state and, eventually, twenty-two others. Los Angeles dropped its plans for a city-run committee. He convinced voters that his committee was sufficient to guide the morals of the entire country. Hays also took action to stem the increasing tide of foreign films that were coming into the country and eating away profits from American studios.

Buoyed by these successes, Hays established a public-relations arm of the MPPDA and ran the organization much as he had the Post Office—with an ironclad fist and dictatorial legislation. He used his clout with the Republican party and the White House to secure politically influential and financially prominent backers for his organization. The Hays Office, as it was informally called, had representatives in every projection room and glancing through every script. Hays's spies were everywhere.

One of Hays's most sweeping acts was to establish a production code for films. The code was lengthy and gave a list of informal rules and guidelines for movie writers, directors, and producers to follow. (A formal code was finally established for the MPPDA in 1930 by a Catholic priest and enforced with threats of nationwide boycotts until 1934, when it was revised. It covered everything from the number of udders on cartoon cows to the length of a kiss.) Religious groups around the country hailed Hays as a hero sent to protect the innocent from the debauchery and decadence of the evil Hollywood. He perpetuated his image by making personal appearances for a hefty fee. He filmed many of his speeches and ordered theaters to run them between the cartoons and the features.

If the moguls planned to use Hays merely to bandage a wounded public image of the industry, believing they could control him and treat him as nothing more than a figurehead, their scheme went sour. They had created a power-hungry monster to whom the studios now had to answer.

But Hays also had enemies. Many Democrats in Washington expressed public outrage that a man so politically partisan should be allowed to dictate the morals of a nation. Many started a petition to force the studios to withdraw their offer. The moment he resigned from the Post Office, many of his so-called reforms (including mandatory "postmaster schools" at taxpayers' expense) were labeled "newfangled notions" and withdrawn.

Hays was keeping close tabs on the second Arbuckle trial, which began on the eleventh of January in San Francisco Superior Court. Jury selection took six days, nearly twice as long as the process for the first trial, and nearly eighty people had been interviewed—it was nearly impossible to find twelve who had not heard of the St. Francis party. Leo Friedman presented the opening arguments for the prosecution, outlining evidence by which he hoped to prove that Virginia Rappé died at the hands of Roscoe Arbuckle. The trial was a disaster from the outset, with witnesses on both sides switching stories.

Much of the testimony was similar to the statements given during the first trial, except for the testimony of Alice Blake, who was called as a witness for the prosecution. When Friedman asked her about charges that she had been mistreated, imprisoned, and intimidated by the district attorney, Blake's memory failed. McNab angrily watched the shenanigans of Friedman and Blake, biting his lip, calling her statements "tortured." Once again there were charges of witness tampering; this time the charges were filed by the defense against Brady's men. The charges were subsequently dropped.

Zey Prevon testified she could not remember if she had lied or not during the first trial. But she also insisted she did not hear Rappé accuse Roscoe of hurting her. Though she began her testimony as a witness for the prosecution, Friedman quickly labeled her "hostile" and asked her to step down.

Another prosecution witness, Dr. Heinrich, now reversed his stand. He said there was a definite possibility that the fingerprints found on the bedroom door were forged!

The defense's strategy this time was to establish Virginia Rappé as a woman of loose morals who drank to excess and slept her way around town. Over loud and continual objections by the prosecution, McNab called witness after witness who claimed to have known of Virginia's wanton character and debauchery.

McNab also objected strenuously to statements by Dr. Francis Wakefield, owner of the sanitarium, who said there were positively signs of external force on Rappé's bladder, and to testimony by Dr. Beardslee, who related incidents told to him about Virginia by Maude Delmont. The prosecution offered to produce Delmont on the stand (a bluff?) but the defense let the matter drop.

The defense made two critical errors, not counting its failure to get Delmont under oath—it did not put Roscoe on the stand again, and McNab did not make a closing speech. McNab later admitted it was a mistake but said, "Roscoe had told his story. It had been printed in all the papers. Though the jurors may not have read those papers, we believed at the time his testimony was unnecessary. We did not dwell on the incidents at the party and Roscoe's alleged role in the incidents leading to Virginia Rappé's illness. Rather, we believed in homing in on Miss Rappé herself."

The jury retired to debate its verdict on February 2. After two days, forty-four hours, and thirteen ballots the group returned in another deadlock. This time the majority had ruled against Roscoe—ten to two for conviction. One juror later admitted he was wavering in his decision to acquit Roscoe, that if another man had voted with the majority, he would have gone along. Technically, one man saved Roscoe from conviction. A third trial was ordered.

While the second trial was under way in San Francisco, Los Angeles was swept up in the clamor of another sensational movie scandal; the murder of Paramount Director William Desmond Taylor.

On February 2, 1922, the director was found murdered on the floor of his bungalow. Listed among the prime suspects were Mabel Normand, Paramount star Mary Miles Minter, and her mother, Charlotte Shelby. The case was a tangled mess of police snafus and cover-ups by the L.A. district attorney. There were rumors of homosexuality, of a nasty love triangle among Taylor, Shelby, and Minter, and there were persistent rumors that Taylor had been murdered in a drug deal that went sour. In any event, the case gave yet another black mark to Zukor's studio and a major black eye to Hollywood.

In March, another scandal hit the papers—movie heart-throb and Paramount star Wallace Reid was undergoing treatment for drug addiction. Reid nearly went insane from the abrupt withdrawal forced upon him in a sanitarium and died the following year.

The Taylor murder and the Reid incident happened right under Hays's nose, and that fact was quickly picked up by Hays's detractors, who claimed that the overseer had little control over the industry he was paid handsomely to bird-dog. In an effort to quell the backlash, Hays stepped up his policing of the studios and their films. He said that stars would "no longer be allowed to act as hooligans with little regard for their American public." He was preparing to take drastic action to show both the studios and the public that he meant business. Hays was closing in on Roscoe Arbuckle regardless of the outcome of the third trial.

Roscoe returned to the courtroom for the third time on March 6. Jury selection lasted seven days. This time McNab left nothing to chance and was very specific and emphatic about Virginia's background, detailing her life as a prostitute in Chicago, a woman who had undergone several abortions, had scores of lovers, had been known to drink and rip off her clothes, and had contracted a number of venereal diseases. Though women in the courtroom gasped, fainted, and stamped their feet to drown out the "vulgarity," McNab got his point across.

The trial was brief. Both sides were exhausted. The

prosecution paraded only six witnesses to the stand. McNab let Arbuckle speak in his own defense. The jury adjourned on April 12.

It returned in less than five minutes with its verdict:

"Acquittal is not enough for Roscoe Arbuckle. We feel that a great injustice has been done him. We feel also that it was only our plain duty to give him this exoneration, under the evidence, for there was not the slightest proof adduced to connect him in any way with the commission of a crime.

"He was manly throughout the case, and told a straightforward story on the witness stand, which we all believed.

"The happening at the hotel was an unfortunate affair for which Arbuckle, so the evidence shows, was in no way responsible.

"We wish him success, and hope that the American people will take the judgment of fourteen men and women who have sat listening for thirty-one days to evidence, that Roscoe Arbuckle is entirely innocent and free from all blame."

Sadly the jury's acquittal and hopes for its acceptance by the American people were in vain. Roscoe came out of a long ordeal bankrupt and deeply in debt. The trial cost him more than $750,000, much of which was paid for through loans from friends (mostly Buster Keaton, Al St. John, and Lew Cody) and Joe Schenck. It cost the state nearly as much.

To pay back some of the debt, Roscoe sold his West Adams home, most of his cars, and other property he had bought as an investment with Lou Anger. Before any of the funds could be returned to Schenck and the others, Roscoe had to settle up with the creditors who had attached his personal and real property. There was little money left, and fortunately none of his friends asked for any of their money back. (Roscoe promised to repay it and allegedly did within a few years.)

Shortly after the acquittal, Roscoe received a summons ordering him to appear in court on charges he violated the Volstead Act. Apparently the government believed he had suffered enough and settled for a $850 fine. But just as the dust settled from one bomb, two others dropped.

The Internal Revenue Service found that Arbuckle owed nearly $100,000 in back taxes. It closed in and attached what was left of his estate and had an outstanding court order to attach any wages the comedian might earn until the debt was settled.

Though that cloud loomed ominously over his head, it was nothing to what was being planned by Adolph Zukor and Will Hays, who were conspiring in Zukor's office to set Roscoe up as a sacrificial lamb.

23

So Roscoe was acquitted—an innocent man and a free man. But was he really?

"By the time the trials were over, Roscoe was completely drained of life," Minta remembered. "It didn't really matter to him anymore that the jury believed he was innocent. Roscoe had already paid for the crime. And the crime here had nothing to do with Roscoe. The crime was committed by Matthew Brady, who wanted to become governor. A horrible man. Fortunately for everyone he never succeeded. But he destroyed Roscoe. There was nothing left of him." Minta moved back to New York.

When word of the verdict reached the press, scores of theaters across the country began rereleasing Roscoe's films. *Gasoline Gus* and *Crazy to Marry* (which had been released on a limited basis in August) garnered full houses in many towns. Theaters were packed with Arbuckle fans and those who wanted to take a look at "Roscoe, the Spectacle." (For example, in Rock Hill, South Carolina, 15,000 people lined the streets to see *Gasoline Gus*. The police were called in. In Buffalo, New York, some theater owners let the public vote, and the overwhelming majority ruled in Arbuckle's favor.) There were plans to release two other features that were in the can prior to the scandal. Few doubted that Roscoe was on his way back. It was only a matter of time and healing wounds between Roscoe and the American public.

It seemed the country was slowly coming around and

accepting Roscoe—even if on a tenuous basis. He was welcomed by old friends (he remained very close with B··ster Keaton and several others throughout the trials). He chatted with former co-workers who were cordial but distant and considered him a pariah in Hollywood. But those who remained close to him heard a story that no juror, no newspaper or radio reporter, nor anyone outside his immediate family and attorneys heard—the story of what really happened at the St. Francis Hotel party.

On the stand, Roscoe testified that he was sitting on the sofa next to Virginia when she suddenly began screaming in pain. But the story that Roscoe told Joe Rock, Minta Durfee, Lew Cody, Adela Rogers St. Johns (through her father Earl Rogers), Alf Goulding, and Joe Schenck not only showed that Roscoe had physical (albeit innocent) contact with Virginia, but also offered an explanation for the hotly debated and cryptic remark in which Virginia accused him of injuring her.

The following story was pieced together from personal interviews, notes found in archives, and stories that have been related secondhand by reliable sources. Each was found independently and each corroborated the other accounts. Because this story was related independently at least six times, there is no reason to doubt its validity. Here, for the first time ever, is Roscoe Arbuckle's own version of the events of that fateful Labor Day weekend.

Roscoe, Lowell Sherman, and Fred Fischbach arrived in San Francisco on Saturday. On Sunday, the three men went for a drive down to the Wharf in Roscoe's Pierce-Arrow car; it was still difficult for Roscoe to sit because of the accident he had had with the acid-soaked rag the night before the trip.

They were driving up Market Street when Fred Fischbach spotted Virginia Rappé and Maude Delmont walking together. Fischbach called to the women from the car and begged Roscoe to pull over. Roscoe told him that the two women were nothing but trouble and he should steer clear. Undaunted, Fischbach yelled over at the two to come up to the St. Francis for a drink on Monday. Arbuckle was upset by Fischbach's actions and the two had a minor argument about it. The matter was dropped until Monday morning.

Roscoe said Fischbach was acting strangely Sunday night and Monday morning. Fischbach invited Ira Fortlois (whom Roscoe called a nightgown salesman) to the suites for no apparent reason. Roscoe told Fischbach that his friend Mae Taub and another woman were expected and that Fortlois's presence would be awkward. Fischbach claimed that the women could try on nightgowns and drum up business for Fortlois. Roscoe brushed the comment aside.

Shortly after noon, Fischbach received a brief phone call, said he had to scout out sea lions, and took the keys to the Pierce-Arrow. He made a quick phone call and took off.

Roscoe was lounging in his pajamas when the phone rang again. It was Fischbach. He said he had run into Al Semnacher, Maude Delmont, and Virginia Rappé in a drugstore and wanted to bring them up to the suites. Roscoe shouted an emphatic "no," that the women were trouble and they would all get thrown out of the hotel if the management found out they were up there. (Virginia had a reputation as a prostitute and Maude Delmont was widely known as a professional co-respondent and troublemaker.) Fischbach told Roscoe he had already invited them and it would be rude to renege on the invitation. Arbuckle slammed down the phone.

Fifteen minutes later, Fischbach phoned again, saying they were in the hotel lobby and coming up. Roscoe again told Fischbach to leave them downstairs but Fischbach reminded him that it would be rude to bring them this far, then turn them away.

"What was I supposed to do?" Roscoe told Joe Rock. "I was backed into a corner. So I told Freddy to bring them up for a little bit, then get rid of them."

Five minutes later Semnacher, Rappé, and Delmont knocked on the door. Fred Fischbach, was nowhere to be found. Semnacher said that Fischbach was out "scouting sea lions" and would be back in about one hour. In what Roscoe described as "the blink of an eye," there was another knock at the door. It was a local bootlegger who dropped off a box filled with bottles of gin, whiskey, rye, orange juice, and soda water. A Victrola was standing outside the door.

Roscoe questioned who had placed the order and Virginia

laughingly claimed she had. He later found out it was Fisch-bach. The liquor started flowing and the party quickly went into high gear.

Lowell Sherman took off with Maude Delmont (who changed into his pajamas) and the two disappeared into his suite for some time. Several other guests arrived and by three o'clock most everyone at the party was drunk and boisterous.

Virginia started doing "high kicks" and soon everyone joined in to see who could kick the highest. While kicking, Roscoe reinjured the burn on his thigh and sat down to rest. Virginia pulled Roscoe's arm to get him up off the sofa. He laughingly obliged.

Everyone who knew Roscoe also knew he was extremely ticklish. For a joke his friends used to shout "Let's tickle Roscoe" or "Let's tickle Fatty" and poke him in the sides. He would double over and usually jerk his knee up toward his stomach. Virginia tickled Roscoe and his knee shot up in a reflex action. Unfortunately, in doing so, it caught Virginia in the abdomen. She screamed in pain, started bleeding, and ran into the bathroom. Roscoe thought little of it until he entered the bathroom to get dressed.

The rest of the story was told in court.

If this story is true, and it appears to be from all accounts, Virginia's remarks, "What did he do to me?" and "He did this to me," make perfect sense. Drunk and in pain, Virginia could not comprehend exactly what had happened, only that she was with Roscoe when "something" happened.

There is also another sidebar to this story. Lowell Sherman, Fred Fischbach, Alf Goulding, Joe Rock, Joe Schenck, Minta Durfee, and Roscoe all have said that Virginia was in town to have an abortion, and that they believed she had that abortion shortly before the party, accounting for the tenderness of her abdomen. As stated before, Wakefield was known "underground" as an abortion clinic, and Delmont's calling of Dr. Rumwell and the subse-quent secret autopsy back this up.

No defense attorney wanted this story to come out in court because it shows Roscoe intoxicated and physically touching Virginia Rappé. According to this version, Roscoe did in-advertently trigger her final illness, though he was clearly innocent of any malicious intent. The real culprit here seems to be Dr. Rumwell who allegedly performed a "hatchet job" abortion.

Everyone who knew Roscoe suspected he was set up. They also suspected that somehow Fischbach was involved. There were too many things pointing to his involvement to be over-looked. But who pulled the strings and why was always a matter of speculation. Most who expressed an opinion suspected Adolph Zukor of masterminding a scheme that backfired into a tragedy.

Zukor had a number of reasons for "getting back" at Roscoe. He had been pushed into a bidding war for Arbuckle's contract. (Zukor openly said he believed there should not have been any debate since he was already releasing Roscoe's films.) That bidding war quadrupled Roscoe's pay and "forced" Zukor to hire another comedian as leverage and as a precaution in case he lost Arbuckle to another studio. Zukor was not a man to spend money freely and hire actors if he did not have to. When asked to appear for Paramount week, Roscoe refused. He pulled pranks that Zukor detested. According to memos, Zukor told Schenck that Arbuckle needed "knocking down a few pegs."

The party was stacked with bootleg booze, a nightgown salesman, an actress who was known to strip, and a woman who would take compromising pictures and say anything in court for the right price. There also needed to be someone who was Zukor's eyes and ears at the party but who would not be implicated. Fischbach seems the likely candidate because of his unusual actions in the suites. After the scandal he directed under a series of aliases, including numerous variations on the spelling of his name and completely new names such as Hibbard.

A popular suspicion is that Zukor intended to obtain compromising photographs either to force Arbuckle to re-negotiate his contract or to use as a weapon against him at a later time. But since the party skidded off into a sickening course, the truth will never be known.

Two more events lend credence to the theory that Zukor was out to get Arbuckle. On March 13, the day the third trial began, Matthew Brady received another $10,000 check, drafted on the Bank of Italy, signed by Zukor and with the cryptic co-signature. Again, the purpose of the check is not clear and it will never be known if this was the only other check sent to Brady.

Then on April 18, Adolph Zukor, Jesse Lasky, and Will Hays huddled together in the Paramount office in New York and drafted a memo that would remain one of the most significant agreements in the history of motion pictures. With Zukor's and Lasky's full cooperation, in a statement written on Famous Players-Lasky stationery, Hays crucified Arbuckle for the sins of Hollywood.

> After consulting at length with Mr. Nicholas Schenck, representing Mr. Joseph Schenck, the producers, and Mr. Adolph Zukor, and Mr. Jesse Lasky of the Famous Players-Lasky Corporation, the distributors, I will state that at my request they have cancelled all showings and all bookings of the Arbuckle films. They do this that the whole matter may have the consideration that its importance warrants, and the action is taken notwithstanding the fact that they had nearly ten thousand contracts in force for the Arbuckle pictures.
>
> Signed Will Hays

Roscoe Arbuckle became the first actor ever blacklisted. The last flicker of light, the final glimmer of hope that the nightmare had ended was snuffed out. Jesse Lasky advised Roscoe to take a six-month vacation to Europe and the Orient until things cooled down. He packed his bags and left.

Much to his surprise Roscoe was well received in his travels. Heads of state and dignitaries invited him to dinner and the local newspapers hailed him as a major star. In Europe, the Labor Day incident was nothing more than an unfortunate set of circumstances. In the Orient, an acquittal meant a man was innocent. The trip bolstered Roscoe's spirits and he returned to Los Angeles with optimism.

While he was away much had happened. Minta had settled into her apartment at 112 East Fifty-seventh Street in New York. Though their marriage was over, Minta had launched a personal campaign to get Roscoe back to the screen. She bombarded Hays with a series of letters pleading with him to lift the ban and clear Roscoe's name.

"Though he said he believes it was a mistake in banning his pictures at least you were honest in doing so—but said he felt if the ban were raised, he would be much better fitted for his work, mentally, morally and physically . . . "

When that did not work she tried the friendly approach.

"Just a little line to say 'hello' . . . I just received a wire from Roscoe and he feels fairly well and mighty glad to get back. Now that Mr. Zukor's Studio is in full blast again and my letters to him have never been answered . . . I was wondering if you could help me out in securing work . . . "

She even offered to meet Hays personally, but all offers were denied. Hays sent back only one letter.

"Dear Mrs. Arbuckle,

"I have nothing to do with Mr. Zukor's decision regarding your or Mr. Arbuckle's employment with his company. It is up to Mr. Zukor. The affair is out of my hands."

Hays was also receiving pressure from other sources. Buster Keaton and Joe Schenck made continual appeals to lift the ban. Theater owners in New England joined together with a chain of independent owners in New York who openly opposed Hays and his tyrannical MPPDA. Fox Films, Warner Bros., and Pathé signed statements saying they would withdraw in protest from the organization, joining Vitagraph, which had already resigned. Hays's group still had the major distributors and some six hundred theaters under its control, and threatened to keep first-run features away from the insurgents. In spite of the threat, Joe Schenck, Buster Keaton, and Norma Talmadge eventually followed the exodus from Hays's organization. The group wrote a letter to Hays.

"The banning of the Arbuckle pictures in April was done wholly on your own initiative, without pressure, endorsement or support of any members of this [MPPDA] committee. There was a generous amount of criticism throughout the country on the action of barring Arbuckle on the ground that there is no law written or unwritten by which you, as an individual, could bring about a situation where another individual is deprived of the means of a livelihood."

Finally, on December 20, 1922, amid a furor of protest from church and women's groups, and a resounding hail from Roscoe's friends and fans, Will Hays lifted the ban. But he would not give Roscoe a full pardon.

> I hope we can start the New Year with no yesterdays.
> My action was simply a declaration that I shall not stand in the way of this man's having a chance to go to work and make good if he can.
> It was not a reinstatement, and did not concern the release of pictures already made.
> I neither sponsor Arbuckle, nor stand in his way.

Joe Schenck announced immediate plans to put Roscoe to work and said there were already scripts in preparation. (Three pictures slated for Arbuckle before the scandal, *The Melancholy Spirit, Thirty Days,* and *The Man from Mexico*, had been given to Will Rogers, Wallace Reid, and John Barrymore respectively. Another picture, *Are You a Mason?*, was eventually shelved.) He said there were plans for six features and ten shorts with $5 million budget. This may have been only talk because no such contract was ever located, nor was any such package ever released. Zukor refused to make a comment on whether he would again try to release the three features Roscoe had made before the San Francisco party.

Word of Roscoe's return to the screen sparked another wave of controversy. Newspapers across the country ran editorials either condemning the offer and painting Arbuckle as a criminal who got off scot-free, or praising the decision but warning of public backlash. There were unconfirmed reports that Schenck and Paramount had backed off because of the protest against releasing the films and that Roscoe was given a cash settlement, which seems unlikely.

Roscoe healed the wound by withdrawing once again and returning to the bottle. Friends said that it seemed the only way Roscoe could escape the emotional tug-of-war was to drink himself into a stupor. He told Minta, "I don't care if I live or die. If I'm lucky I'll just pass out and never wake up. Life isn't worth living anymore. I can't take it anymore."

24

"I am not only wholly innocent, but more than that. There is a higher law which deals with the spiritual side of mankind, and surely this Christmas time should not be the season when the voice of the pharisee is heard in the land.

"No one ever saw a picture of mine that was not clean. No one ever saw a picture of mine that was not wholesome. No one will ever see such a picture of mine. I claim the right of work and service.

"The sentiment of every church on Christmas Day will be peace on earth and good will toward all mankind. What will be the attitude the day after Christmas to me?"

Roscoe had had enough. He issued this statement in his own defense, tired of the haggling over his right to work or to remain unjustly banished forever. The statement echoed his frustration, and it opened the eyes of his friends and business associates who immediately swung into action to bring the comedian back to the screen.

Nicholas Schenck 1540 Broadway New York NY Jan 22, 1923.

"R can not accept a flat salary as he owes too much money to the government for back income tax and other people. We have excellent comedian here Poddles Hanneford [sic] whom R could direct in two reelers that would not cost over twenty-thousand including Rs salary which would be one thousand per week. Arrange with a distributing company

251

through association if necessary to distribute and
finance comedies and prints and then fifty for R
and fifty for distributing company. In this way no
one will lose any money. I am quite sure R will have
a chance to get on his feet. Please get quick action on
this proposition. Also wire me result of conference
with———'

Signed Joe Schenck

The above telegram clearly indicates that friends were
working for Roscoe on two fronts—the first to get Hays to
back off on his still-raging campaign against Arbuckle, the
second to find him work that would bring in a decent salary
and skirt the IRS.

Poodles Hanneford was a major star with the Sells-Floto
Circus and came from a long line of circus performers. He
had been touring the United States with Billy Sunday and
making quite a mark. The Schencks apparently believed he
had a future in two-reelers and courted him with an offer.
Roscoe wrote and directed and possibly produced the Hanneford comedies, which were produced through a company
called Reel Comedies and distributed by Educational. His
credit either as Arbuckle or William Goodrich (which he later
adopted as a pseudonym) does not appear.

Buster Keaton's widow, Eleanor (whom he married in
1940, seven years after divorcing Natalie), said the problem
with credits rested squarely with Hays.

"A lot of that had to do with the Hays Office. And Zukor
wouldn't help him. Zukor was only interested in money and
not in helping Roscoe. They figured they owed him enough to
hire him under a phony name, but didn't have the guts to hire
him up front with his own name."

While the Schencks were busy getting Roscoe behind the
cameras, attorney Gavin McNab was trying to put Roscoe
back before the public. He hired the comedian to star in a
two-reeler titled *Handy Andy*, which McNab financed on his
own. There were rumors Joe Schenck may have been a
backer, but this has never been confirmed. Whether the
Poodles Hanneford deal persuaded Arbuckle to direct, or if
continued pressure from Hays forced his hand, Roscoe

suspended work on *Handy Andy* in February. The fate of the picture is not known. Some believe it was scrapped; others suspect it was released only in Europe. The first belief seems the most credible because any return to the screen, even in Europe, would have been heralded by significant fanfare in the press.

There was a major ban put on any comment on Roscoe— very little about his work either before or behind the camera was written. He made only one brief statement that he was going to direct, then nothing more was said. The lack of publicity on Roscoe seems to say more than if he had been fully documented at this time. Someone was keeping his name out of the papers.

The controversy over Roscoe's return to the industry, even as a director, was fueled by Will Hays, who let it be known that the "bad boy of Hollywood" was not yet through. In spite of his lifting of the ban, Hays was relentless and ruthless in blackening Arbuckle's reputation. He solicited letters from associates and prominent and influential people asking them to speak out against the comedian.

One of the most verbose condemnations came from William Jennings Bryan in a letter to Hays.

"It is kind of you to take the time to write me about the Arbuckle case. I have as much sympathy as anybody can have for a reformed man. But it did not seem to me that Arbuckle's statement showed either a sense of guilt or a determination to reform. His acquittal only relieved him of the penalty that attaches to a crime.

"The evidence showed a depravity entirely independent of the question of actual murder. As long as his character must be measured by such orgies as that in which he played the leading part, there is no reason why he should be given another chance. Whenever he repents and reforms in his habits he will find the public charitable to a fault and anxious to forgive. So far as I have seen utterances from him, he does not return like the Prodigal Son but comes running back with a song of victory upon his lips and enquiring for the fatted calf."

By this time almost everyone knew that the name Roscoe Arbuckle was dead in motion pictures. He needed a new name, even to direct, and that was only if the producers involved would acknowledge his work in films at all.

While the front offices argued over where and how he should work, Roscoe returned to the one area that, to him, signified happiness: on stage, before live audiences in vaudeville. His friends, Keaton among them, warned that he might not be well received and the experience might crush what spark remained in him. But Roscoe believed a small tour was the shot in the arm he needed. He packed his bags and headed for Chicago.

He signed for an eight-week engagement at a local night-club, reportedly earning a salary of more than two thousand a week—double the offer from the Schencks to direct. Arbuckle needed the money inasmuch as he was still trying to clear out his personal debts. He opened in the Marigold Gardens in June of 1923 to a packed house. Many were gawkers but most were fans who heard self-effacing jokes and saw old comedy gags. He received standing ovations after each performance.

After hours Roscoe visited the downtown Chicago haunts, the nightclubs on State Street and Division Street. He spent hours sitting alone, drinking, listening to music. His favorite musicians were Snaggs Maroone and His Highnote High-landers. They usually closed down the clubs at two o'clock in the morning. Roscoe often was the last to leave.

Several Chicago newspapers ran headlines and editorials against Roscoe, but he had seen and heard it all so many times, he was oblivious; it seemed he was finally starting to mellow after the nightmare in San Francisco.

The Hollywood community had clearly rallied behind Roscoe by the time he returned from Chicago. Director James Cruze cast Roscoe in an all-star feature called *Hollywood*, produced by Paramount. The film was a not-so-funny spoof on life in Tinsel Town. Roscoe played a cameo role as an out-of-work actor in a casting director's office. A sign hangs in the window reading CLOSED. Some of Roscoe's friends saw the role as a jab at Hollywood, others saw it as an ironic humiliation because it rubbed the comedian's nose in his problem.

Working incognito kept him busy, put money in his

pocket, and reunited him with the woman who was to become his second wife, Doris Deane. Deane was an actress from New York who moved to Hollywood in 1923. She picked up bit parts and co-starring work in comedies at Metro, Universal, and Educational, some of which Roscoe was assigned to direct.

In spite of Roscoe's heavy drinking, Doris saw a man who was gentle and big-hearted, desperately in need of love. In Doris, Roscoe saw a strong woman who served as a refuge from the bitterness of the outside world. The two quickly became inseparable, and formed a tight foursome with Buster Keaton and Natalie Talmadge, his first wife.

Roscoe wrote Minta that he had fallen in love with Doris and wanted to marry her. Minta had met Doris several times and the two had got along quite well. Minta told Roscoe that if he was to marry anyone, she was happy it was Doris Deane. She initiated divorce proceedings from New York in November of 1923.

With Roscoe's personal life on the mend and his directing career building, Buster stepped in and hired his friend to direct *Sherlock, Jr.* Buster had continually consulted Roscoe on most of his films, working out gags and directing ideas, but this was to be the first official directing job for Roscoe. It proved to be a disaster.

Eleanor Keaton said his spirit was gone. "He was so bitter, and so hurt and so torn up that nothing was funny. Buster just had to take him off the film. He was so broken he wasn't getting things done right, he couldn't tell what was funny and what wasn't funny. He snapped at everyone. Buster just wasn't able to use him. It was sad. But they remained close friends until the end. Buster used him on other pictures, but he didn't get credit."

Roscoe allegedly returned to Educational, anonymously directing the Al St. John comedies (for which St. John, and later Grover Jones, received credit.) It was not until 1925 that Roscoe finally started receiving credit for directing, and the name on the credits was William Goodrich.

Buster Keaton thought the name was funny; funnier still was the nickname Keaton took from it—Will B. Good, prophetic as well as concise. The nickname stuck and was

widely accepted throughout the industry as the alias of
Roscoe Arbuckle.

A fan magazine described the "new" Roscoe. "Today
then, Fatty Arbuckle, the hilarious comedian, is gone.
Instead, there is a big fat fellow behind a director's desk in a
Hollywood office, the door of which bears a name that
doesn't even remotely resemble Roscoe Arbuckle.

"There's no grin on his face. It's almost always serious.
There are lines there that weren't on that cherubically asinine
countenance that beamed from the screen in the old "Fatty'
comedies.

"He works hard. When he's casting his comedies, he
makes a point of picking the names of old-timers he used to
know. He's particularly happy when he can give a few days'
work to some fellow who's had the breaks against him.

"He doesn't court publicity. Now and then, a writer or an
editor will say: 'What can we do for you to help you,
Roscoe?' He says nothing."

With steady work, Roscoe was able to hang on to his West
Adams house, stop the foreclosure proceedings in the nick of
time, and pay off his debts. The home was relatively empty,
but it was now his, free and clear. He was a working director
and accepted as "one of the gang" by almost everyone in
Hollywood—as long as he stayed out of the limelight. He
wanted to return to a normal life, which was for him in front
of an audience.

He accepted a three-month contract to tour with the
Pantages Circuit. (Early accounts of Roscoe's life claim the
tour was one year in length, which was impossible because of
his commitments to Educational. A look at the chronology of
the Arbuckle/Educationals would back the shorter schedule.
Newspaper accounts also show the agreement was for twelve
weeks.)

His old friend and early benefactor, Alexander Pantages,
was more than happy to get Roscoe on stage. He called
Roscoe "the funniest man alive" and signed him to a cross-
country tour. Once again he received a standing ovation in
every house he played. There were some detractors who
believed he should not be allowed to appear, and a petition
was filed in Long Beach to keep the comedian off the stage.

The ban was rejected after a heated battle before a packed chamber.

Roscoe met up with Minta in Atlantic City, New Jersey. He had been booked into the Palais Royal Cabaret; Minta was playing at a theater down the street with Will Morrissey's Newcomers Troupe. They had not seen one another in quite some time and agreed to meet for dinner and a few drinks. They both checked out of their respective hotels and booked a suite together. Roscoe also suggested they reunite as a performing team, but after some discussion he realized that it would do Minta more harm than good.

"There was no romance there really. We felt like old friends getting together. Nothing more than that. I knew he was in love with Doris."

Roscoe continued to pick up the hotel bill for Minta after he left for Philadelphia. After her show closed, Minta returned to her apartment in New York. In January of 1925, she left for Paris and divorced Roscoe.

It was Roscoe's idea to send Minta to Paris to avoid yet another scandal. The French did not consider divorce as shocking as the still-Puritanical Americans did. In fact, many Americans traveled to Paris for that reason in the 1920s. Roscoe could not go with Minta because of his work commitment, but agreed to pay for her trip, her attorneys, and any luxuries she might need, including jewelry, dresses, and a fur coat. Though Roscoe was barely out of debt, he had not yet learned how to handle money—he still spent it as fast as he made it.

The decree was granted on January 27, 1925. Roscoe was now free to marry Doris Deane.

Doris's parents were initially apprehensive about their daughter marrying Roscoe—the scandal was well known and they were familiar with the Hays Office and the unspoken ban against Roscoe appearing on screen. The emotional scars were apparent and Arbuckle had been drinking heavily. He was not already an alcoholic but he was well on his way.

But they also noticed the love between the two and after they got to know Roscoe, gave him their daughter's hand with their blessing. The wedding was held on May 16, at the Deanes' San Marino home. Buster Keaton was the best man;

257

matron of honor was Buster's wife Natalie. Joe Schenck helped Roscoe in a fatherly capacity, doing everything from giving advice to helping plan some of the details of the wedding.

The reception was held at the Keaton home. Instead of moving into Roscoe's West Adams place, the couple rented a house owned by Joe Schenck as investment property. The marriage was off to a shaky start, mostly due to Roscoe's skittishness around strangers and continued pummeling from pushy newspaper reporters. He suffered from exaggerated mood swings—aloof and distant one moment, drunk, depressed, and quarrelsome the next. The strain had eaten away at him. But Doris had faith he would eventually come around and again become the Roscoe whom millions of movie fans had seen and who she believed was still locked away inside a tormented soul.

In *The Day the Laughter Stopped*, Doris Deane recalls a party in Beverly Hills. Roscoe was playing his ukulele and enjoying himself when a strange woman came up to him and asked why he was called Fatty. The woman then said to Roscoe, "This isn't a very lively party. I bet that one you gave in the St. Francis was better." Doris said Roscoe froze and told the woman to go away. She said he often introduced himself as Roscoe C. Arbuckle; the "C" was not for Conkling, his real middle name, but for Crucified.

He kept to himself and his small circle of friends. He went to work and came home. Roscoe quickly became a recluse and found Doris the only company he needed outside of his male friends. Socializing was confined to Lew Cody (who was married to Mabel Normand at this time) and Buster Keaton and his wife.

On September 2, Cody invited Roscoe to join The Masquers, an all-male club of vaudeville, burlesque, and film actors who got together for fun, socializing, and charity work, and to help one another find jobs in their field. Roscoe was elected to join on September 28 and finally made an official member on October 7, 1925, just five months after the club was founded. He was the 216th member.

The group organized a show called *Public Revels*, a comedy and song revue in which men played both male and female roles. The play consisted of eight separate sketches including an elaborate number by the world-famous female impersonator Julian Eltinge playing the femme fatale to Warner Baxter. It was billed as a spoof on Hollywood, "a travesty exposing the frills and frailties of the Cinema Capitol [sic]," and was booked in the Hollywood High School auditorium.

Just hours before the show was to open on October 17, School Board Secretary William Sheldon and other board members stormed the auditorium and rescinded its permit for the play. It gave only one reason for its decision—Roscoe Arbuckle.

The group said that "in the interest of the school children of Los Angeles, he should not be permitted to appear on the school stage, in view of the unenviable notoriety which has attached to the former comedian."

The Masquers responded quickly. They sent a curt note back to the board. "Mr. Arbuckle is a member of this club, and the club stands back of him to a man." Troupers stick together, probably the most loyal group of people that could be found anywhere. No matter what personal problems might arise, when one of their own was in trouble, actors always banded together to help. They agreed the show would go on, with Arbuckle, no matter where they had to perform. "The Masquers has no quarrel with anyone, but we stand back of our members. And Roscoe Arbuckle will play."

They eventually secured a contract with the Philharmonic Auditorium and the show played to standing-room-only houses, delayed only one week by the board's action.

By the spring of the following year, one of Roscoe's most vocal detractors made an about-face and gave him one of the biggest career boosts since the scandal. William Randolph Hearst offered Arbuckle a chance to direct Marion Davies in her new musical feature *The Red Mill*. But the opportunity soured into one of his most bitter experiences in nearly five years.

25

Buster Keaton approached Marion Davies about hiring Roscoe to direct her next feature. He told her the break would do Roscoe a world of good. While she considered the idea, she invited Roscoe and Doris to the Hearst Castle—San Simeon. Davies was a very warm and gentle woman, and people who knew her claim the invitation was very likely her way of trying to apologize for and undo some of the damage caused by Hearst's newspaper campaign against the comedian.

In any event, Davies encouraged Hearst to hire Roscoe (as William Goodrich) to direct *The Red Mill*, which was being made through Cosmopolitan Productions—a company set up by Hearst primarily for Marion Davies—and released by MGM. The movie was based on the 1906 Victor Herbert operetta of the same name, and starred Davies, Owen Moore, and Louise Fazenda. It started production in the fall of 1906 and was a disaster from the beginning.

Reports got back to Hearst that Roscoe was not handling his job, that there were unspecified problems and disruptions on the set. Exactly what was going on was never published and many suspect the real problem was more Hearst's suspicious nature and distrust of Roscoe than any lack of skill on Arbuckle's part. Days into the production, Hearst hired MGM director King Vidor to sit in on the set and "help" Roscoe. Arbuckle was ordered to consult with Vidor about every setup and shot, and Roscoe immediately knew he was being squeezed out. Vidor had great respect for Arbuckle and

260

the ordeal he had suffered and felt awkward and uneasy about the entire situation. But he had to follow orders. The film itself was a box-office disaster.

Word quickly ran through the industry that Roscoe was incompetent and incapable as a feature director, and though unfounded, the rumor proved to be another terrible blow. No matter where he turned there was someone or something to knock him down.

Once again his benefactor Joe Schenck intervened to give Roscoe another chance. At his insistence, Arbuckle was hired to direct *Special Delivery*, starring Eddie Cantor with William Powell. The film was plagued by problems—among them Will Hays's demand to rewrite the story line, which involved a spoof on a mail robbery. The dour Hays did not find any aspersions on the Post Office the least bit humorous. And once again an "assistant' director was brought in to supervise Roscoe—comedian Larry Semon. It was one knock-down too many for Arbuckle, who said he had had it with films. He signed up for another twelve-week stint with Pantages.

Roscoe was earning better than twelve hundred dollars a week and was financially secure though emotionally shattered. Word that he was a soft touch followed him throughout his tour and he doled out ten, twenty, or fifty dollars to any performer with a hard-luck story. His generosity did not stop at money. He also did what he could to help other talented, struggling performers; chief among them was a young comedian named Bob Hope.

While in Cleveland, Roscoe saw Hope performing on stage and immediately recognized his potential as more than a two-stepping song and dance jokester. Hope was quick on his feet, bantering with the audience, throwing back one-liners and asides as quickly as the audience could toss them out. Hope played to the crowd, and he made it look easy and natural.

Roscoe knew the young comedian would be a major star if he had the right break. He called him "one of the most clever hoofers I'd ever seen . . . he can dance, sing and ad-lib jokes playing to the audience . . . he belonged in Hollywood." Arbuckle contacted Joe Schenck and other friends in Los

Angeles and instructed Hope to do the same. He followed Arbuckle's orders and eventually headed west.

Roscoe headed to New York where he opened in *Baby Mine* on June 9 at Chanin's Forty-sixth Street Theater. The play scored one of the biggest successes yet for Arbuckle, and his friends turned out to show their support.

The *New York World Telegram* gave this review:

> Many notables, especially from the film world where Fatty once ranked so highly, were on hand for auld lang cinema to see the manager, John Tuerk, ease him back into public favor via the stage door. There was a general atmosphere about the theatre of "give the guy a hand." or "give him an even break." When Fatty made his first entrance, looking very spick and span in a neatly pressed suit, he got such a spirited hand from the audience that his face acquired that schoolgirl complexion all over.
>
> It might be said at once that Fatty was the best thing in the show . . . you find yourself anticipating every development as the feather brained young wife tries to bring back her estranged young husband by palming off his paternal instincts [by claiming] an adopted child as his own.
>
> The audience laughed cordially at times—justifiably so at Fatty's antics—but more of their gaiety seemed to spring from the heart rather than the midriff . . . the only blush raised was that on Fatty at his welcoming reception. That crackling greeting seemed to embarrass him considerably for a moment, and then he proceeded to act with his customary 250 pounds of aplomb. He has always had a good deal of poise, and he seemed to have lost neither this nor his weight while directing pictures obscurely under the name of William Goodrich.

The *New York Tribune* also gave Roscoe high marks for *Baby Mine* and details an unusual speech he made after the second curtain call.

Ladies and Gentlemen—but that sounds too formal, and I wonder if I may call you just friends. I'm glad to be back. I thought at first I wouldn't be able to make it, because I was motoring from Hempstead last night in one of those little drive-yourself cars —you know, the kind they sing about: "Although You Belong to Somebody Else, Tonight You Belong to Me."

A motorcycle cop overtook me and waved me to the side. I said I didn't believe he was a cop because he had no whistle. He said he didn't need one because he had asthma. He led me to the station house and I faced a fellow behind the bench. He looked familiar. I asked how he was feeling and he said, "Fine—$25." But when I told him I was Fatty Arbuckle, he rubbed it off and said I had trouble enough already, and I could take the money and get.

On the way out, a little girl asked me to tell her how to get in the movies and I answered I wished she would tell me. She said I ought to be on the screen and I said I intended to be if I had to turn into a fly and climb on.

"But I should be serious and ask you, if you like our play, tell the neighbors . . . this night gives me the thrill of my life. I've had other thrills, but never before so large an audience—there were only—let's see—just twelve men facing me when I got my last big thrill.

Again, as he successfully built up one part of his life, another crashed down around him. His marriage to Doris Deane was on the rocks. They quarreled bitterly, snapped at one another, and went for periods without speaking. Doris said she never blamed Roscoe. It was simply the strain and pressure from the ongoing struggle to rebuild his life. She believed any other man would have fared far worse given the same set of hellish circumstances. They divorced in August of 1928.

He began reinvesting his money in real estate and business ventures. The most prominent was the Plantation Club, a nightclub in Culver City. Everyone who was anyone in the entertainment industry swarmed to the club, drinking, eating, and dancing to the orchestra. Often Roscoe would get up onstage and invite friends to do the same. It was one happy family and quite often a free-for-all fun time. The money poured in and it looked like Roscoe had a winner.

He also went into a silent partnership with Charlie Chaplin. They invested $75,000 each into a fifty-three room, Spanish villa-type hotel, the Montecito Inn, in Montecito near Santa Barbara. The stars' names did not appear anywhere in the publicity campaign, and the construction company of Seaman's and Sebastian (which picked up the other $175,000 in building costs) was listed as the owner. Montecito was a quiet, sophisticated oceanside community and the builders believed it would not welcome anyone from Hollywood (especially Arbuckle). Even today the hotel advertises only Chaplin, not Arbuckle, as the original owner, and even that is disputed by many in the town. But if there is any doubt that the original co-owners were Arbuckle and Chaplin, one has only to look at the grand-opening invitation list—it reads like a who's who in Hollywood. Certainly an "ordinary" hotel would not draw such a stellar Hollywood crowd.

Once again the fates were against Roscoe. The Plantation Club had been bucking opposition from the Culver City community. It was declared a public nuisance. The stock-market crash of 1929 and the subsequent Depression put an abrupt halt to free spending and luxury hotels. Roscoe was forced to shut down the Plantation Club in 1930. He lost nearly his entire investment in the Montecito Inn. The double blow nearly forced him into bankruptcy.

Roscoe apparently saw the need to purge himself of the scandal. While a writer at RKO for comedian Louis John Bartels and his "Traveling Salesman Comedies," Arbuckle scripted his version of the St. Francis incident and the subsequent blacklisting. Though the storylines are metaphoric, it is clear who and what Roscoe was writing about.

In *That's My Line*, the lead character is a nightgown sales-man (possibly suggested by the Fortlois character who sold nightgowns, who innocently wanders into a small Mexican town (Roscoe innocently wandering into San Francisco).

There he is set up by a married woman (Delmont?) and seduced (Rappé?) Two of the woman's male friends chase the salesman and try to kill him with daggers in the back (Zukor? Hays?). The salesman finally runs away wearing a suit of armor to ward off any future attacks (Roscoe?). One title card was also revealing. The salesman asks, "Why is everyone mad at me? What did I do?"

In his next film, *Beach Pajamas*, the lead is once again a traveling salesman who runs into a matronly woman (Delmont?) and her niece (Rappé?) who use him to break a wedding engagement. The niece lures the salesman to her hotel room (the St. Francis?) under the ruse of wanting to try on a swimming suit (again Fortlois and his nightgowns, which were used as a ruse to get Rappé and Delmont into the room). She gets behind a dressing screen, undresses, and signals to send the soon-to-be jilted fiancé over to catch her in a compromising state with the salesman.

These two plot lines certainly lay to rest any doubt as to whether or not Roscoe knew he was set up. It is apparent he had a clear and complete understanding of what had happened to him and who was responsible.

It seemed that once he wrote these stories he was free to move on. Roscoe finally found one light at the end of the dark tunnel—Addie Oakley Dukes McPhail, a beautiful young actress who was already established in Hollywood. She seemed to be the spark that Roscoe so desperately needed and the two hit it off from the start. Those who knew Addie said that she was the perfect match for Roscoe and the woman he seemed to be waiting for. She told several people that she never saw the emotionally "dead" man that so many others had described. She found a wonderful, warm man with a very loving nature. It may be that Addie brought out the best in him too. But either way, his meeting Addie seemed to be his good-luck charm. His life and his luck turned around.

In February of 1932, Roscoe received a phone call from Jack Warner. It was the chance he had waited for since Labor Day of 1921—he was asked to return to pictures, in front of the cameras, starring in his own two-reelers as Roscoe Arbuckle! The series would consist of six two-reelers with the possibility of expanding into features. The eleven years of torment and punishment for a crime he did not commit had finally ended.

Roscoe told a movie magazine, "It's kinda like home to me, you know—pictures. I can promise they'll be good, clean, wholesome pictures. Broad comedy, with something for the children."

With the security of what appeared to be a major screen comeback, Roscoe and Addie McPhail married on June 21, 1932. She gave up her acting career to be with the man she loved. Roscoe returned to his other love—screen comedy.

His director on the series was his old friend Alf Goulding, who recalled that first reunion with Roscoe. "He was living in a hotel in Central Park with his wife. He told me, 'You got to know that we can still make pictures.' . . . Roscoe was a big, innocent baby . . . one of the finest fellows I ever met."

The first picture they made together at the Warner Bros./Brooklyn studio was *Hey, Pop!*, which co-starred Bill Heyes, already a veteran actor at age twelve. Roscoe saw him in vaudeville and went backstage to offer him the role.

The plot centered around an orphan boy abandoned in a restaurant in which Roscoe was employed as the cook. Arbuckle recycled many of the gags he used so successfully in his other comedies from Keystone and Comique (mostly relying on bits from *The Butcher Boy* and borrowing quite heavily from Chaplin's *The Kid*).

Heyes lived with Roscoe for two weeks during the shooting. Arbuckle treated him like a kid brother and took him to Coney Island and other places such as Luna Park every night. Everywhere they went, they were mobbed by fans who wanted autographs. Roscoe always obliged.

"We always got free rides at the parks. There was never any hint of that scandal, it was all forgotten. It never seemed to appear either with the crowds or in public, at least with Arbuckle. All the outward scars seemed to be healed," Heyes said.

Roscoe never stepped in to direct; he respected Goulding's capabilities and maintained his place as an actor. There was only one problem that seemed to surface during production

—drinking. Though it never affected Arbuckle's perform-ance, the bottle was always present on the set. Heyes's father would hold Roscoe's scotch or whiskey bottle off camera, and Roscoe would take a sip or two during each break.

Bill Heyes said he looked up to Roscoe and never wanted to disappoint him. "We shot that picture in two weeks. The principal shooting was done in one week, and pickups the next week. I remember being called back to reshoot the ending of the film, but the main part was done in two weeks. There were no problems on the set—ever. Everyone seemed to know their stuff."

The release of the picture was delayed for several weeks by a lawsuit, initiated by Heyes's manager, Irene Taylor Schultz, who was seeking $25,000 in damages. Though she was in a psychiatric hospital when Heyes's father negotiated the deal for *Hey, Pop!*, Schultz insisted she was owed commission. The breach-of-contract suit was filed against Warners/Vitaphone and eventually settled out of court.

The suit angered the front offices, which wanted to cash out Heyes's contract with the studio. It offered Heyes's father two or three thousand dollars in Warners stock as a settlement, but still feeling the effects of the crash, he opted for the money instead. A short time later the price of Warners stock soared.

His second film was *Buzzin' Around*, and for this one he brought back his nephew Al St. John to co-star. The comedy was a story about a country boy who invents a solution that makes glass unbreakable. St. John accidentally switches it with moonshine and Roscoe winds up in big trouble when he starts demolishing a porcelain collection.

Alf Goulding says the film was slated to be released in England but was withdrawn by exhibitors who said they did not believe the public was ready to accept Arbuckle. But the American public welcomed him with open arms and the Warners series continued to receive a strong showing at the box office.

While the films were going well, Arbuckle's health began to deteriorate. He complained of an irregular heartbeat and would often have to rest between takes. He refused medical treatment, and especially cautioned everyone against leaking

267

any word of his condition to Addie, whom he did not want to worry.

In his second to last film, *Tamalio*, Roscoe runs a strenuous footrace against Charles Judels, who was cast as a Mexican general. Even with careful editing, Roscoe looks drawn and flushed and is obviously struggling to catch his breath. Unfortunately, the film itself was abysmal. Its release was held until after his next film, *In the Dough*, a vulgar comedy in which Roscoe is chased by gangsters, which pokes fun at a woman with a speech impediment—an unfortunate legacy for Roscoe's last screen performance.

The day he finished shooting *In the Dough*, he celebrated his one-year wedding anniversary with Addie. They celebrated with New York restaurant owner Billy LaHiff, and two friends. The dinner was relaxing and Roscoe was in great spirits. Afterward, Roscoe and Addie returned to their suite at the Park Central Hotel at Fifty-fifth Street and Seventh Avenue in Manhattan and Roscoe went to bed. When Addie called to him he did not answer.

Roscoe died in his sleep at 2:30 A.M. on June 29, 1933. The cause of death was given as angina pectoris and coronary sclerosis—heart disease. Buster Keaton said that Roscoe actually died of a broken heart.

A wake was held on Friday at 1:00 P.M. at Campbell's Funeral Home on Broadway and Sixty-sixth. His body was laid out in the gold room—the same room in which Rudolph Valentino had been waked seven years earlier. Thousands of mourners lined the street to pay their last respects. The crowd was solemn and orderly.

A funeral service was held the following day at the local Elks' Lodge. Roscoe was cremated at Fresh Pond Cemetery in New York.

Alf Goulding said, "He was on the threshold of winning back the public and he was on the threshold of becoming a big star again." They had been planning a five-reel feature comedy for Roscoe when he died and reportedly had contracts from Warners for another series of pictures.

He had also just signed a contract for another vaudeville tour, which was set to open the following Monday in St. Louis. If he had lived, Roscoe certainly would have been back on top, reestablishing himself as America's favorite comedian. Ultimately fate was against him. It seemed that from the very beginning Roscoe could never shake the dark shadow that haunted his life.

ROSCOE "FATTY" ARBUCKLE: A FILMOGRAPHY

Compiled by Samuel A. Gill
Copyright © 1990 by Samuel A. Gill

An index to the films of Roscoe "Fatty" Arbuckle, produced between 1909 and 1933, and including those made under his pseudonym William Goodrich.

This filmography is arranged chronologically by release date. It includes the following information in this order: final release title; working title (in parentheses), release date(s); copyright date(s); date the picture was finished or print shipped; number of reels; film length in feet; sound or color (when applicable); series or brand name; identification number; copyright claimant; production company; distribution company; production credits; cast; production information; variant spellings and alternate titles.

This filmography includes short and feature-length productions, films for which Arbuckle worked in a variety of capacities—actor, director, writer, adapter and possibly producer—and films for which Arbuckle used both his real name and the pseudonym William Goodrich.

271

ABBREVIATIONS

adapt	adapter	play	playwright
art dir	art director	pres	presented by
assoc pro	associate producer	pro	producer
asst dir	assistant director	r	release date
c	copyright date	scen	scenarist
cam	cameraman	scen ed	scenario editor
cc	copyright claimant	sd	sound
cont	continuity writer	sd rec	sound recorder
dance dir	dance director	sets	sets designer
dia	dialogue writer	story	story writer
dir	director	sup	supervisor
dist	distributor	sup dir	supervising director
fs	date finished or shipped	titl	title writer
film ed	film editor	ward	wardrobe designer
music	music composer	writ	writer

SELIG

Arbuckle's Selig pictures were produced by the Selig Polyscope Company at the Selig western studio at 1845 Allesandro Street in Los Angeles (Edendale), California.

BEN'S KID (Selig, 1909, r1 Jul 1909. 1 reel. 1,000 feet. Selig Polyscope Company (pro). Francis Boggs (dir). James Crosby (cam). Roscoe Arbuckle, Thomas Santschi, Harry Todd.

MRS. JONES' BIRTHDAY (Selig, 1909). r30 Aug 1909. 1/2 reel. 540 feet. Selig Polyscope Company (pro). Roscoe Arbuckle. Released on same reel with WINNING A WIDOW (450 feet).

MAKING IT PLEASANT FOR HIM. (Selig, 1909), r29 Nov 1909. 1/2 reel. 380 feet. Selig Polyscope Company (pro). Roscoe Arbuckle. Released on same reel with BROUGHT TO TERMS (615 feet).

THE SANITARIUM (Selig, 1910). r10 Oct 1910. 1 reel. 1,000 feet. Selig Polyscope Company (pro). Roscoe Arbuckle, Nick Cogley, George Hernandez.

ALAS! POOR YORICK (Selig, 1913). r21 Apr 1913. c17 Apr 1913. 1/2 reel. Selig Polyscope Company (pro/cc). Colin Campbell (dir/writ). Wheeler Oakman, Thomas Santschi, Lillian Hayward, Hobart Bosworth, John Lancaster, Frank Clark, Roscoe Arbuckle. Released on same reel with CANTON, CHINA (educational subject).

UNIVERSAL–NESTOR

Arbuckle worked four weeks in Nestor Comedies under the supervision of Al E. Christie, produced for and distributed by the Universal Film Manufacturing Company. Titles have not been found for these comedies, which were supposedly filmed in February-March 1913 at the Universal Studio on Sunset Boulevard and Gower Street in Hollywood, California.

MUTUAL–KEYSTONE

Keystone comedies were produced by the Keystone Film Company under the supervision of Mack Sennett and distributed by the Mutual Film Corporation on a state-rights basis. Arbuckle's comedies from 1913 to 1915 were produced at the Keystone studio at 1712 Allesandro Street in Los Angeles (Edendale), California, and filmed at the studio and in the general Los Angeles vicinity. A few comedies were filmed on location in other areas, such as FATTY AND MABEL AT THE SAN DIEGO EXPOSITION and MABEL AND FATTY VIEWING THE WORLD'S FAIR AT SAN FRANCISCO.

THE GANGSTERS (THE FEUD) (Keystone, 1913). r29 May 1913. fs 24 Apr 1913. 1 reel. Keystone Film Company (pro). Mutual Film Corporation (dist). Henry Lehrman (dir). Roscoe Arbuckle, Fred Mace, Ford Sterling, Hank Mann, Al St. John. Variants: GANGSTERS; THE GANGSTER.

PASSIONS, HE HAD THREE (COUNTRY BOYS) (Keystone, 1913). r5 Jun 1913. fs3 May 1913. 1/2 reel. Keystone Film Company (pro). Mutual Film Corporation (dist). Henry Lehrman (dir). Roscoe Arbuckle, Mabel Normand. Variants: PASSIONS—HE HAD THREE; PASSIONS! HE HAD THREE; POSSUMS, HE HAD THREE.

HELP! HELP! HYDROPHOBIA! (THE CHEMIST) (Keystone, 1913). r5 June 1913. fs3 May 1913. 1/2 reel. Keystone Film Company (pro). Mutual Film Corporation (dist). Henry Lehrman (dir). Roscoe Arbuckle, Peggy Pearce. Variants: HELP HELP HYDROPHOBIA; HELP, HELP, HYDROPHOBIA!

THE WAITERS' PICNIC (THE CHEFF [sic]) (Keystone, 1913). r16 June 1913. fs15 May 1913. 1 reel. Keystone Film Company (pro). Mutual Film Corporation (dist). Mack Sennett (dir). Roscoe Arbuckle, Mabel Normand, Ford Sterling, Hank Mann, Al St. John. Variant: THE WAITER'S PICNIC.

A BANDIT (A BANDIT) (Keystone, 1913). r23 June 1913. fs21 May 1913. 1/2 reel. Keystone Film Company (pro). Mutual Film Corporation (dist). Mack Sennett (dir). Roscoe Arbuckle, Nick Cogley.

PEEPING PETE (THE PEEP HOLE) (Keystone, 1913). r23 June 1913. fs21 May 1913. 1/2 reel. Keystone Film Company (pro). Mutual Film Corporation (dist). Mack Sennett (dir). Roscoe Arbuckle, Mack Sennett, Ford Sterling, Nick Cogley.

FOR THE LOVE OF MABEL (THE MELO-DRAME) (Keystone, 1913). r30 June 1913. fs6 June 1913. 1 reel. Keystone Film Company (pro). Mutual Film Corporation (dist). Henry Lehrman (dir). Roscoe Arbuckle, Mabel Normand. Variant: FOR THE LOVE OF MABEL.

THE TELLTALE LIGHT (THE MIRROR) (Keystone, 1913). r10 Jul 1913. fs16 June 1913. 1 reel. Keystone Film Company (pro). Mutual Film Corporation (dist). Mack Sennett (dir). Roscoe Arbuckle, Mabel Normand, Alice Davenport, Charles Avery. Variant: THE TELL-TALE LIGHT.

A NOISE FROM THE DEEP (A NEW TRICK) (Keystone, 1913). r17

Jul 1913. fs23 Jun 1913. 1 reel. Keystone Film Company (pro). Mutual Film Corporation (dist). Mack Sennett (dir). Roscoe Arbuckle, Mabel Normand.

LOVE AND COURAGE (RUBES) (Keystone), 1913). r21 Jul 1913. fs25 Jun 1913. 1/2 reel. Keystone Film Company (pro). Mutual Film Corporation (dist). Henry Lehrman (dir). Roscoe Arbuckle, Mabel Normand.

PROF. BEAN'S REMOVAL (HOUSE MOVING) (Keystone, 1913). r31 Jul 1913. fs11 Jul 1913. 1 reel. Keystone Film Company (pro). Mutual Film Corporation (dist). Henry Lehrman (dir). Roscoe Arbuckle, Mabel Normand, Ford Sterling. Variant: PROFESSOR BEAN'S REMOVAL.

THE RIOT (THE RIOT) (Keystone, 1913). r11 Aug 1913. fs25 Jul 1913. 1 reel. Keystone Film Company (pro). Mutual Film Corporation (dist). Mack Sennett (dir). Roscoe Arbuckle, Mabel Normand, Ford Sterling.

MABEL'S NEW HERO (THE BALOON [sic]) (Keystone, 1913). r28 Aug 1913. fs Aug 1913. 1 reel. Keystone Film Company (pro). Mutual Film Corporation (dist). Mack Sennett (dir). Roscoe Arbuckle, Mabel Normand. Also known as FATTY AND THE BATHING BEAUTIES.

FATTY'S DAY OFF (THE INVALID) (Keystone, 1913). r1 Sep 1913. fs1 Aug 1913. 1/2 reel. Keystone Film Company (pro). Mutual Film Corporation (dist). Wilfred Lucas (dir). Roscoe Arbuckle.

MABEL'S DRAMATIC CAREER (THE ACTRESS) (Keystone, 1913). r8 Sep 1913. fs12 Aug 1913. 1 reel. Keystone Film Company (pro). Mutual Film Corporation (dist). Mack Sennett (dir). Roscoe Arbuckle, Mabel Normand, Mack Sennett, Alice Davenport, Ford Sterling, Virginia Kirtley, Charles Avery, Mack Swain. Also known as HER DRAMATIC DEBUT.

THE GYPSY QUEEN (THE GYPSY) (Keystone, 1913). r11 Sep

275

1913. fs16 Aug 1913. 1 reel. Keystone Film Company (pro). Mutual Film Corporation (dist). Mack Sennett (dir). Roscoe Arbuckle, Mabel Normand.

THE FATAL TAXICAB (THE TAXICAB) (Keystone, 1913). r18 Sep 1913. fs21 Aug 1913. 1 reel. Keystone Film Company (pro). Mutual Film Corporation (dist). Mack Sennett (dir). Roscoe Arbuckle, Mabel Normand, Ford Sterling. Variant: THE FAITHFUL TAXICAB.

WHEN DREAMS COME TRUE (THE SNAKE) (Keystone, 1913). r22 Sep 1913. fs26 Aug 1913. 1 reel. Keystone Film Company (pro). Mutual Film Corporation (dist). Mack Sennett (dir). Roscoe Arbuckle, Mabel Normand, Ford Sterling.

MOTHER'S BOY (THE BEARS) (Keystone, 1913). r25 Sep 1913. fs1 Sep 1913. 1 reel. Keystone Film Company (pro). Mutual Film Corporation (dist). Henry Lehrman (dir). Roscoe Arbuckle, Nick Cogley. Variants: MOTHER'S BOYS; MOTHERS BOY.

TWO OLD TARS (YACHTING) (Keystone, 1913). r20 Oct 1913. fs22 Sep 1913. 1 reel. Keystone Film Company (pro). Mutual Film Corporation (dist). Henry Lehrman (dir). Roscoe Arbuckle, Nick Cogley. Original title, THE SEA DOGS, changed to TWO OLD TARS, probably to avoid confusion with a Broncho two-reeler titled THE SEA DOG (r21 May 1913). Also known as THE SEA DOGS.

A QUIET LITTLE WEDDING (INTERRUPTED WEDDING) (Keystone, 1913). r23 Oct 1913. fs25 Sep 1913. 1 reel. Keystone Film Company (pro). Mutual Film Corporation (dist). Wilfred Lucas (dir). Roscoe Arbuckle, Minta Durfee.

THE SPEED KINGS (Keystone, 1913). r30 Oct 1913. 1 reel. Keystone Film Company (pro). Mutual Film Corporation (dist). Wilfred Lucas (dir). Roscoe Arbuckle, Teddy Tetzlaff, Earl Cooper, Mabel Normand, Ford Sterling, Paul Jacobs. Filmed at automobile race track in Santa Monica. Variants: SPEED KINGS; THE SPEED KING; TEDDY TETZLAFF AND EARL

COOPER, SPEED KINGS; TEDDY TELZAFF AND EARL COOPER, SPEED KINGS.

FATTY AT SAN DIEGO (A JEALOUS HUSBAND) (Keystone, 1913). r3 Nov 1913. fs9 Oct 1913. 1 reel. Keystone Film Company (pro). Mutual Film Corporation (dist). George Nichols (dir). Roscoe Arbuckle, Minta Durfee, Phyllis Allen.

WINE (WINE MAKING) (Keystone, 1913). r13 Nov 1913. fs18 Oct 1913. 1 reel. Keystone Film Company (pro). Mutual Film Corporation (dist). George Nichols (dir). Roscoe Arbuckle, Minta Durfee. Ford Sterling.

FATTY JOINS THE FORCE (FREAK COWARD) (Keystone, 1913). r24 Nov 1913. fs25 Oct 1913. 1 reel. Keystone Film Company (pro). Mutual Film Corporation (dist). George Nichols (dir). Roscoe Arbuckle, Minta Durfee, Dot Farley.

THE WOMAN HATERS (YACHTING) (Keystone, 1913). r1 Dec 1913. fs4 Oct 1913. 1 reel. Keystone Film Company (pro). Mutual Film Corporation (dist). Henry Lehrman (dir). Roscoe Arbuckle, Nick Cogley. Variant: THE WOMAN HATER.

RIDE FOR A BRIDE (THE GOLF BALL) (Keystone, 1913). r8 Dec 1913. fs1 Nov 1913. 1 reel. Keystone Film Company (pro). Mutual Film Corporation (dist). George Nichols (dir). Roscoe Arbuckle, Edgar Kennedy. Variant: A RIDE FOR A BRIDE.

FATTY'S FLIRTATION (THE MASHER) (Keystone, 1913). r18 Dec 1913. fs13 Nov 1913. 1/2 reel. Keystone Film Company (pro). Mutual Film Corporation (dist). George Nichols (dir). Roscoe Arbuckle, Mabel Normand, Minta Durfee, Hank Mann.

HIS SISTER'S KIDS (THE DOCTOR'S CAT) (Keystone, 1913). r20 Dec 1913. fs12 Nov 1913. 1 reel. Keystone Film Company (pro). Mutual Film Corporation (dist). George Nichols (dir). Roscoe Arbuckle, Keystone Cops.

HE WOULD A HUNTING GO (HUNTING STORY) (Keystone, 1913). r 29 Dec 1913. fs30 Nov 1913. 1 reel. Keystone Film Company (pro). Mutual Film Corporation (dist). George Nichols (dir). Roscoe Arbuckle, Grover Ligon.

A MISPLACED FOOT (COMEDY OF ERRORS) (Keystone, 1914). r1 Jan 1914, fs3 Dec 1913. 1/2 reel. Keystone Film Company (pro). Mutual Film Corporation (dist). Wilfred Lucas (dir). Roscoe Arbuckle, Mabel Normand, Minta Durfee.

THE UNDER SHERIFF (THE SHERIFF) (Keystone, 1914). r8 Jan 1914. fs17 Dec 1913. 1 reel. Keystone Film Company (pro). Mutual Film Corporation (dist). George Nichols (dir). Roscoe Arbuckle.

A FLIRT'S MISTAKE (THE HINDOO) (Keystone, 1914). r12 Jan 1914. fs18 Dec 1913. 1 reel. Keystone Film Company (pro). Mutual Film Corporation (dist). George Nichols (dir). Roscoe Arbuckle.

IN THE CLUTCHES OF THE GANG (THE DISGUISED MAYOR) (Keystone, 1914). r17 Jan 1914. fs 11 Dec 1913. 2 reels. Keystone Film Company (pro). Mutual Film Corporation (dist). George Nichols (dir). Roscoe Arbuckle, Ford Sterling, George Nichols, Rube Miller, Edgar Kennedy, Hank Mann, George Jeske, Al St. John. Variants: IN THE CLUTCHES OF A GANG.

REBECCA'S WEDDING DAY (THE SISTERS) (Keystone, 1914). r24 Jan 1914. fs31 Dec 1913. 1 reel. Keystone Film Company (pro). Mutual Film Corporation (dist). George Nichols (dir). Roscoe Arbuckle. Variant: REBECKAS WEDDING DAY.

A ROBUST ROMEO (THE WOLF) (Keystone, 1914). r12 Feb 1914. fs22 Jan 1914. 1 reel. Keystone Film Company (pro). Mutual Film Corporation (dist). George Nichols (dir). Roscoe Arbuckle.

'TWIXT LOVE AND FIRE (THE FINISH) (Keystone, 1914). r23 Feb 1914. fs4 Feb 1914. 1 reel. Keystone Film Company (pro).

Mutual Film Corporation (dist). George Nichols (dir). Roscoe Arbuckle, Peggy Pearce. This picture should not be confused with the Keystone split-reel picture 'TWIXT LOVE AND FIRE, directed by Henry Lehrman and released 19 May 1913.

A FILM JOHNNIE (A MOVIE BUG) (Keystone, 1914). r4 Mar 1914. fs11 Feb 1914. 1 reel. Keystone Film Company (pro). Mutual Film Corporation (dist). George Nichols (dir). Roscoe Arbuckle, Charles Chaplin, Minta Durfee, Virginia Kirtley. Also known as MOVIE NUT; MILLION DOLLAR JOB.

TANGO TANGLES (A MIDNIGHT DANCE) (Keystone, 1914). r9 Mar 1914. fs17 Feb 1914. 1/2 reel. Keystone Film Company (pro). Mutual Film Corporation (dist). Mack Sennett (dir). Roscoe Arbuckle, Charles Chaplin, Ford Sterling, Chester Conklin, Minta Durfee. Referred to variously as 1/2 reel, 3/4 reel, 1 reel. Variant: TANGO TANGLE: Also known as CHARLIE'S RECREATION: MUSIC HALL.

HIS FAVORITE PASTIME (THE DRUNK) (Keystone, 1914). r16 Mar 1914. fs19 Feb 1914. 1 reel. Keystone Film Company (pro). Mutual Film Corporation (dist). George Nichols (dir). Roscoe Arbuckle, Charles Chaplin, Peggy Pearce, Harry McCoy, Hank Mann, Edgar Kennedy. Original release date changed from 12 Mar 1914 to 16 Mar 1914. Also known as THE BONEHEAD; CHARLIE IS THIRSTY.

A RURAL DEMON (A HORSE) (Keystone, 1914). r19 Mar 1914. fs25 Feb 1914. 1 reel. Keystone Film Company (pro). Mutual Film Corporation (dist). Mack Sennett, Henry Lehrman (dirs). Roscoe Arbuckle. Original release date changed from 14 Mar 1914 to 19 Mar 1914.

ARBUCKLE AS DIRECTOR

Arbuckle received his first credit as director with BARNYARD FLIRTATIONS; and with the exception of a few comedies directed by Charles Chaplin (THE MASQUERADER, THE ROUNDERS), and Mack Sennett (THE LITTLE TEACHER) and co-directed by Ferris Hartman (THE WAITERS' BALL), Arbuckle received official credit as director of his own comedies from 1914 to 1920 for Mutual-Keystone, Triangle-Keystone, and Comique. Several individuals who assisted Arbuckle with direction on set and never received official credit include Charles Avery (ca. 1914–1915), Andy Anderson (ca. 1916), Harry Williams (ca. 1916), Frank Griffin)1917), Herbert Warren (1917–1918), Buster Keaton (1917–1919), Al St. John (1917–1919), and Glen Cavender (1918).

BARNYARD FLIRTATIONS (THE FARMER'S TOE) (Keystone, 1914). r28 Mar 1914. fs7 Mar 1914. 1 reel. Keystone Film Company (pro). Mutual Film Corporation (dist). Roscoe Arbuckle (dir). Roscoe Arbuckle. Variant: BARNYARD FLIRTATION.

CHICKEN CHASER (NEW YARD LOVERS) (Keystone, 1914). r2 Apr 1914. fs13 Mar 1914. 1 reel. Keystone Film Company (pro). Mutual Film Corporation (dist). Roscoe Arbuckle (dir). Roscoe Arbuckle, Keystone Cops. Variants: THE CHICKEN CHASER. Also known as NEW YARD LOVERS.

A BATH HOUSE BEAUTY (BATHING PICTURE) (Keystone, 1914). r13 Apr 1914. fs26 Mar 1914. 1 reel. Keystone Film Company (pro). Mutual Film Corporation (dist). Roscoe Arbuckle (dir). Variants: A BATHHOUSE BEAUTY; A BATHING BEAUTY.

WHERE HAZEL MET THE VILLAIN (BURGLARS UNION) (Keystone, 1914). r23 Apr 1914. fs6 Apr 1914. 1 reel. Keystone Film Company (pro). Mutual Film Corporation (dist). Roscoe Arbuckle (dir). Mabel Normand. Variant: WHEN HAZEL MET THE VILLAIN.

A SUSPENDED ORDEAL (HUNG BY A HOOK) (Keystone, 1914). r9 May 1914. fs23 Apr 1914. 1 reel. Keystone Film Company (pro). Mutual Film Corporation (dist). Roscoe Arbuckle (dir). Roscoe Arbuckle, Minta Durfee. Variant: SUSPENDED ORDEAL.

THE WATER DOG (THE RESCUE) (Keystone, 1914). r18 May 1914. fs2 May 1914. 1 reel. Keystone Film Company (pro). Mutual Film Corporation (dist). Roscoe Arbuckle (dir). Roscoe Arbuckle.

THE ALARM (FIREMAN'S PICNIC) (Keystone, 1914). r28 May 1914. fs16 May 1914. 2 reels. Keystone Film Company (pro). Mutual Film Corporation (dist). Roscoe Arbuckle (dir). Roscoe Arbuckle, Mabel Normand, Al St. John, Hank Mann.

THE KNOCK-OUT (FIGHTING DEMON) (Keystone, 1914). r11 Jun 1914. fs29 May 1914. 2 reels. Keystone Film Company (pro). Mutual Film Corporation (dist). Roscoe Arbuckle, Charles Chaplin, Minta Durfee, Edgar Kennedy, Mack Swain, Al St. John, Hank Mann, Alice Howell, George "Slim" Summerville, Charles Parrott (later known as Charley Chase), Mack Sennett, Eddie Cline, Joe Bordeau. Variant: THE KNOCKOUT. Also known as COUNTED OUT; THE PUGILIST.

FATTY AND THE HEIRESS (LOVE AND MONEY) (Keystone, 1914). r25 June 1914. fs14 Jun 1914. 1 reel. Keystone Film Company (pro). Mutual Film Corporation (dist). Roscoe Arbuckle (dir). Roscoe Arbuckle. Referred to variously as 1 reel, 2 reels.

FATTY'S FINISH (FATTY'S FLIRTATION) (Keystone, 1914). r2 Jul 1914. fs19 June 1914 1 reel. Keystone Film Company (pro). Mutual Film Corporation (dist). Roscoe Arbuckle (dir). Roscoe Arbuckle.

LOVE AND BULLETS (THE ASSASSIN) (Keystone, 1914). r4 Jul 1914. fs22 Jun 1914. 1 reel. Keystone Fiom Company (pro). Mutual Film Corporation (dist). Roscoe Arbuckle (dir). Roscoe Arbuckle, Charles Murray. Also known as THE TROUBLE MENDER.

A ROWBOAT ROMANCE (BOATING) (Keystone, 1914). r6 Jul 1914. fs23 Jun 1914. 1 reel. Keystone Film Company (pro). Mutual Film Corporation (dist). Roscoe Arbuckle (dir). Roscoe Arbuckle. Variants: ROW-BOAT ROMANCE; ROW BOAT ROMANCE.

THE SKY PIRATE (UP IN THE AIR) (Keystone, 1914). r18 Jul 1914. fs4 Jul 1914. 1 reel. Keystone Film Company (pro). Mutual Film Corporation (dist). Roscoe Arbuckle (dir). Roscoe Arbuckle. Variant: A SKY PIRATE.

THOSE HAPPY DAYS (CAST ADRIFT) (Keystone, 1914). r23 Jul 1914. fs11 Jul 1914. 1 reel. Keystone Film Company (pro). Mutual Film Corporation (dist). Roscoe Arbuckle (dir). Roscoe Arbuckle.

THAT MINSTREL MAN (FANNY'S JEWELS) (Keystone, 1914). r17 Aug 1914. fs4 Aug 1914. 1 reel. Keystone Film Company (pro). Mutual Film Corporation (dist). Roscoe Arbuckle (dir). Roscoe Arbuckle, Ford Sterling. Referred to variously as 1 reel, 2 reels.

THOSE COUNTRY KIDS (THE RURAL RIVALS) (Keystone, 1914). r20 Aug 1914. fs5 Aug 1914. 1 reel. Keystone Film Company (pro). Mutual Film Corporation (dist). Roscoe Arbuckle (dir). Roscoe Arbuckle, Mabel Normand.

FATTY'S GIFT (HIS BABY) (Keystone, 1914). r24 Aug 1914. fs8 Aug 1914. 1 reel. Keystone Film Company (pro). Mutual Film Corporation (dist). Roscoe Arbuckle (dir). Roscoe Arbuckle.

THE MASQUERADER (QUEEN OF THE MOVIES) (Keystone, 1914). r27 Aug 1914. fs12 Aug 1914. 1 reel. Keystone Film Company (pro). Mutual Film Corporation (dist). Charles Chaplin (dir). Roscoe Arbuckle, Charles Chaplin, Charles Parrott, Harry McCoy, Minta Durfee, Cecile Arnold, Charles Murray, Fritz Schade, Vivian Edwards, Chester Conklin. Also known as PUTTING ONE OVER; THE FEMALE IMPERSONATOR; THE PICNIC; HIS NEW PROFESSION; CHARLIE AT THE STUDIO; CHARLIE THE ACTOR.

A BRAND NEW HERO (THE CHIEF'S DAUGHTER) (Keystone, 1914). r5 Sep 1914. fs18 Aug 1914. 1 reel. Keystone Film Company (pro). Mutual Film Corporation (dist). Roscoe Arbuckle (dir). Roscoe Arbuckle.

THE ROUNDERS (THE TWO DRUNKS) (Keystone, 1914). r7 Sep 1914. fs21 Aug 1914. 1 reel. Keystone Film Company (pro). Mutual Film Corporation (dist). Charles Chaplin (dir). Roscoe Arbuckle, Charles Chaplin, Minta Durfee, Phyllis Allen, Al St. John, Charles Parrott, Fritz Schade, Dixie Chene, Edgar Kennedy, Wallace Macdonald. Also known as REVELRY; TWO OF A KIND; OH, WHAT A NIGHT.

LOVER'S LUCK (THE THREE LOVERS) (Keystone, 1914). r19 Sep 1914. fs29 Aug 1914. 1 reel. Keystone Film Company (pro). Mutual Film Corporation (dist). Roscoe Arbuckle (dir). Roscoe Arbuckle. Variant: LOVERS LUCK.

FATTY'S DEBUT (SAVING LIZZIE) (Keystone, 1914). r26 Sep 1914. fs4 Sep 1914. 1 reel. Keystone Film Company (pro). Mutual Film Corporation (dist). Roscoe Arbuckle (dir). Roscoe Arbuckle. Also known as FATTY BUTTS IN.

FATTY AGAIN (THE STAR) (Keystone, 1914). r3 Oct 1914. fs10 Sep 1914. 1 reel. Keystone Film Company (pro). Mutual Film Corporation (dist). Roscoe Arbuckle (dir). Roscoe Arbuckle, Minta Durfee, Charles Murray. Also known as FATTY THE FOURFLUSHER.

THEIR UPS AND DOWNS (THE BALOON [sic]) (Keystone, 1914). r5 Oct 1914. fs12 Sep 1914. 1 reel. Keystone Film Company (pro). Mutual Film Corporation (dist). Roscoe Arbuckle (dir). Roscoe Arbuckle.

ZIP, THE DODGER (THE AFRICAN DODGER) (Keystone, 1914). r17 Oct 1914. fs19 Sep 1914. 1 reel. Keystone Film Company (pro). Mutual Film Corporation (dist). Roscoe Arbuckle (dir). Roscoe Arbuckle. Variant: ZIP THE DODGER.

LOVERS' POST OFFICE (LOVER'S POSTOFFICE) (Keystone,

1914). r2 Nov 1914. c2 Nov 1914. fs15 Oct 1914. 1 reel.
Keystone Film Company (pro/cc). Mutual Film Corporation
(dist). Roscoe Arbuckle (dir). Roscoe Arbuckle, Mabel
Normand. First Arbuckle Keystone comedy to be copy-
righted. Variants: LOVERS' POST-OFFICE; LOVER'S
POSTOFFICE; LOVERS POST OFFICE.

AN INCOMPETENT HERO (THE WRONG ROOM) (Keystone,
1914). r12 Nov 1914. c12 Nov 1914. fs25 Oct 1914. 1 reel.
Keystone Film Company (pro/cc). Mutual Film Corporation
(dist). Roscoe Arbuckle (dir). Roscoe Arbuckle, Minta
Durfee. Variant: IN INCOMPETENT HERO.

FATTY'S JONAH DAY (PARK TROUBLES) (Keystone, 1914). r16
Nov 1914. c16 Nov 1914. fs29 Oct 1914. 1 reel. Keystone
Film Company (pro/cc). Mutual Film Corporation (dist).
Roscoe Arbuckle (dir). Roscoe Arbuckle, Mabel Normand,
Phyllis Allen. Variants: FATTY'S HOODOO DAY.

FATTY'S WINE PARTY (ONLY A DOLLAR) (Keystone, 1914). r21
Nov 1914. c21 Nov 1914. fs6 Nov 1914. 1 reel. Keystone Film
Company (pro/cc). Mutual Film Corporation (dist). Roscoe
Arbuckle (dir). Roscoe Arbuckle, Mabel Normand, Syd
Chaplin.

THE SEA NYMPHS (CATALINA STORY) (Keystone, 1914). r23
Nov 1914. c21 Nov 1914. fs12 Sept 1914. 2 reels. Keystone
Film Company (pro/cc). Mutual Film Corporation (dist).
Roscoe Arbuckle (dir). Roscoe Arbuckle, Mabel Normand,
Mack Swain. Variant: SEA NYMPHS.

LEADING LIZZIE ASTRAY (THE COUNTRY GIRL) (Keystone,
1914). r30 Nov 1914. c30 Nov 1914. fs18 Nov 1914. 1 reel.
Keystone Film Company (pro/cc). Mutual Film Corporation
(dist). Roscoe Arbuckle (dir). Roscoe Arbuckle, Minta
Durfee, Mack Swain, George "Slim" Summerville. Variant:
LEADING LIZZIE ESTRAY.

SHOTGUNS THAT KICK (FATTY'S BIRTHDAY PRESENT) (Keystone, 1914). r3 Dec 1914. c3 Dec 1914. fs20 Nov 1914. 1 reel.

Keystone Film Company (pro/cc). Mutual Film Corporation (dist). Roscoe Arbuckle (dir). Roscoe Arbuckle.

FATTY'S MAGIC PANTS (THE BORROWED DRESS) (Keystone, 1914). r14 Dec 1914. c14 Dec 1914. fs2 Dec 1914. 1 reel. Keystone Film Company (pro/cc). Mutual Film Corporation (dist). Roscoe Arbuckle (dir). Roscoe Arbuckle, Minta Durfee, Bert Roach, Harry McCoy, Charles Parrott, Al St. John, George "Slim" Summerville. Variant: FATT'S MAGIC PANTS. Also known as FATTY'S SUITLESS DAY.

FATTY AND MINNIE-HE-HAW (THE SQUAW'S MAN) (Keystone, 1914). r21 Dece 1914. c19 Dec 1914. fs8 Oct 1914. 2 reels. Keystone Film Company (pro/cc). Mutual Film Corporation (dist). Roscoe Arbuckle (dir). Roscoe Arbuckle, Minta Durfee, Princess Minnie. Variants: FATTY AND MINNIE HE-HAW.

MABEL AND FATTY'S WASH DAY (MABEL'S FLIRTATION) (Keystone, 1915). r14 Jan 1915. c14 Jan 1915. fs4 Jan 1915. 1 reel. Keystone Film Company (pro/cc). Mutual Film Corporation (dist). Roscoe Arbuckle (dir). Roscoe Arbuckle, Mabel Normand. Original title, MABEL'S FLIRTATION, changed to MABEL AND FATTY'S WASH DAY. Variant: MABEL'S AND FATTY'S WASH DAY.

FATTY AND MABEL'S SIMPLE LIFE (THE RUNAWAY AUTO) (Keystone, 1915). r18 Jan 1915. c16 Jan 1915. fs4 Jan 1915. 2 reels. Keystone Film Company (pro/cc). Mutual Film Corporation (dist). Roscoe Arbuckle (dir). Roscoe Arbuckle, Mabel Normand. Variants: FATTY'S AND MABEL'S SIMPLE LIFE; MABEL AND FATTY'S SIMPLE LIFE.

FATTY AND MABEL AT THE SAN DIEGO EXPOSITION (FATTY & MABEL AT THE FAIR) (Keystone, 1915). r23 Jan 1915. c23 Jan 1915. fs11 Jan 1915. 1 reel. Keystone Film Company (pro/cc). Mutual Film Corporation (dist). Roscoe Arbuckle (dir). Roscoe Arbuckle, Mabel Normand, Frank Hayes. Variants: FATTY AND MABEL; FATTY AND MABEL (AT THE SAN DIEGO EXPOSITION); FATTY AND MABEL AT SAN DIEGO EXPO.

MABEL, FATTY AND THE LAW (NO FLIRTING ALLOWED) (Keystone, 1915). r28 Jan 1915. c28 Jan 1915. fs18 Jan 1915. 1 reel. Keystone Film Company (pro/cc). Mutual Film Corporation (dist). Roscoe Arbuckle (dir). Roscoe Arbuckle, Mabel Normand, Minta Durfee, Harry Gribbon, Frank Hayes, Al St. John. Variants: MABLE, FATTY AND THE LAW; FATTY, MABEL AND THE LAW; Also known as FATTY'S SPOONING DAYS.

FATTY'S NEW ROLE (GERMAN SALOON STORY) (Keystone, 1915). r1 Feb 1915. c1 Feb 1915. fs22 Jan 1915. Keystone Film Company (pro/cc). Mutual Film Corporation (dist). Roscoe Arbuckle (dir). Roscoe Arbuckle. Referred to variously as 1 reel, 2 reels.

MABEL AND FATTY'S MARRIED LIFE (MONKEY SCARE) (Keystone, 1915). r11 Feb 1915. c11 Feb 1915. fs29 Jan 1915. Keystone Film Company (pro/cc). Mutual Film Corporation (dist). Roscoe Arbuckle (dir). Roscoe Arbuckle, Mabel Normand. Variant: FATTY AND MABEL'S MARRIED LIFE.

FATTY'S RECKLESS FLING (DISAPPEARING BED STORY) (Keystone, 1915). r4 Mar 1915. c4 Mar 1915. fs24 Feb 1915. 1 reel. Keystone Film Company (pro/cc). Mutual Film Corporation (dist). Roscoe Arbuckle (dir). Roscoe Arbuckle, Ted Edwards. Variant: FATTY'S WRECKLESS FLING.

FATTY'S CHANCE ACQUAINTANCE (FATTY'S WIFE'S HUSBAND) (Keystone, 1915). r8 Mar 1915. c8 Mar 1915. fs27 Feb 1915. 1 reel. Keystone Film Company (pro/cc). Mutual Film Corporation (dist). Roscoe Arbuckle (dir). Roscoe Arbuckle, Minta Durfee, Frank Hayes.

LOVE IN ARMOR (SUIT OF ARMOR STORY) (Keystone, 1915). r11 Mar 1915. c11 Mar 1915. fs3 Mar 1915. 1 reel. Keystone Film Company (pro/cc). Mutual Film Corporation (dist). Roscoe Arbuckle (dir). Roscoe Arbuckle, Charles Parrott, Max Davidson.

THAT LITTLE BAND OF GOLD (BEFORE AND AFTER MARRIAGE)

(Keystone, 1915). r15 Mar 1915. c13 Mar 1915. fs17 Feb 1915. 2 reels. Keystone Film Company (pro/cc). Mutual Film Corporation (dist). Roscoe Arbuckle (dir). Roscoe Arbuckle, Mabel Normand, Alice Davenport, Ford Sterling, May Emory, Phyllis Allen, Vivian Edwards, Al St. John, Dora Rodgers, Dixie Chene. Filmed at a local courthouse, the interior of the Republic Theater in Los Angeles, and at the Keystone studio.

FATTY'S FAITHFUL FIDO (FATTY THE TOUGH) (Keystone, 1915). r20 Mar 1915. c20 Mar 1915. fs14 Mar 1915. Keystone Film Company (pro/cc). Mutual Film Corporation (dist). Roscoe Arbuckle (dir). Roscoe Arbuckle, Minta Durfee, Al St. John, Glen Cavender, Frank Hayes, Ted Edwards, Luke (dog). Variants: FATTY'S FAITHFUL WIFE; FATTY'S FATAL FIDO.

WHEN LOVE TOOK WINGS (FATTY'S LAST RIDE) (Keystone, 1915). r1 Apr 1915. c1 Apr 1915. fs25 Mar 1915. 1 reel. Keystone Film Company (pro/cc). Mutual Film Corporation (dist). Roscoe Arbuckle (dir). Roscoe Arbuckle.

WISHED ON MABEL (GOLDEN GATE PARK STORY) (Keystone, 1915). r19 Apr 1915. c19 Apr 1915. fs9 Apr 1915. 1 reel. Keystone Film Company (pro/cc). Mutual Film Corporation (dist). Roscoe Arbuckle (dir). Roscoe Arbuckle, Mabel Normand.

MABEL AND FATTY VIEWING THE WORLD'S FAIR AT SAN FRANCISCO, CAL. (THE FRISCO STORY) (Keystone, 1915). r22 Apr 1915. c22 Apr 1915. fs16 Apr 1915. 1 reel. Keystone Film Company (pro/cc). Mutual Film Corporation (dist). Roscoe Arbuckle (dir). Roscoe Arbuckle, Mabel Normand, Ernestine Schumann-Heink. Variant: FATTY AND MABEL VIEWING THE WORLD'S FAIR AT SAN FRANCISCO.

MABEL'S WILFUL WAY (IDORA PARK STORY) (Keystone, 1915). r1 May 1915. c1 May 1915. fs23 Apr 1915. 1 reel. Keystone Film Company (pro/cc). Mutual Film Corporation (dist). Roscoe Arbuckle (dir). Roscoe Arbuckle, Mabel Normand.

MISS FATTY'S SEASIDE LOVERS (BY THE SEA) (Keystone, 1915). f15 May 1915. c15 May 1915. fs7 May 1915. 1 reel. Keystone Film Company (pro/cc). Mutual Film Corporation (dist). Roscoe Arbuckle (dir). Roscoe Arbuckle, Harold Lloyd. Variant: MISS FATTY'S SEASIDE LOVER.

THE LITTLE TEACHER (SMALL TOWN TEACHER) (Keystone, 1915). r21 Jun 1915. c21 Jun 1915. fs25 May 1915. 2 reels. Keystone Film Company (pro/cc). Mutual Film Corporation (dist). Roscoe Arbuckle (dir). Roscoe Arbuckle, Mabel Normand, Owen Moore, Mack Sennett, Harry McCoy. Also known as SMALL TOWN BULLY.

FATTY'S PLUCKY PUP (DOG AND VILLAIN STORY) (Keystone, 1915). f28 Jun 1915. c28 Jun 1915. fs10 Jun 1915. 2 reels. Keystone Film Company (pro/cc). Mutual Film Corporation (dist). Roscoe Arbuckle (dir). Roscoe Arbuckle, Luke (dog). Also known as FATT'S PLUCKY PUP; FOILED BY FIDO.

FATTY'S TINTYPE TANGLE (CAUGHT ON THE SCREEN) (Keystone, 1915). r26 Jul 1915. c26 Jul 1915. fs14 Jul 1915. 2 reels. Keystone Film Company (pro/cc). Mutual Film Corporation (dist). Roscoe Arbuckle (dir). Roscoe Arbuckle, Louise Fazenda, Edgar Kennedy, Luke (dog). Variants: FATTY'S TIN TYPE TANGLE; FIDO'S TIN-TYPE-TANGLE; FIDO'S TINTYPE TANGLE.

TRIANGLE–KEYSTONE

Triangle-Keystone comedies were produced by the Keystone Film Company under the supervision of Mack Sennett and distributed by the Triangle Film Corporation on a block-booking basis. Arbuckle's Triangle-Keystone comedies of 1915 were produced at the Keystone studio at 1712 Allesandro Street in Los Angeles (Edendale), California, and filmed at the studio and in the general Los Angeles vicinity.

Arbuckle's Triangle-Keystone comedies of 1916 were produced at the Keystone studio at 1712 Allesandro Street in Los Angeles (Edendale), California, and at the Eastern Triangle studios in Fort Lee, New Jersey; their production locations are identified in the filmography at the end of each entry.

FICKLE FATTY'S FALL (FATTY'S WAY) (Keystone, 1915). f14 Nov 1915; and 28 Nov 1915. c1 Nov 1915; and 15 Nov 1915. fs12 Oct 1915. 2 reels. Keystone Film Company (pro). Triangle Film Corporation (dist/cc). Roscoe Arbuckle (dir). Roscoe Arbuckle, Minta Durfee, Phyllis Allen, Al St. John, Glen Cavender, Ivy Crosthwaite, Fritz Schade, Bobby Dunn.

THE VILLAGE SCANDAL (Keystone, 1915). r12 Dec 1915. c18 Nov 1915; and 13 Dec 1915. 2 reels. Keystone Film Company (pro). Triangle Film Corporation (dist/cc). Roscoe Arbuckle (dir). Roscoe Arbuckle, Raymond Hitchcock, Flora Zabelle, Al St. John, Harry McCoy.

FATTY AND THE BROADWAY STARS (FATTY'S DREAM) (Keystone, 1915). r1 Dec 1915; and 20 Dec 1915. fs23 Nov 1915. 2 reels. Keystone Film Company (pro). Triangle Film Corporation (dist/cc). Roscoe Arbuckle (dir). Roscoe Arbuckle, Ivy Crosthwaite, Al St. John, Mack Sennett, Joe Weber, Lew Fields, William Collier, Sr., Joe Jackson, Sam Bernard, Bert Clark, Fred Mace, Chester Conklin, Charles Murray, Mack Swain, Mae Busch, Ford Sterling, Hank Mann, Alice Davenport, Harry Gribbon, Glen Cavender, Wayland Trask, Minta Durfee, Edgar Kennedy, Harry Booker, Louis Hippe, Polly Moran, George "Slim" Summerville, Bobby Vernon, Keystone Cops (as it was usually spelled then).

FATTY AND MABEL ADRIFT (HOUSE AT SEA) (Keystone, 1916). r9 Jan 1916. c10 Jan 1916; and 14 Jan 1916. fs24 Dec 1915. 3 reels. Color (tinted and toned). Keystone Film Company (pro). Triangle Film Corporation (dist/cc). Roscoe Arbuckle (dir). Roscoe Arbuckle, Mabel Normand, Frank Hayes, May Wells, Al St. John, Wayland Trask, James Bryant, Joe

Bordeau, Glen Cavender, Luke (dog). Filmed at Pacific Ocean and at Keystone studio in Los Angeles, California.

HE DID AND HE DIDN'T (LOVE AND LOBSTERS) (Keystone, 1916). r30 Jan 1916. c9 Feb 1916. 2 reels. Keystone Film Company (pro). Triangle Film Corporation (dist/cc). Roscoe Arbuckle (dir). Roscoe Arbuckle, Mabel Normand, William Jefferson, Al St. John, Joe Bordeau. Filmed at Eastern Triangle studios in Fort Lee, New Jersey. Also known as LOVE AND LOBSTERS.

THE BRIGHT LIGHTS (THE LURE OF BROADWAY) (Keystone, 1916). r20 Feb 1916. c14 Feb 1916; and 10 Mar 1916. 2 reels. Keystone Film Company (pro). Triangle Film Corporation (dist/cc). Roscoe Arbuckle (dir). Roscoe Arbuckle, Mabel Normand, Minta Durfee, William Jefferson, Al St. John, Joe Bordeau. Filmed at Eastern Triangle studios in Fort Lee, New Jersey. Also known as THE LURE OF BROADWAY.

HIS WIFE'S MISTAKE (THE WRONG MR. STOUT) (Keystone, 1916). r2 Apr 1916, c2 Apr 1916; and 19 Apr 1916. 2 reels. Keystone Film Company (pro). Triangle Film Corporation (dist/cc). Roscoe Arbuckle (dir). Roscoe Arbuckle, William Jefferson, Minta Durfee, Arthur Earle, Al St. John, Betty Gray. Working title THE WRONG MR. STOUT was a Keystone inside joke referring to studio manager George Walter Stout. Filmed at Eastern Triangle studios in Fort Lee, New Jersey.

THE OTHER MAN (Keystone, 1916). r16 Apr 1916. c16 Apr 1916. 2 reels. Keystone Film Company (pro). Triangle Film Corporation (dist/cc). Roscoe Arbuckle (dir). Roscoe Arbuckle, Irene Wallace, Minta Durfee, Horace J. Haine, Al St. John, William Jefferson, Lillian Shaffner, Joe Bordeau. Filmed at Eastern Triangle studios in Fort Lee, New Jersey.

THE MOONSHINERS (THE MOONSHINER) (Keystone, 1916). r14 May 1916. No copyright. 2 reels. Keystone Film Company (pro). Triangle Film Corporation (dist). Roscoe Arbuckle (dir). Al St. John, Alice Lake, Horace J. Haine, Joe Bordeau, Mike Eagan, Bert Franc. Filmed at Dover in the

New Jersey countryside while at Eastern Triangle studios in Fort Lee, New Jersey. Variant: THE MOONSHINER.

THE WAITERS' BALL (THE WAITERS BALL) (Keystone, 1916). r25 Jun 1916. No copyright. fs8 Aug 1916. 2 reels. Keystone Film Company (pro). Triangle Film Corporation (dist). Roscoe Arbuckle, Ferris Hartman (dirs). Roscoe Arbuckle, Corinne Parquet, Al St. John, Joe Bordeau, Robert Maximilian, Kate Price, Alice Lake. Filmed at Eastern Triangle studios in Fort Lee, New Jersey. Variants: THE WAITERS BALL; THE WAITER'S BALL.

A RECKLESS ROMEO (HIS ALIBI) (Keystone, 1916). rJuly? 1916. No copyright. fs13 Sep 1916. 2 reels. Keystone Film Company (pro). Triangle Film Corporation (dist). Roscoe Arbuckle (dir). Filmed at Keystone studio in Los Angeles, California.

A CREAMPUFF ROMANCE (Keystone, 1916). rJuly? 1916. No copyright. 2 reels. Keystone Film Company (pro). Triangle Film Corporation (dist). Roscoe Arbuckle (dir). Roscoe Arbuckle, Alice Lake, Al St. John. Filmed at Keystone studio in Los Angeles, California. Variant: A CREAM PUFF ROMANCE. Also known as HIS ALIBI: A RECKLESS HERO.

COMIQUE

The Paramount-Arbuckle Comedies were produced by the Comique Film Corporation under the supervision of Joseph M. Schenck and distributed through Famous Players-Lasky Corporation by Paramount Pictures (Famous Players-Lasky Exchanges) on an open-booking basis. Famous Players-Lasky considered Arbuckle an affiliate or allied producer. The Paramount-Arbuckle Comedies were produced at several studios in New York and California; their production locations are identified in the filmography at the end of each entry.

THE BUTCHER BOY (Comique, 1917). r23 Apr 1917. 2 reels.

Paramount-Arbuckle Comedy No. A-3101. Comicque [sic] Film Corporation (pro/cc). Paramount Pictures (dist). Roscoe Arbuckle (dir/writ). Joe Roach (story). Herbert Warren (scen ed). Frank D. Williams (cam). Roscoe Arbuckle, Buster Keaton, Al St. John, Josephine Stevens, Arthur Earle, Agnes Neilson, Joe Bordeau, Luke (dog). Filmed at Norma Talmadge Film Corporation studios at 318 East 48th Street in New York.

A RECKLESS ROMEO (Comique, 1917). r21 May 1917. No copyright. 2 reels. Paramount-Arbuckle Comedy No. A-3102. Comicque [sic] Film Corporation (pro). Paramount Pictures (dist). Roscoe Arbuckle (dir/writ). Joe Roach (story). Herbert Warren (scen ed). Frank D. Williams (cam). Roscoe Arbuckle, Buster Keaton, Al St. John, Alice Lake, Corinne Parquet, Agnes Neilson. Filmed at Palisades Park amusement resort and at Norma Talmadge Film Corporation studios at 318 East 48th Street in New York.

THE ROUGH HOUSE (Comique, 1917). r25 Jun 1917. c20 Jun 1917. 2 reels. Paramount-Arbuckle Comedy No. A-3103. Comicque [sic] Film Corporation (pro/cc). Paramount Pictures (dist). Roscoe Arbuckle (dir/writ). Joe Roach (story). Herbert Warren (scen ed). Frank D. Williams (cam). Roscoe Arbuckle, Buster Keaton, Al St. John, Alice Lake. Filmed at Norma Talmadge Film Corporation studios at 318 East 48th Street in New York. Variants: A ROUGH HOUSE; ROUGH HOUSE

HIS WEDDING NIGHT (Comique, 1917). r20 Aug 1917; and 30 Aug 1917. c20 Aug 1917. 2 reels. Paramount-Arbuckle Comedy No. A-3104. Comicque [sic] Film Corporation (pro/cc). Paramount Pictures (dist). Roscoe Arbuckle (dir/writ). Joe Roach (story). Herbert Warren (scen ed). George Peters (cam). Roscoe Arbuckle, Buster Keaton, Al St. John, Alice Mann, Arthur Earle. Filmed at Selznick Studios (old Biograph studios) at 796 East 176th Street in New York.

OH, DOCTOR! (Comique, 1917). r30 Sep 1917. c19 Sep 1917. 2

reels. Paramount-Arbuckle Comedy No. A-3105. Comicque [sic] Film Corporation (pro/cc). Paramount Pictures (dist). Roscoe Arbuckle (dir/writ). Herbert Warren (scen ed). Jean Havez (scen). George Peters (cam). Roscoe Arbuckle, Buster Keaton, Al St. John, Alice Mann. Filmed at Selznick Studios (old Biograph studios) at 796 East 176th Street in New York; and at Coney Island amusement park. Variants: OH DOCTOR; OH DOCTOR!

FATTY AT CONEY ISLAND (Comique, 1917). r29 Oc 1917. c11 Oct 1917. 2 reels. Paramount-Arbuckle Comedy No. A-3106. Comicque [sic] Film Corporation (pro/cc). Paramount Pictures (dist). Roscoe Arbuckle (dir/writ). Herbert Warren (scen ed). George Peters (cam). Roscoe Arbuckle, Buster Keaton, Al St. John, Alice Mann, Agnes Neilson, James Bryant, Joe Bordeau. Filmed at Selznick Studios (old Biograph studios) at 796 East 176th Street in New York; and at Coney Island amusement Park. Variants: FATTY IN CONEY ISLAND; CONEY ISLAND.

A COUNTRY HERO (Comique, 1917). r10 Dec 1917. c13 Dec 1917. 2 reels. Paramount-Arbuckle Comedy No. A-3107. Famous Players-Lasky Corporation (cc). Comique Film Corporation (pro). Paramount Pictures (dist). Roscoe Arbuckle (dir/writ). Herbert Warren (scen ed). George Peters (cam). Roscoe Arbuckle, Buster Keaton, Al St. John, Alice Lake, Joe Keaton. Filmed at Jazzville, a rural village set built for Arbuckle at Horkheimer Brothers' Balboa Amusement Producing Company studios on Sixth and Alamitos streets in Long Beach, California. Variant: COUNTRY HERO.

OUT WEST (Comique, 1918). r20 Jan 1918. c29 Feb 1918. 2 reels. Paramount-Arbuckle Comedy No. A-3108. Comique Film Corporation (pro/cc). Paramount Pictures (dist). Roscoe Arbuckle (dir/writ). Herbert Warren (scen ed). Natalie Talmadge (scen). George Peters (cam). Roscoe Arbuckle, Buster Keaton, Al St. John, Alice Lake. Filmed at Horkheimer Brothers' Balboa Amusement Producing Company studios on Sixth and Alamitos streets in Long Beach and at Mad Dog Gulch, a Western mining-camp set built for Arbuckle in the San Gabriel Canyon near Los Angeles.

THE BELL BOY (Comique, 1918). r18 Mar 1918. c7 Mar 1918. 2 reels. Paramount-Arbuckle Comedy No. A-3109. Famous Players-Lasky Corporation (cc). Comique Film Corporation (pro). Paramount Pictures (dist). Roscoe Arbuckle (dir/writ). Herbert Warren (scen ed). George Peters (cam). Roscoe Arbuckle, Buster Keaton, Al St. John, Alice Lake, Joe Keaton, Charles Dudley. Filmed at Ouchgosh, a rural village set built for Arbuckle at Horkheimer Brothers' Balbao Amusement Producing Company studios on Sixth and Alamitos streets in Long Beach, California.

MOONSHINE (Comique, 1918). r13 May 1918. c6 May 1918. 2 reels. Paramount-Arbuckle Comedy No. A-3110. Famous Players-Lasky Corporation (cc). Comique Film Corporation (pro). Paramount Pictures (dist). Roscoe Arbuckle (dir/writ). Herbert Warren (scen ed). George Peters (cam). Roscoe Arbuckle, Buster Keaton, Al St. John, Charles Dudley, Alice Lake, Joe Bordeau. Filmed in the San Gabriel Canyon near Los Angeles; and at Horkheimer Brothers' Balboa Amusement Producing Company studios on Sixth and Alamitos streets in Long Beach, California. The Horkheimers' Balboa Amusement Producing Company ceased operations April 1918 while MOONSHINE was in production, but Arbuckle continued to use the studio for his own productions under the name Comique Film Corporation studios, Roscoe Arbuckle Comedy Company.

GOOD NIGHT, NURSE! (Comique, 1918). c8 Jul 1918. c22 Jun 1918. 2 reels. Paramount-Arbuckle Comedy No. A-3111. Famous Players-Lasky Corporation (cc). Comique Film Corporation (pro). Paramount Pictures (dist). Roscoe Arbuckle (dir/writ). Herbert Warren (scen ed). George Peters (cam). Roscoe Arbuckle, Buster Keaton, Al St. John, Alice Lake, Kate Price, Joe Keaton. Filmed at Arrowhead Hot Springs health resort and at Comique Film Corporation studios (old Balboa studios) on Sixth and Alamitos streets in

Long Beach, California. Variants: GOOD NIGHT NURSE; GOOD NIGHT, NURSE; GOODNIGHT NURSE.

THE COOK (Comique, 1918) r15 Sep 1918. c20 Aug 1918. 2 reels. Paramount-Arbuckle Comedy No. A-3112. Comique Film Corporation (pro/cc). Paramount Pictures (dist). Roscoe Arbuckle (dir/writ). Roscoe Arbuckle, Buster Keaton, Al St. John, Alice Lake, Glen Cavender. Filmed at Comique Film Corporation studios (old Balboa studios) on Sixth and Alamitos streets in Long Beach, California. Original release date changed from 18 Aug 1918 to 15 Sep 1918.

THE SHERIFF (Comique, 1918). r24 Nov 1918. No copyright. 2 reels. Paramount-Arbuckle Comedy No. A-3113. Comique Film Corporation (pro). Paramount Pictures (dist). Roscoe Arbuckle (dir/writ). Roscoe Arbuckle, Betty Compson, Mario Bianchi, Glen Cavender. Filmed at Diando Film Corporation studios (old Kalem studios) on Verdugo Road in Glendale, California.

LIBERTY LOAN AND VICTORY FILMS

UNITED STATES FOURTH LIBERTY LOAN DRIVE (U.S. Gov't, 1918). rNov 1918. Picture made by different studios to aid the Fourth Liberty Loan Drive; supervised by E.L. Hyman, Director of Pictures Division of the Commission on Training Camp Activities, for distribution to all Liberty Theaters throughout the United States. Roscoe Arbuckle, Douglas Fairbanks, Geraldine Farrar, Mary Pickford, Wallace Reid, William S. Hart, Elsie Ferguson, George M. Cohan, Lillian Gish, Dorothy Dalton, William Faversham, Mabel Normand, Harold Lockwood, Edith Storey, Emily Stevens, Alice Brady, Norma Talmadge, William Farnum, Mae Murray, Pauline Frederick, Mae Marsh, Madge Kennedy, Tom Moore, Sessue Hayakawa.

CANADIAN VICTORY LOAN DRIVE (Canadian Gov't, 1918). rNov 1918. Picture produced by Famous Players-Lasky

Corporation for the Canadian government's 1918 Victory Loan Campaign during October–November 1918. Roscoe Arbuckle, Elsie Ferguson, William S. Hart, Mary Pickford, Douglas Fairbanks, Wallace Reid, Lillian Gish, Dorothy Dalton, Mack Sennett players.

COMIQUE

CAMPING OUT (Comique, 1918). r5 Jan 1919. c31 Dec 1918. 2 reels. Paramount-Arbuckle Comedy No. A-3114. Famous Players-Lasky Corporation (cc). Comique Film Corporation (pro). Paramount Pictures (dist). Roscoe Arbuckle (dir/writ). Roscoe Arbuckle, Al St. John, Alice Lake. Filmed in and around Avalon on Catalina Island. Also known as CAMPING.

THE PULLMAN PORTER (Comique, 1919). r16 Feb 1919. No copyright. No Paramount-Arbuckle Comedy Number assigned. Comique Film Corporation (pro). Paramount Pictures (dist). Roscoe Arbuckle (dir/writ). Roscoe Arbuckle.

LOVE (Comique, 1919). r2 Mar 1919. c21 Feb 1919. 2 reels. Paramount-Arbuckle Comedy No. A-3115. Famous Players-Lasky Corporation (cc). Comique Film Corporation (pro). Paramount Pictures (dist). Roscoe Arbuckle (dir/writ). Vincent Bryan (scen). Roscoe Arbuckle, Al St. John, Winifred Westover. Filmed at Comique Film Corporation studios at 1723 Allesandro Street in Los Angeles (Edendale), California. Original release date changed from 16 Feb 1919 to 2 Mar 1919.

THE BANK CLERK (Comique, 1919), r5 Apr 1919. No copyright. 2 reels. No Paramount-Arbuckle Comedy Number assigned. Comique Film Corporation (pro). Paramount Pictures (dist). Roscoe Arbuckle (dir/writ). Roscoe Arbuckle, Molly Malone. Filmed at Comique Film Corporation studios at 1723 Allesandro Street in Los Angeles (Edendale), California.

A DESERT HERO (Comique, 1919). r1 Jun 1919; and 15 Jun 1919. c13 Jun 1919. 2 reels. Paramount-Arbuckle Comedy No. A-3116. Famous Players-Lasky Corporation (cc). Comique Film Corporation (pro). Paramount Pictures (dist). Roscoe Arbuckle (dir/writ). Jean Havez (scen). Roscoe Arbuckle, Al St. John, Molly Malone, Monte Collins, Sr. Filmed in the hills near Glendale, California, and at the Comique Film Corporation studios at 1723 Allesandro Street in Los Angeles (Edendale), California.

BACK STAGE (Comique, 1919). r7 Sep 1919. c20 Aug 1919. Color (tinted). Famous Players-Lasky Corporation (cc). Comique Film Corporation (pro). Paramount Pictures (dist). Roscoe Arbuckle (dir/writ). Jean Havez (scen). Roscoe Arbuckle, Buster Keaton, Al St. John, Molly Malone, John Coogan. Filmed at Comique Film Corporation studios at 1723 Allesandro Street in Los Angeles (Edendale), California.

THE HAYSEED (Comique, 1919). r26 Oct 1919. c13 Oct 1919. 2 reels. Famous Players-Lasky Corporation (cc). Comique Film Corporation (pro). Paramount Pictures (dist). Roscoe Arbuckle (dir/writ). Jean Havez (scen). Roscoe Arbuckle, Buster Keaton, Al St. John, Molly Malone. Filmed at Henry Lehrman studios (Thomas H. Ince studios) in Culver City, California.

THE GARAGE (Comique, 1920). r11 Jan 1920. c15 Dec 1919. 2 reels. Famous Players-Lasky Corporation (cc). Comique Film Corporation (pro). Paramount Pictures (dist). Roscoe Arbuckle (dir/writ). Jean Havez (scen). Elgin Lessley (cam). Roscoe Arbuckle, Buster Keaton, Molly Malone, Harry McCoy, Daniel Crimmins, Luke (dog). Filmed at Henry Lehrman studios (Thomas H. Ince studios) in Culver City, California. Also known as FIRE CHIEF.

FAMOUS PLAYERS-LASKY

The Paramount feature-length pictures starring Arbuckle

were produced by the Famous Players-Lasky Corporation under the supervision of Jesse L. Lasky and distributed by Paramount Pictures (Famous Players-Lasky Exchanges). Famous Players-Lasky no longer considered Arbuckle an affiliate or allied producer. Arbuckle's feature pictures were produced at the Lasky ranch and the Lasky studio at 1520 Vine Street in Hollywood, California.

THE ROUND UP (Famous Players-Lasky, 1920). r10 Oct 1920. c26 Aug 1920. 7 reels. 6,417 feet. Paramount Production No. 323 (#2011). Famous Players-Lasky Corporation (pro/cc). Paramount Pictures (dist). Jesse L. Lasky (pres). George Melford (pro/dir). Edmund Day (play). Tom Forman (scen). Paul Perry (cam). Lon Megargee (art titl). Roscoe Arbuckle, Tom Forman, Irving Cummings, Mabel Julienne Scott, Jean Acker, Guy Oliver, Lucien Littlefield, Fred W. Huntley, Wallace Beery, Jane Wolfe, George Kuwa, Edward Sutherland, Buster Keaton (bit as an Indian). Picture produced between 22 Dec 1919 and 11 Feb 1920.

THE LIFE OF THE PARTY (Famous Players-Lasky, 1920). r12 Dec 1920. c8 Nov 1920. 5 reels. 4,944 feet. Paramount Production No. 342 (#2029). Famous Players-Lasky Corporation (pro/cc). Paramount Pictures (dist). Jesse L. Lasky (pres). Joseph Henabery (dir). Dick Johnston (ass dir). Irvin S. Cobb (story: *Saturday Evening Post*). Walter Woods (scen). Karl Brown (cam). Roscoe Arbuckle, Viora Daniel, Winifred Greenwood, Roscoe Karns, Julia Faye, Frank Campeau, Allen Connor, Frederick Starr, Ben Lewis. Picture produced between 15 Apr and 22 May 1920.

BREWSTER'S MILLIONS (Famous Players-Lasky, 1921). rJan 1921. c4 Jan 1921. 6 reels. 5,502 feet. Color (tinted and toned). Paramount Production No. 355. Famous Players-Lasky Corporation (pro/cc). Paramount Pictures (dist). Jesse L. Lasky (pres). Frank E. Woods (sup). Joseph Henabery (dir). Dick Johnston (asst dir). George Barr McCutcheon (story: novel). Winchell Smith (play). Walter Woods (scen). Karl Brown (cam). Wilfred Buckland (art dir). Roscoe Arbuckle, Betty Ross Clark, Fred W. Huntley,

Marian Skinner, James Corrigan, Jean Acker, Charles Ogle, Neely Edwards, William Boyd, L.J. McCarthy, Parker J. McConnell, John McFarland, Walter A. Coughlin. This picture should not be confused with the BREWSTER'S MILLIONS produced by Jesse L. Lasky Feature Play Company and released in 1914. Picture produced between 29 Jul 1920 and 20 Oct 1920.

THE DOLLAR A YEAR MAN (Famous Players-Lasky, 1921). r3 Apr 1921. c3 Apr 1921. 5 reels. 4,606 feet. Color (tinted and toned). Paramount Production No. 363 (#2061). Famous Players-Lasky Corporation (pro/cc). Paramount Pictures (dist). James Cruze (dir). Vernon Keays (asst dir). Walter Woods (story/scen). Karl Brown (cam). Roscoe Arbuckle, Lila Lee, Winifred Greenwood, Jean M. Dumont, Edward Sutherland, Edwin Stevens, Henry Johnson. Variant: THE DOLLAR-A-YEAR MAN. Picture produced between 16 Oct and 6 Nov 1920.

THE TRAVELING SALESMAN (Famous Players-Lasky, 1921). r5 Jun 1921. c2 Jun 1921. 5 reels. 4,514 feet. Paramount Production No. 350 (#2076). Famous Players-Lasky Corporation (pro/cc). Paramount Pictures (dist). Joseph Henabery (dir). James Grant Forbes (play). Walter Woods (scen). Karl Brown (cam). Roscoe Arbuckle, Betty Ross Clark, Frank Holland, Wilton Taylor, Lucille Ward, Jim Blackwell, Richard Wayne, George C. Pearce, Robert Dudley, Gordon Rogers. This picture should not be confused with THE TRAVELING SALESMAN produced by Famous Players Film Company, presented by Daniel Frohman and released by Paramount Pictures in 1916. Picture produced between 10 Jun 1920 and 12 Jul 1920; completed before BREWSTER'S MILLIONS and THE DOLLAR A YEAR MAN, but released later.

GASOLINE GUS (Famous Players-Lasky, 1921). r20 Aug 1921. No Copyright. 5 reels. Color (tinted and toned). Paramount Production No. 378 (#2112). Famous Players-Lasky Corporation (pro). Paramount Pictures (dist). Jesse L. Lasky (pres). Frank E. Woods (sup). James Cruze (dir). Vernon

Keays (asst dir). George Patullo (story: *Saturday Evening Post*). Walter Woods (adapt/scen). Karl Brown (cam). Roscoe Arbuckle, Lila Lee, Charles Ogle, Theodore Lorch, Wilton Taylor, Knute Erickson, Fred W. Huntley. Adapted from two Patullo stories, "Gasoline Gus" and "Drycheck Charlie," which appeared in *Saturday Evening Post*. Picture produced between 21 May 1921 and 14 Apr 1921. Withdrawn from United States distribution in September 1921.

CRAZY TO MARRY (THREE MILES OUT) (Famous Players-Lasky, 1921). r28 Aug 1921. c28 Aug 1921. 5 reels, 4,693 feet; 4,761; or 5,402 feet. Color (tinted and toned). Paramount Production No. 372 (#2098). Famous Players-Lasky Corporation (pro/cc). Paramount Pictures (dist). Jesse L. Lasky (pres). Frank E. Woods (sup). James Cruze (dir). Vernon Keays (asst dir). Frank Condon (story). Walter Woods (scen). Karl Brown (cam). Max Parker (art dir). Roscoe Arbuckle, Lila Lee, Lura Anson, Edwin Stevens, Lillian Leighton, Bull Montana, Allen Durnell, Sidney Bracy, Genevieve Blinn, Clarence Burton, Henry Johnson, Charles Ogle, Jackie Young, Lucien Littlefield. Picture produced between 17 Jan 1921 and 19 Feb 1921; completed before GASOLINE GUS , but released later. Also known as THREE MILES OUT.

LEAP YEAR (SKIRT SHY) (Famous Players-Lasky, 1921, unreleased). r (scheduled) 1921. No copyright. 5 reels. 4,767 feet. Paramount Production No. 389 (#2128). Famous Players-Lasky Corporation (pro). Paramount Pictures (dist). Adolph Zukor (pres). James Cruze (dir). Vernon Keays (asst dir). Sarah Y. Mason (story). Walter Woods (scen). Karl Brown (cam). Roscoe Arbuckle, Mary Thurman, Lucien Littlefield, Harriet Hammond, Maude Wayne, Clarence Geldart, Winifred Greenwood, Allen Durnell, Gertrude Short, John McKinnon. Picture produced between 16 May 1921 and 9 Jun 1921 under the working title SHOULD A MAN MARRY? Picture completed and title changed to SKIRT SHY, but not released in the United States. Picture released in Europe 26 Mar 1922 as LEAP YEAR. Also known as THIS IS SO SUDDEN.

FREIGHT PREPAID (VIA FAST FREIGHT) (Famous Players-Lasky, 1921, unreleased). r (scheduled) 1921. No copyright. 5 reels. Paramount Production No. 397 (#2176). Famous Players-Lasky Corporation (pro). Paramount Pictures (dist). James Cruze (dir). Curtis Benton (story). Roscoe Arbuckle, Lila Lee, Nigel Barrie, Herbert Standing, Raymond Hatton. Picture produced between 18 Jul 1921 and 13 Aug 1921 under the working title VIA FAST FREIGHT. Exterior scenes filmed on location in Chicago. Picture completed and title changed to FREIGHT PREPAID, but not released in the United States. Picture released in Europe 18 Jun 1922. Also known as FAST FREIGHT; THE FAST FREIGHT; HANDLE WITH CARE.

"THE MELANCHOLY SPIRIT." r (scheduled) 1922. Famous Players-Lasky Corporation (pro). Picture begun with Arbuckle in September 1921 under the working title THE MELANCHOLY SPIRIT. Production under the supervision of Frank E. Woods, directed by James Cruze from an original story by James Cruze and A.B. Barringer, scenario by Walter Woods, and camera by Karl Brown. Production was suspended, story revised under the title, EK, A FIGHTING SOUL, and picture given to Will Rogers, with Lila Lee, Alan Hale, John Fox, George Nichols, Emily Rait, Knute Erikson. Title changed to ONE GLORIOUS DAY and picture released in 5 reels by Paramount Pictures on 5 Feb 1922.

"THIRTY DAYS" r (scheduled) 1922. Famous Players-Lasky Corporation (pro). Picture intended for Arbuckle, but given to Wallace Reid, with Wanda Hawley, Charles Ogle, Cyril Chadwick, Herschel Mayall, Helen Dunbar, Carmen Phillips, Kalla Pasha, Robert Brower. Picture produced between 24 Aug 1922 and 9 Sep 1922; released as THIRTY DAYS in 5 reels by Paramount Pictures on 10 Dec 1922.

"THE MAN FROM MEXICO" r (scheduled) 1922. Famous Players-Lasky Corporation (pro). Picture intended for Arbuckle as remake of MAN FROM MEXICO (Famous Players, 1914) starring John Barrymore and based upon the Henry A. Du Souchet stage play, THE MAN FROM MEXICO. Picture given to Richard Dix, with Lois Wilson, Nat Pendleton,

Douglas MacPherson, Gunboat Smith, Joseph Kilgour, Tom Findley, Edna May Oliver. Title changed to LET'S GET MARRIED and picture released in 7 reels by Paramount Pictures on 29 Mar 1926.

"ARE YOU A MASON?" r (scheduled) 1922. Famous Players-Lasky Corporation (pro). Picture intended for Arbuckle as a remake of ARE YOU A MASON? (Famous Players, 1915) starring John Barrymore and based upon the Leo Ditrichstein stage play ARE YOU A MASON? Picture rights sold by Paramount to Twickenham Film Studios in London in 1934 for ARE YOU A MASON?) UNIVERSAL-OLYMPIC, 1934). RIGHTS WERE BOUGHT BACK IN 1941 FOR POSSIBLE FEATURE FOR BOB HOPE OR JACK BENNY, BUT PICTURE WAS NOT PRODUCED.

MC NAB

Arbuckle's attorney Gavin McNab and associates financed the following two-reel picture to be Arbuckle's first starring role in films after the scandal:

"HANDY ANDY." r (scheduled) 1923. No copyright. 2 reels. Gavin McNab (pro). Herman Raymaker (dir). Roscoe Arbuckle, Molly Malone. Arbuckle suspended work on this production in February 1923 and announced his return to the screen as director, not as comedian. Picture may have been completed but was not released in the United States.

FAMOUS PLAYERS-LASKY

HOLLYWOOD (Famous Players-Lasky, 1923). r19 Aug 1923. c10 Jul 1923. 8 reels, 8,100 feet. Paramount Production No. 477. Famous Players-Lasky Corporation (pro/cc): Paramount Pictures (dist). Jesse L. Lasky (pres). James Cruze (dir). Frank Condon (story). Tom Geraghty (adapt). Karl Brown (cam). Hope Drown, Luke Cosgrave, George K. Arthur, Ruby Lafayette, Harrison Gordon, Bess Flowers, Eleanor Lawson, King Zany, Roscoe Arbuckle (bit as man who walks up to casting director's window to have it slammed in his face with the word "Closed"). Picture produced between 15 Feb 1923 and 3 May 1923.

EDUCATIONAL

Educational's first Tuxedo Comedies starring Ned Sparks, Harry Tighe, and Poodles Hanneford were produced by Reel Comedies, Inc., and distributed by the Educational Film Exchanges. Arbuckle began his affiliation with Reel Comedies in February 1923 and may have worked as director, writer, supervising director, and/or producer on these pictures.

EASTER BONNETS (Educational, 1923). r26 Aug 1923. No Copyright. 2 reels. Tuxedo Comedies. Reel Comedies (pro). Educational Film Exchanges (dist). Ned Sparks, Harry Tighe, Marion Harlan, Doris Deane. First release in the Tuxedo Comedies series.

FRONT! (Educational, 1923). r17 Oct 1923. No copyright. 2 reels. Tuxedo Comedies. Reel Comedies (pro). Educational Film Exchanges (dist). Poodles Hanneford.

NO LOAFING (Educational, 1923). r25 Nov 1923. No copyright. 2 reels. Tuxedo Comedies. Reel Comedies (pro). Educational Film Exchanges (dist). Poodles Hanneford.

ONE NIGHT IT RAINED (Educational, 1924). r20 Jan 1924. No copyright. 2 reels. Tuxedo Comedies. Reel Comedies (pro). Educational Film Exchanges (dist). Ned Sparks, Harry Tighe, Doris Deane.

THE NEW SHERIFF (Educational, 1924). r16 Mar 1924. No copyright. 2 reels. Tuxedo Comedies. Reel Comedies (pro). Educational Film Exchanges (dist). Poodles Hanneford.

METRO

SHERLOCK, JR. (Metro, 1924). r21 Apr 1924. c22 Apr 1924. 5 reels. Joseph M. Schenck (pro/cc). Metro Pictures Corporation (dist). Buster Keaton (dir). Jean Havez, Joseph Mitchell, Clyde Bruckman (writs/adapts). Fred Gabourie (sets). Clare West (ward). Elgin Lessley, Byron Houck (cam). Buster Keaton, Kathryn McGuire, Joe Keaton, Ward Crane, Erwin Connelly, Jane Connelly, Ford West, George Davis, Horace Morgan, John Pattrick, Ruth Holley. According to Keaton, Arbuckle directed this picture's first few days of production until personal problems on set forced Keaton to assume full control as director. According to Doris Deane, Arbuckle wrote and directed this picture as well as other Keaton pictures for which he was not given screen credit.

EDUCATIONAL

THE BONEHEAD (Educational, 1924). r18 May 1924. No copyright. 2 reels. Tuxedo Comedies. Reel Comedies (pro). Educational Film Exchanges (dist). Poodles Hanneford.

ARBUCKLE AS DIRECTOR OF AL ST. JOHN

Educational's series of Tuxedo Comedies starring Al St. John was produced by Reel Comedies, Inc., and distributed by the Educational Film Exchanges. Al St. John received official credit as director and writer for his first four Tuxedo Comedies, and Grover Jones received credit as director for St. John's three remaining Tuxedo Comedies. According to Doris Deane, Arbuckle was director on set and writer for all Tuxedo Comedies starring Al St. John.

HIS FIRST CAR (Educational, 1924). r27 Jul 1924. No copyright. 2 reels. Tuxedo Comedies. Reel Comedies (pro). Educational Film Exchanges (dist). Al St. John (dir/writ). Al St. John, Doris Deane, Leon Holmes, George Davis, Blanche Payson. Al St. John's first picture in the Tuxedo Comedies series.

NEVER AGAIN (Educational, 1924). r24 Aug 1924. c24 Aug 1924. 2 reels. Tuxedo Comedies. Reel Comedies (pro/cc). Educational Film Exchanges (dist). Al St. John (dir/writ). Al St. John, Doris Deane, Blanche Payson.

STUPID BUT BRAVE (Educational, 1924). r26 Oct 1924. c27 Oct 1924. 2 reels. Tuxedo Comedies. Reel Comedies (pro/cc). Educational Film Exchanges (dist). Al St. John (dir/writ). Al St. John, Doris Deane.

LOVEMANIA (Educational, 1924). r28 Dec 1924. c28 Dec 1924. 2 reels. Tuxedo Comedies. Reel Comedies (pro/cc). Educational Film Exchanges (dist). Al St. John (dir/writ). Al St. John, Doris Deane, George Davis, Glen Cavender.

DYNAMITE DOGGIE (Educational, 1925). rMar 1925. c6 Apr 1925. 2 reels. Tuxedo Comedies. Reel Comedies (pro/cc). Educational Film Exchanges (dist). Grover Jones (dir). Al St. John.

THE IRON MULE (Educational, 1925). r12 Apr 1925. c4 May 1925. 2 reels. Tuxedo Comedies. Reel Comedies (pro/cc). Educational Film Exchanges (dist). Grover Jones (dir). Al St. John, Doris Deane, George Davis, Glen Cavender, Burlesque of John Ford's THE IRON HORSE (Fox, 1924).

CURSES (Educational, 1925). rMay 1925. c21 May 1925. 2 reels. Tuxedo Comedies. Reel Comedies (pro/cc). Educational Film Exchanges (dist). Grover Jones (dir). Al St. John.

ARBUCKLE DIRECTING AS WILLIAM GOODRICH

Arbuckle adopted the pseudonym William Goodrich and used this name from 1925 to 1932. Tuxedo Comedies starring Johnny Arthur were produced by Goodwill Comedies, Inc. Arbuckle worked as director and writer on this series, and may have been producer and/or supervising director. Lloyd Hamilton Comedies were produced by the Lloyd Hamilton Corporation and the Lupino Lane Comedies by Lupino Lane

Comedy Corporation. These three series were distributed by Educational Film Exchanges and produced at the Educational studio at 7250 Santa Monica Boulevard in Los Angeles.

THE TOURIST (Educational, 1925). r20 Sep 1925. c24 Sep 1925. 2 reels. Tuxedo Comedies. Educational Film Exchanges (dist/cc). Goodwill Comedies (pro). William Goodrich (dir). Johnny Arthur, Helen Foster. First of the Tuxedo Comedies starring Johnny Arthur.

THE MOVIES (Educational, 1925). r4 Oct 1925. c13 Oct 1925. 2 reels. Hamilton Comedies. Educational Film Exchanges (dist/cc). Lloyd Hamilton Corporation (pro). William Goodrich (dir/writ). Lloyd Hamilton, Marcella Daley, Arthur Thalasso, Frank Jonasson, Glen Cavender. Filmed at Montmartre Cafe on Hollywood Boulevard and at the Educational studio in Los Angeles.

METRO-GOLDWYN-MAYER

GO WEST (Metro-Goldwyn-Mayer, 1925). r1 Nov 1925. c23 Nov 1925. New York premier 25 Oct 1925. 7 reels. 6,293 feet. Buster Keaton Productions (pro/cc). Metro-Goldwyn-Mayer (dist). Joseph M. Schenck (pro/pres). Buster Keaton (dir/story). Raymond Cannon (scen). Elgin Lessley, Bert Haines (cam). Buster Keaton, Howard Truesdale, Kathleen Myers, Ray Thompson, Roscoe Arbuckle (bit as big lady in department store), Babe London ("her" daughter), Brown Eyes (cow).

EDUCATIONAL

CLEANING UP (Educational, 1925). r22 Nov 1925. c2 Jan 1926. Tuxedo Comedies. Educational Film Exchanges (dist/cc). Goodwill Comedies (pro). William Goodrich (dir/writ). Johnny Arthur, George Davis.

THE FIGHTING DUDE (Educational, 1925). r6 Dec 1925. c29 Dec 1925. 2 reels. Lupino Lane comedies. Educational Film Exchanges (dist/cc). Lupino Lane Comedy Corporation (pro). William Goodrich (dir/writ). Lupino Lane, Virginia Vance, Wallace Lupino, Glen Cavender, George Davis.

MY STARS (Educational, 1926) r17 Jan 1926. c17 Mar 1926. 2 reels. Tuxedo Comedies. Educational Film Exchanges (dist/cc). Goodwill Comedies (pro). William Goodrich (dir/writ). Johnny Arthur, Virginia Vance, Florence Lee, Glen Cavender, George Davis.

HOME CURED (Educational, 1926). r14 Mar 1926. c14 Mar 1926. 2 reels. Tuxedo Comedies. Christie Film Company [sic] (cc). Goodwill Comedies (pro). Educational Film Exchanges (dist). William Goodrich (dir). Vernon Keays (asst dir). Donna Barrel (story). Byron Houck (cam). Johnny Arthur, Virginia Vance, Glen Cavender, George Davis.

FOOL'S LUCK (Educational, 1926). r21 Mar 1926. c22 Jun 1926. 2 reels. Lupino Lane Comedies. Educational Film Exchanges (dist/cc). Lupino Lane Comedy Corporation (pro). William Goodrich (dir/writ). Bert Houck (cam) Lupino Lane, Virginia Vance, George Davis, Jack Lloyd.

HIS PRIVATE LIFE (Educational, 1926). r16 May 1926. c10 May 1926. 2 reels. Lupino Lane Comedies. Educational Film Exchanges (dist/cc). Lupino Lane Comedy Corporation (pro). William Goodrich (dir/writ). Lupino Lane, Virginia Vance, Glen Cavender, George Davis.

ONE SUNDAY MORNING (Educational, 1926). r12 Dec 1926. c14 Dec 1926. 2 reels. Hamilton Comedies. Educational Film Exchanges (dist/cc). Lloyd Hamilton Corporation (pro). William Goodrich (dir/writ). William Nobles (cam). Lloyd Hamilton.

PEACEFUL OSCAR (Educational, 1927). r30 Jan 1927. c30 Jan 1927. 2 reels. Educational-Hamilton Comedy. Educational Film Exchanges (dist/cc). Lloyd Hamilton Corporation (pro). William Goodrich (dir). Lloyd Hamilton.

METRO-GOLDWYN-MAYER

THE RED MILL (Metro-Goldwyn Mayer, 1927). r29 Jan 1927. c2 Mar 1927. 7 reels. 6,337 feet. Metro-Goldwyn-Mayer Corporation (dist/cc). Cosmopolitan Productions (pro). William Goodrich, King Vidor (dirs). Victor Herbert, Henry Martyn Blossom (musical comedy play). Frances Marion (adpt/scen). Joe Farnham (titl). Hendrik Sartov (cam). Cedric Gibbons, Merrill Pye (sets). Daniel J. Gray (film ed). Andre-ani (ward). Marion Davies, Owen Moore, Louise Fasenda, George Siegmann, Karl Dane, J. Russell Powell, Snitz Edwards, William Orlamond, Fred Gambold, Ignatz (mouse). Due to William R. Hearst's dissatisfaction with Arbuckle's direction, King Vidor was brought onto the film and finished it with Arbuckle. Arbuckle alone, as William Goodrich, received official credit as director.

FAMOUS PLAYERS-LASKY

SPECIAL DELIVERY (Famous Players-Lasky, 1927). r6 May 1927. c26 Mar 1927. 6 reels. 5,524 feet. Paramount Production No. 630. Famous Players-Lasky Corporation (pro/cc). Paramount Pictures (dist). Adolph Zukor, Jesse L. Lasky (pres). B.P. Schulberg (assoc pro). William Goodrich (dir). Henry Hathaway, Vernon Keays (asst dirs). Eddie Cantor (story). John Goodrich (adapt/const/scen). George Marion, Jr. (titl). Henry Hallenberger (cam). Louis D. Lighton (editor-in-chief). Eddie Cantor, Jobyna Ralston, William Powell, Louis Stern, Mabel Julienne Scott, Donald Keith, Jack Dougherty, Victor Potel, Paul Kelly, Mary Carr, Doris Deane. Picture produced between 27 Dec 1926 and 4 Feb 1927.

RKO RADIO

Arbuckle started work with RKO Radio Pictures on January 21, 1930, working as a writer in the scenario department, where he stayed until April 19, 1930. Scripts or films on which he worked at this period are not presently known. He returned to the RKO studios on May 9, 1930, where he worked as gagman, uncredited, on the Wheeler and Woolsey feature comedy HALF SHOT AT SUNRISE. Arbuckle remained at work on the script of this film until June 28, 1930, at which time he left the studio. He did not return until 1931, at which time he began work for RKO Pathé as director and writer on the "Traveling Man Comedies" series starring Louis John Bartels.

HALF SHOT AT SUNRISE (RKO, 1930). r4 Oct 1930. c25 Sep 1930. Sd (Photophone). 10 reels. 7,059 feet. Production No. 505. RKO Radio Pictures (pro/cc). RKO Distributing Corp (dist). William Le Baron (pro). Henry Hobart (assoc pro). Paul Sloane (dir). James Ashmore Creelman, Jr. (story/scen). Anne Caldwell, Ralph Spence (dia). Nick Musuraca (cam). Arthur Roberts (film ed). Mary Read (dance dir). Hugh McDowell (sd rec). Harry Tierney, Anne Caldwell (music & lyrics). Bert Wheeler, Robert Woolsey, Dorothy Lee, Hugh Trevor, Edna May Oliver, Eddie De Lange, E.H. Calvert, Alan Roscoe, John Rutherford, George MacFarlane, Roberta Robinson, Leni Stengel. Arbuckle worked as gagman, uncredited, on this picture. Picture produced between 30 Jun 1930 and 8 August 1930.

EDUCATIONAL

The Lloyd Hamilton Talking Comedies (later Lloyd Hamilton Comedies), Ideal Talking Comedies (later Ideal Comedies), Mermaid Comedies, and Cameo Comedies were produced by Educational Pictures, Inc., distributed by Educational Film Exchanges, and produced at the Educational studio at 7250 Santa Monica Boulevard in Los Angeles.

WON BY A NECK (Educational, 1930). r5 Oct 1930. c5 Oct 1930; and 1 Mar 1931. 2 reels. Sd. Lloyd Hamilton Talking Comedies. Educational Film Exchanges (dist/cc). Educational Pictures (pro). William Goodrich (dir). Ralph Nelson (asst dir). Tom Whiteley (story). Harry McCoy,

Walter DeLeon (cont/dia). Dwight Warren (cam). Lloyd
Hamilton.

SI, SI, SENOR (Educational, 1930). r21 Sep 1930. c26 Oct 1930.
2 reels. Sd. Ideal Talking Comedies. Educational Film
Exchanges (dist/cc). Educational Pictures (pro). William
Goodrich (dir). Tom Patricola, Joe Phillips, Chiquita,
Carmel Guerrox. Variant: SI SI SENOR.

UP A TREE (Educational, 1930). c30 Nov 1930. c27 Dec 1930.
2 reels. S. Lloyd Hamilton Talking Comedies. Educational
Film Exchanges (dist/cc). Educational Pictures (pro).
William Goodrich (dir/story). Ralph Nelson (asst dir). Harry
McCoy, Jimmy Starr (cont/dia). Dwight Warren (cam).
Lloyd Hamilton, Dell Henderson, Addie McPhail.

THREE HOLLYWOOD GIRLS (Educational, 1931). r4 Jan 1931.
c4 Jan 1931. 2 reels. Sd. Ideal Comedies. Educational Film
Exchanges (dist/cc). Educational Pictures (pro). William
Goodrich (dir). Ralph Nelson (asst dir), Katharine Scola,
Sherman L. Lowe (story). James Gleason, Ernest Pagano,
Jack Townley (cont/dia). Dwight Warren (cam). Leota Lane,
Rita Flynn, Phyllis Crane, Eddie Nugent, Ford West,
Florence Oberle. First picture in the "Hollywood Girls"
series.

MARRIAGE ROWS (Educational, 1931). r18 Jan 1931. c18 Jan
1931. 2 reels. Sd. Lloyd Hamilton Talking Comedies. Educa-
tional Film Exchanges (dist/cc). Educational Pictures (pro).
William Goodrich (dir/story). Ralph Nelson (asst dir).
Walter Reed (cont/adapt). Dwight Warren (cam). Lloyd
Hamilton, Al St. John, Addie McPhail, Doris Deane, Edna
Marion.

PETE AND REPEAT (Educational, 1931). r1 Mar 1931. c1 Mar
1931. 2 reels. Sd. Ideal Comedies. Educational Film Exchanges (dist/cc). Educational Pictures (pro). William
Goodrich (dir). George Jeske, Joey Mack, A. Gold (story).
Ernest Pagano, Jack Townley (cont/dia). "Bud" Harrison

and Peenie Elmo ("Seben 'n' Leben," vaudeville blackface comics).

EX-PLUMBER (Educational, 1931). r8 Mar 1931. c8 Mar 1931. Sd. Lloyd Hamilton Comedies. Educational Film Exchanges (dist/cc). Educational Pictures (pro). William Goodrich (dir/writ). Ralph Nelson (asst dir). Walter Reed (cont/dia). Dwight Warren (cam). Lloyd Hamilton, Addie McPhail, Stanley Blystone, Mitchell Lewis, Amber Norman, Polly Christy.

CRASHING HOLLYWOOD (Educational, 1931). r5 Apr 1931. c5 Apr 1931. 2 reels. Sd. Ideal Comedies. Educational Film Exchanges (dist/cc). Educational Pictures (pro). William Goodrich (dir). Ralph Nelson (asst dir). Ernest Pagano, Jack Townley (story/cont/dia). Dwight Warren (cam). Virginia Brooks, Rita Flynn, Phyllis Crane, Eddie Nugent, Wilbur Mack, Walter Merrill. Second picture in the "Hollywood Girls" series.

WINDY RILEY GOES HOLLYWOOD (Educational, 1931). r3 May 1931. c3 May 1931. 2 reels. Sd. Mermaid Comedies. Educational Film Exchanges (dist/cc). Educational Pictures (pro). William Goodrich (dir). Ken Kling (story). Ernest Pagano, Jack Townley (cont/dia). Louise Brooks, Jack Shutta, William Davidson, Wilbur Mack, Dell Henderson, Walter Merrill, E.H. Allen. Picture based upon Ken Kling's syndicated comic strip *Windy Riley*. Picture included guest appearances by E.H. Allen, General Manager of Educational studio.

THE BACK PAGE (Educational, 1931). r24 May 1931. c24 May 1931. 2 reels. Sd. Mermaid Comedies. Educational Film Exchanges (dist/cc). Educational Pictures (pro). William Goodrich (dir). Ernest Pagano, Jack Townley (story/cont/dia). George Chandler, Virginia Brooks, Wheeler Oakman, George MacFarlane, Ethel Davis. Burlesque of THE FRONT PAGE (United Artists, 1931).

THE LURE OF HOLLYWOOD (Educational, 1931). r5 Jul 1931.

c5 Jul 1931. 2 reels. Sd. Ideal Comedies. Educational Film Exchanges (dist/cc). Educational Pictures (pro). William Goodrich (dir). Ernest Pagano, Jack Townley (story/dia). Virginia Brooks, Rita Flynn, Phyllis Crane, George Chandler, Bryant Washburn. Third picture in the "Hollywood Girls" series.

RKO PATHÉ

The RKO Pathé "Traveling Man Comedies" and "Gay Girls Comedies" were produced by RKO Pathé Pictures, inc., distributed by RKO Pathé Distributing Corporation, and produced at the RKO Pathé studios at 9336 Washington Boulevard in Culver City, California.

THAT'S MY LINE (RKO Pathé, 1931). r13 Jul 1931. c13 Jul 1931. 2 reels. Sd. Traveling Man Comedies. Production No. 194. RKO Pathé Distributing Corporation (dist/cc). RKO Pathé Pictures (pro). Lew Lipton (sup). William Goodrich (dir/story/adapt). Albert Benham (asst dir). Ewart Adamson (cont). Harry Forbes, Robert Palmer (cam). Fred Maguire (film ed). Louis John Bartels, Paul Hurst, Doris McMahon, Gino Corrado, Bert Young, Al Thompson, Glen Cavender, James Bryant, Teddy Mangean, Billy Arnold, William Armstrong, Oscar Smith, William McCall, Gene Lewis, William LeMaire, Patricia Caron, Dorothy Granger. First picture in the "Traveling Man Comedies" series (sometimes called "Traveling Salesman Comedies"). Picture produced between 18–24 Apr 1931.

EDUCATIONAL

HONEYMOON TRIO (Educational, 1931). r30 Aug 1931. c30 Aug 1931. 1 reel. Sd. Cameo Comedies. Educational Film Exchanges (dist/cc). Educational Pictures (pro). William Goodrich (dir). Ernest Pagano, Jack Townley, Harrison Jacobs (story/dia). Walter Catlett, Al St. John. Dorothy Granger.

UP POPS THE DUKE (Educational, 1931). r20 Sep 1931. c20 Sep 1931. 2 reels. Sd. Mermaid Comedies. Educational Film Exchanges (dist/cc). Educational Pictures (pro). William Goodrich (dir). Ernest Pagano, Jack Townley (story/dia). George Chandler, Pauline Wagner, Helen Bolton.

RKO PATHÉ

BEACH PAJAMAS (RKO Pathé, 1931). r28 Sep 1931. c28 Sep 1931. 2 reels. Sd. Traveling Man Comedies. Production No. 203. RKO Pathé Distributing Corporation (dist/cc). RKO Pathé Pictures (pro). Lew Lipton (sup). William Goodrich (dir/story/adapt). William Mull (asst dir). Henry R. Symonds, Hal Yates, Nick Barrows, E.A. Brown, Charles Callahan (cont). Dwight Warren (cam). Walter Thompson (film ed). Louis John Bartels, Addie McPhail, Marion Douglass, Charlotte Mineau, Vernon Dent, James Finlayson, Evelyn De Shields, George Billings, Charles Moore, Al Thompson, Claude Paton, Clarence Wertz, Bob Smith, Bert Young, George Billings. Second picture in the "Traveling Man Comedies" series. Picture produced between 1–5 June 1931.

TAKE 'EM AND SHAKE 'EM (RKO Pathé, 1931). r28 Sep 1931. c28 Sep 1931. 2 reels. Sd. Gay Girls Comedies. Production No. 204. RKO Pathé Distributing Corporation (dist/cc). RKO Pathé Pictures (pro). Lew Lipton (sup). William Goodrich (dir). Albert Benham (asst dir). Beatrice Van (story). Ralph Ceder (cont). Ted McCord (cam). John Link (film ed). June MacCloy, Marion Shilling, Gertrude Short, Charles Judels, Arthur Hoyt, Frank Marlowe. Second Picture in the "Gay Girls Comedies" series (sometimes called "Sugar Snatchers" series). Arbuckle was scheduled to direct the first picture in the series, JUNE FIRST, but was replaced by Don Gallaher before production began. Picture produced between 3 June 1931 (Marion Shilling test) and 8–11 Jun 1931. Shilling's test was directed and photographed by cameraman Ted McCord.

EDUCATIONAL

THAT'S MY MEAT (Educational, 1931). r4 Oct 1931. c4 Oct 1931. 1 reel. Sd. Cameo Comedies. Educational Film Exchanges (dist/cc). Educational Pictures (pro). William Goodrich (dir). Ernest Pagano, Jack Townley, Johnnie Grey (story/dia). Al St. John.

ONE QUIET NIGHT (Educational, 1931). r25 Oct 1931. c25 Oct 1931. 1 reel. Sd. Cameo Comedies. Educational Film Exchanges (dist/cc). Educational Pictures (pro). William Goodrich (dir). Ernest Pagano, Jack Townley (story/dia). Jacobs (story/dia).

QUEENIE OF HOLLYWOOD (Educational, 1931). r8 Nov 1931. c8 Nov 1931. 2 reels. Sd. Ideal Comedies. Educational Film Exchanges (dist/cc). Educational Pictures (pro). William Goodrich (dir). Ernest Pagano, Jack Townley (story/dia). Virginia Brooks, Rita Flynn, Jeanne Flarrin. Fourth picture in the "Hollywood Girls" series.

ONCE A HERO (Educational, 1931). r22 Nov 1931. C22 Nov 1931. 2 reels. Sd. Mermaid Comedies. Educational Film Exchanges (dist/cc). Educational Pictures (pro). William Goodrich (dir). Ernest Pagano, Jack Townley (story/dia). Emerson Treacy.

THE TAMALE VENDOR (Educational, 1931). r26 Nov 1931. c26 Nov 1931. 2 reels. Sd. Ideal Comedies. Educational Film Exchanges (dist/cc). Educational Pictures (pro). William Goodrich (dir). Ernest Pagano, Jack Townley (story/dia). Tom Patriocola.

IDLE ROOMERS (Educational, 1931). r29 Nov 1931. c29 Nov 1931. 1 reel. Sd. Cameo Comedies. Educational Film Exchanges (dist/cc). Educational Pictures (pro). William Goodrich (dir). Ernest Pagano, Jack Townley (story/dia).

SMART WORK (Educational, 1931). r27 Dec 1931. c27 Dec 1931. 1 reel. Sd. Cameo Comedies. Educational Film Exchanges (dist/cc). Educational Pictures (pro). William Goodrich (dir). Ernest Pagano, Jack Townley (story/dia). Billy Dooley, Addie McPhail.

MOONLIGHT AND CACTUS (Educational, 1932). r10 Jan 1932. c10 Jan 1932. 2 reels. Sd. Ideal Comedies. Educational Film Exchanges (dist/cc). Educational Pictures (pro). William Goodrich (dir). Ernest Pagano, Jack Townley (story/dia). Tom Patriocola.

KEEP LAUGHING (Educational, 1932). r24 Jan 1932. c24 Jan 1932. 2 reels. Sd. Mermaid Comedies. Educational Film Exchanges (dist/cc). Educational Pictures (pro). William Goodrich (dir). Ernest Pagano, Jack Townley (story/dia). Monte Collins, Jr., Addie McPhail, Bryant Washburn, Phyllis Crane, Jack Shaw, Dorothy Granger, Richard Malaby, George Davis.

ANYBODY'S GOAT (Educational, 1932). r24 Jan 1932. c24 Jan 1932. 1 reel. Sd. Cameo Comedies. Educational Film Exchanges (dist/cc). Educational Pictures (pro). William Goodrich (dir). Ernest Pagano, Jack Townley (story/dia).

BRIDGE WIVES (Educational, 1932). r21 Feb 1932. c21 Feb 1932. 1 reel. Sd. Cameo Comedies. Educational Film Exchanges (dist/cc). Educational Pictures (pro). William Goodrich (dir). Ernest Pagano, Jack Townley (story/dia). Al St. John.

HOLLYWOOD LUCK (Educational, 1932). r13 Mar 1932. c13 Mar 1932. 2 reels. Sd. Ideal Comedies. Educational Film Exchanges (dist/cc). Educational Pictures (pro). William Goodrich (dir). Ernest Pagano, Jack Townley (story/dia). Virginia Brooks, Rita Flynn, Frances Dean, Clarence Norstrom, Fern Emmett, Addie McPhail.

MOTHER'S HOLIDAY (Educational, 1932). r20 Mar 1932. c20 Mar 1932. 1 reel. Sd. Cameo Comedies. Educational Film Exchanges (dist/cc). Educational Pictures (pro). William Goodrich (dir). Walter Catlett (story).

IT'S A CINCH (Educational, 1932). r27 Mar 1932. c27 Mar 1932. 2 reels. Sd. Mermaid Comedies. Educational Film Exchanges (dist/cc). Educational Pictures (pro). William Goodrich (dir). Ernest Pagano, Jack Townley (story/dia). Monte Collins, Jr., Phyllis Crane.

HOLLYWOOD LIGHTS (Educational, 1932). r8 May 1932. c8 May 1932. 2 reels. Sd. Ideal Comedy. Educational Film Exchanges (dist/cc). Educational Pictures (pro). William Goodrich (dir). Ernest Pagano, Jack Townley (story/dia).

RKO PATHÉ

GIGOLETTES (RKO Pathé, 1932). r23 May 1932. c6 Apr 1932. 2 reels. Sd. Gay Girls Comedies. Production No. 224. RKO Pathé Pictures (pro/cc). RKO Pathé Distributing Corporation (dist). Lew Lipton (sup). William Goodrich (dir). Albert Benham (asst dir). Beatrice Van (story). H. Jackson (cam). Fred Maguire (film ed). June MacCloy, Marion Shilling, Gertrude Short, Roderick O'Farrell, Jerry Mandy, Charles Dorety, Bud Jamison, Heinie Conklin, Arthur Thalasso, Bud Fine, Herman Bing. Fifth picture in the "Gay Girls Comedies" series. Picture produced between 24–27 Aug 1931, with added scenes directed by Ralph Ceder, assisted by Bert Gilroy and photographed by George Meehan on 19 Sep 1931.

NIAGARA FALLS (RKO Pathé, 1932). r27 June 1932. c16 Jul 1932. 2 reels. Sd. Gay Girls Comedies. Production No. 227. RKO Pathé Pictures (pro/cc). RKO Pathé Distributing Corporation (dist). Lew Lipton (sup). William Goodrich (dir). Bert Gilroy (asst dir). Ewart Adamson (story). Ted McCord (cam). Walter Thompson (film ed). June MacCloy, Marion Shilling, Gertrude Short, Eddie Nugent, Emerson Treacy, Jessie Perry, Ernest Hilliard, Isabelle Withers, Violet Barlow. Sixth and last picture in the "Gay Girls Comedies" series. Picture produced between 2–5 Sep 1931 with scenes re-recorded on 29 Sep and 1 Oct 1931.

VITAPHONE

Vitaphone's Big V Comedies starring Arbuckle were produced by the Vitaphone Corporation under the supervision of Sam Sax, distributed by Warner Bros., and produced at the Vitaphone studio in Brooklyn, New York.

HEY, POP! (Vitaphone, 1932). r12 Nov 1932. c12 Dec 1932. 2 reels. Sd. Big V Comedies, No. 4. Production No. 1466-67. The Vitaphone Corporation (pro/cc). Warner Bros. (dist). Alf Goulding (dir). Jack Henley, Glen Lambert (story). E.P. DuPar (cam). David Mendoza (music). Roscoe Arbuckle, Billy Heyes, Florence Auer, Jack Shutta, Dan Wolheim, Milton Wallace, Leo Hoyt, Herschel Mayall, Connie Almy, J.F. Lee. Picture produced between 25–31 Aug 1932.

BUZZIN AROUND (Vitaphone, 1933). r4 Feb 1933. c22 Mar 1933. 2 reels. Sd. Big V Comedies, No. 9. Production No. 1509-10. The Vitaphone Corporation (pro/cc). Warner Bros (dist). Alf Goulding (dir). Jack Henley, Glen Lambert (story). E.P. DuPar (cam). David Mendoza (music). Roscoe Arbuckle, Al St. John, Dan Coleman, Alice May Tuck, Tom Smith, Al Ochs, Harry Ward, Gertrude Mudge, Fritz Hubert, Donald MacBride, Pete (dog).

HOW'VE YOU BEAN? (Vitaphone, 1933). r24 Jun 1933. c3 Jul 1933. 2 reels. Sd. Big V. Comedies, No. 11. Production No. 1525–26. The Vitaphone Corporation (pro/cc). Warner Bros (dist). Alf Goulding (dir). Jack Henley, Glen Lambert (story). E.P. DuPar (cam). David Mendoza (music). Roscoe Arbuckle, Mildred Van Dorn, Fritz Hubert, Jean Hubert, Edmund Elton, Dora Mills Adams, Paul Clare, Charles Howard, Herbert Warren. Picture produced between 16–22 Dec 1932.

CLOSE RELATIONS (Vitaphone, 1933). r30 Sep 1933. c12 Sep 1933. 2 reels. Sd. Big V Comedies (New Series), No. 2. Production No. 1556–57. The Vitaphone Corporation (pro/cc). Warner Bros. (dist). Ray McCarey (dir). Jack Henley, Glen Lambert (story). E.P. DuPar (cam). David Mendoza (music).

Roscoe Arbuckle, Charles Judels, Mildred Van Dorn, Harry Shannon, Shemp Howard, Hugh O'Connell, Jack Harwood, Hershel Mayall. Picture produced between 22–27 May 1933.

IN THE DOUGH (Vitaphone, 1933). r25 Nov 1933. c15 Nov 1933. 2 reels. Sd. Big V Comedies (New Series), No. 5. Production No. 1568-69. The Vitaphone Corporation (pro/cc). Warner Bros. (dist). Ray McCarey (dir). Jack Henley (story). E.P. DuPar (cam). David Mendoza (music). Roscoe Arbuckle, Dexter McReynolds, Marie Marion, Ralph Sanford, Fred Harper, Gracie Worth, Lionel Stander, Shemp Howard, Lawrence O'Sullivan, Ethel Davis, Dan Coleman, Bud Grey. Picture produced between 22–28 June 1933. Arbuckle's last produced film, completed shortly before his death, but released before TOMALIO.

TOMALIO (Vitaphone, 1933). r30 Dec 1933. c13 Feb 1934. 2 reels. Sd. Big V Comedies (New Series), No. 7. Production No. 1537-38. The Vitaphone Corporation (pro/cc). Warner Bros. (dist). Ray McCarey (dir). Jack Henley, Glen Lambert, (story). E.P. DuPar (cam). David Mendoza (music). Roscoe Arbuckle, Charles Judels, Phyllis Holden, Fritz Hubert, Phillip Ryder, Jerry Bergen, Pierre de Ramey, Clyde Veaux, Clarence Rock, Aristides De Leoni, John Barclay, Lew Kessler, Joe McCauley, Dermar Poppen. Picture produced 7–13 Apr 1933, completed before CLOSE RELATIONS and IN THE DOUGH, but released as Arbuckle's last film.

FILMOGRAPHY ACKNOWLEDGMENTS

The filmography was compiled with the assistance and co-operation of many individuals to whom the compiler expresses his gratitude: David A. Yallop, Minta Durfee, Doris Deane, Addie McPhail, King Vidor, Babe London, Mrs. Al St. John, Anthony Slide, Leonard Maltin, John and Dorothy Hampton, David Bradley, Kenneth Munden, Sam E. Brown, Mike Hawks, Mildred Simpson, Anne Schlosser, Ned Comstock, Leith Adams, Brigitte Keuppers; library staffs of the American Film Institute, Kansas City Public Library,

Library of Congress, The Museum of Modern Art, University of California at Los Angeles, University of Southern California, and University of Texas at Austin; the compiler's family and not just two but three parents, Florence L. Gill, Dr. George L. Gill and Joan Gunter Gill; a very special friend Stacey M. Endres; Dr. Linda Harris Mehr and the heroic staff of the Academy Foundation's Margaret Herrick Library, whom the compiler has had the rare pleasure and privilege of calling his friends and colleagues; and to a patient, loyal, and trusting friend, Andy Edmonds.